Poses for Artists Vol. 1
Justin R. Martin

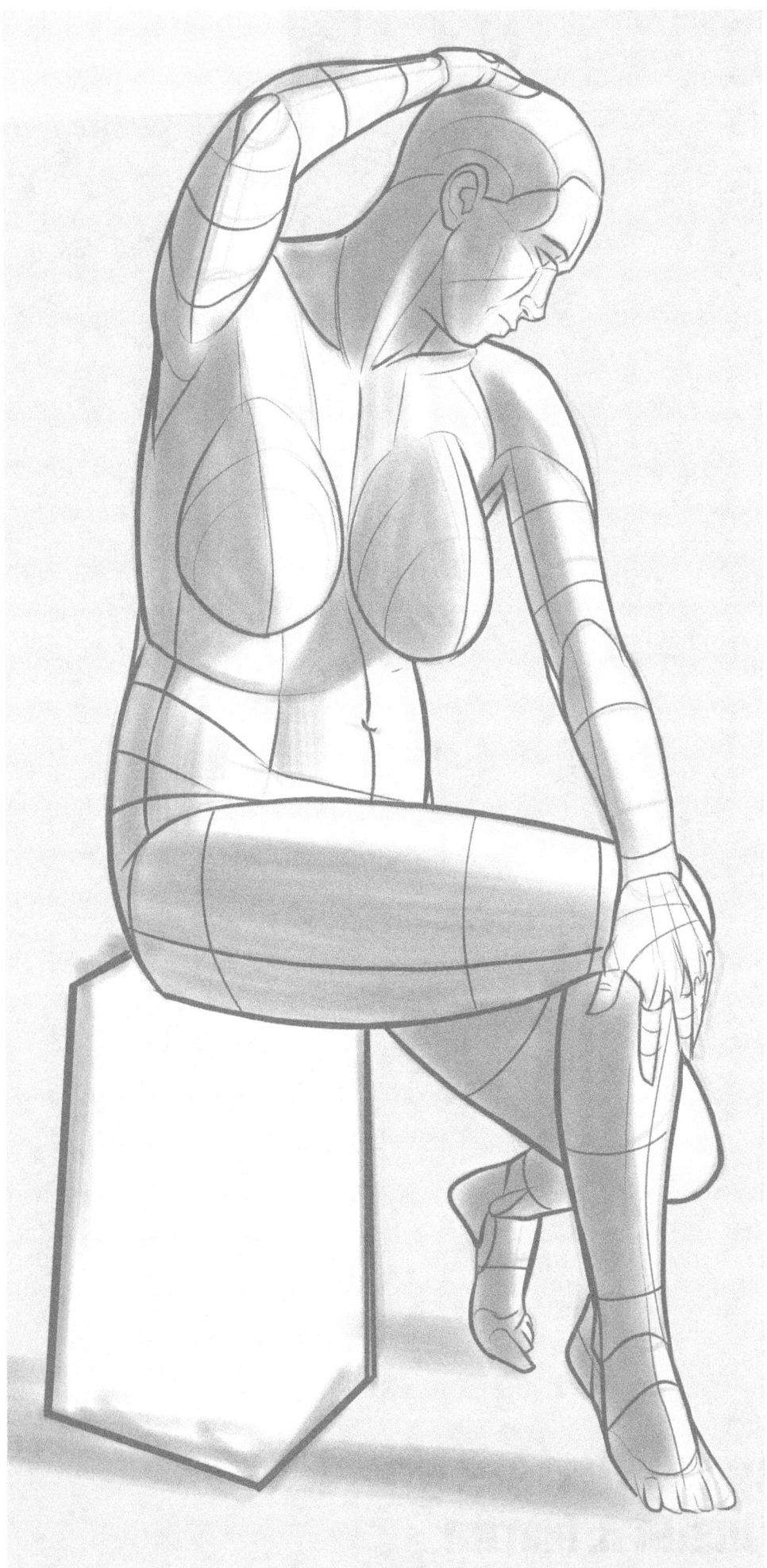

Poses for Artists VOL 1

Published by Eagel Ink Factory/ Justin Martin © 2016 Justin Martin.

special thanks to Sergio Aragones, Terri Martin, Tavin Martin, Sarah Martin, August Tarantino and Paul Roberts

P.O. Box 2105
Edwards, CO

81632

POSEmuse.com

First Edition, 2016

ISBN 978-1530106110
ISBN 1530106117

CONTENTS
- Dynamic Poses
- Sitting Poses

Dynamic Poses

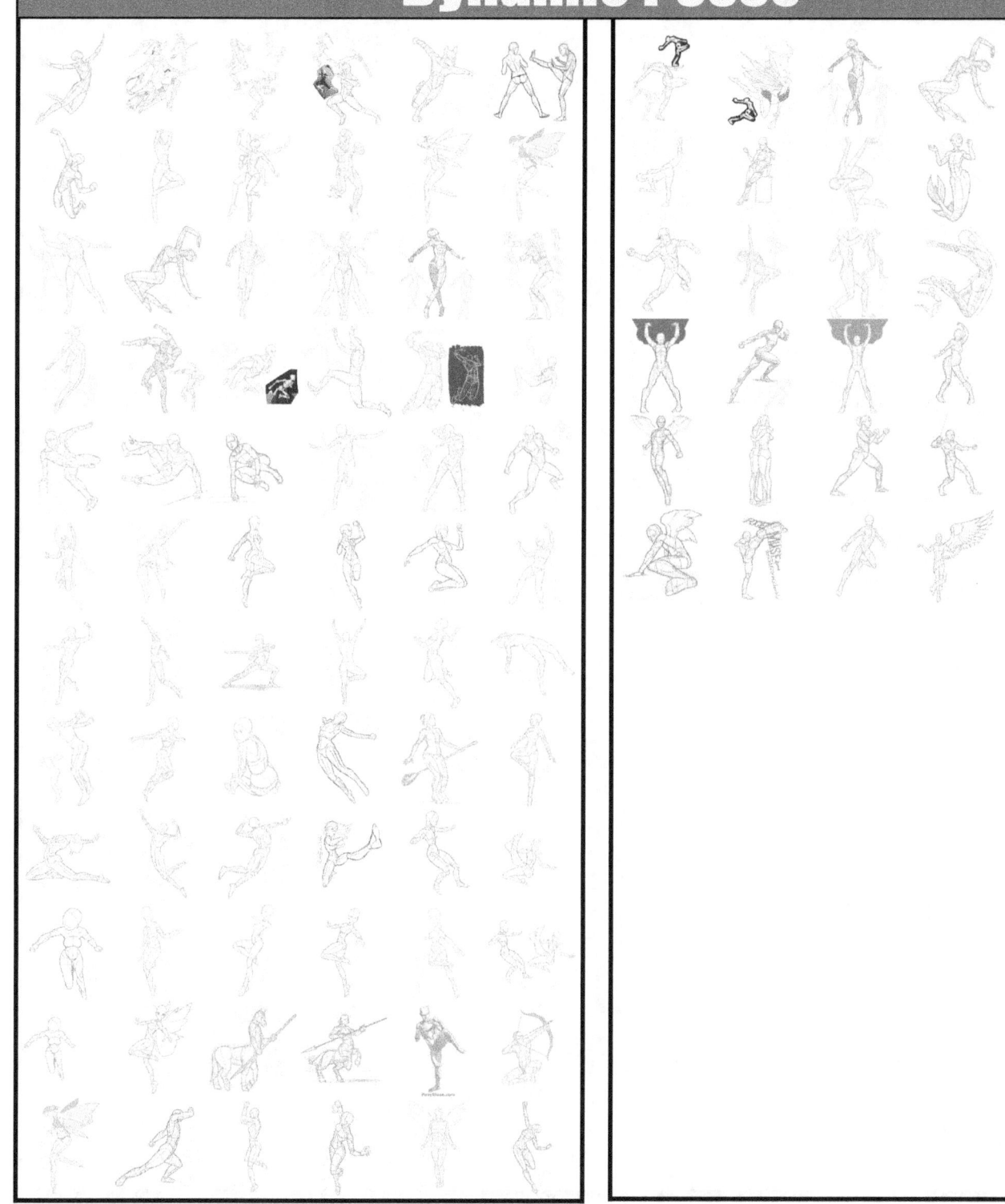

Sitting Poses

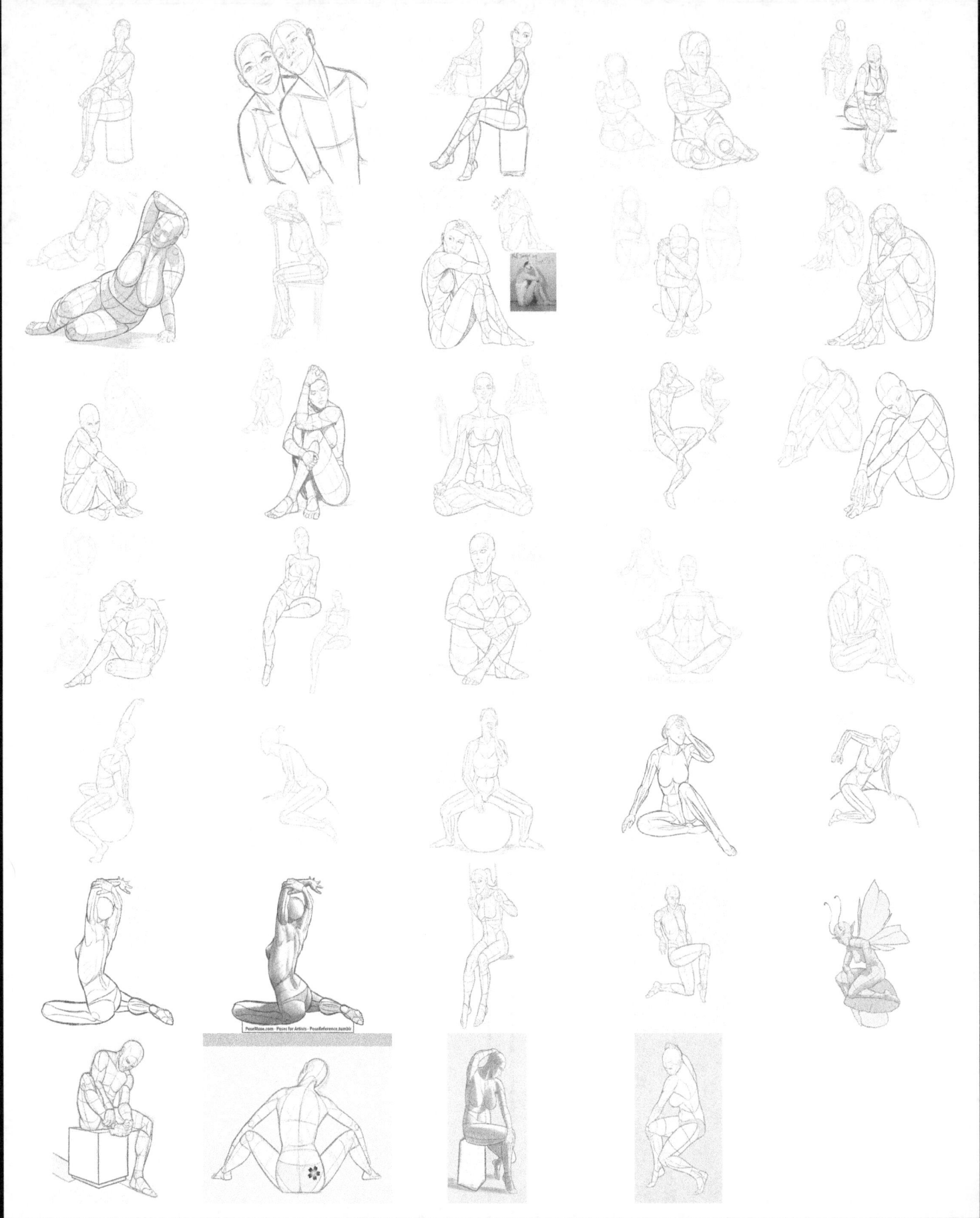

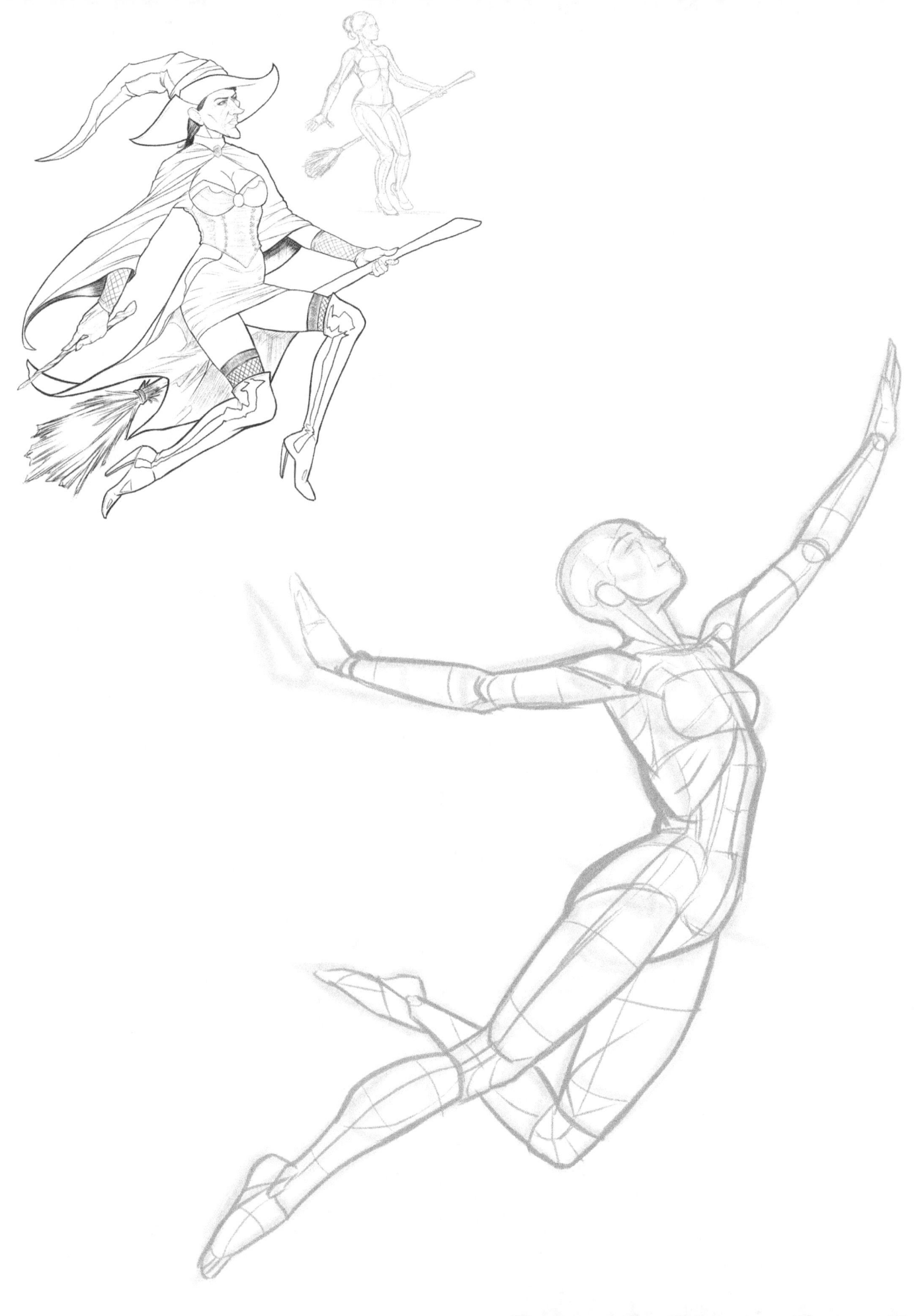

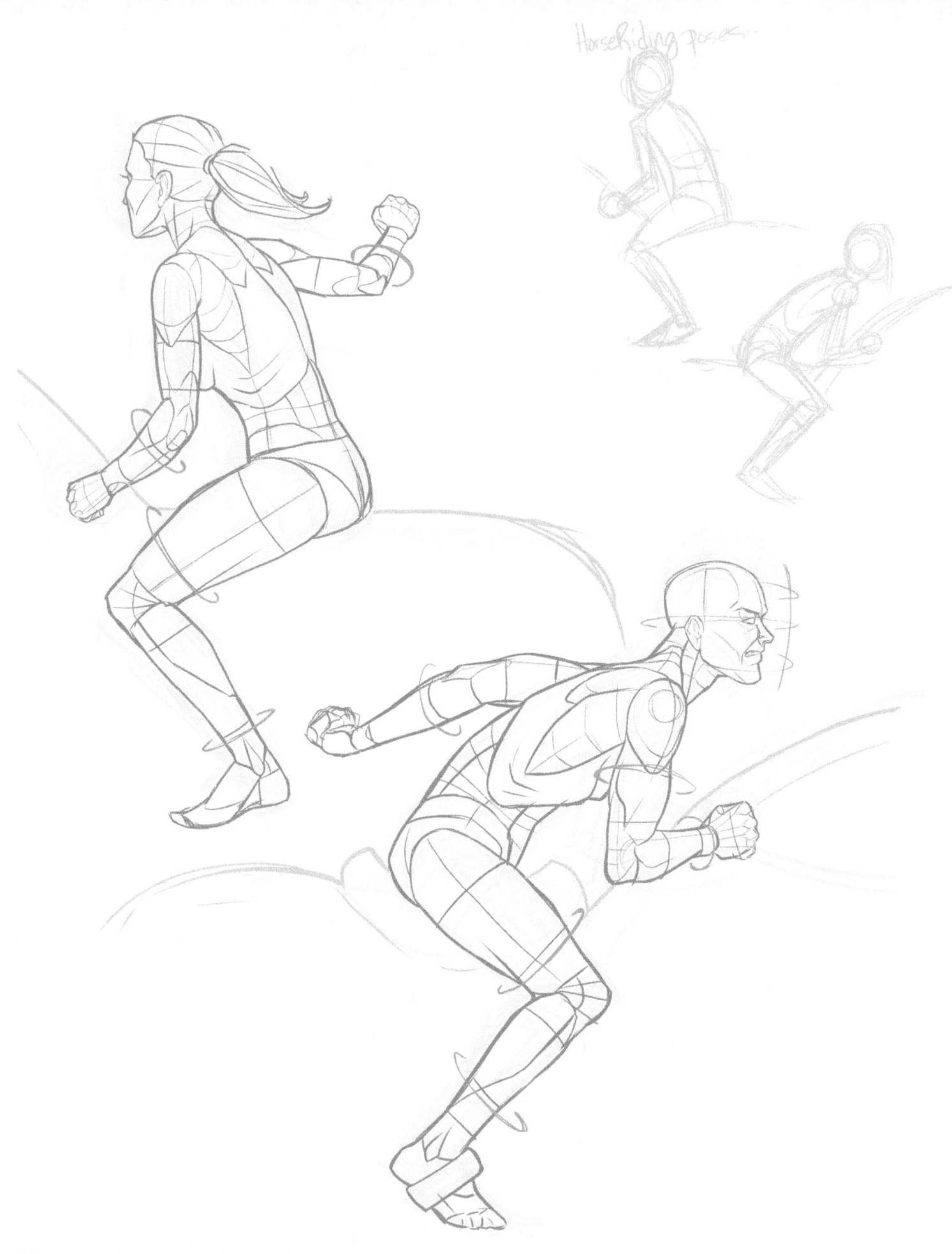

HorseRiding poses.

Dynamic Poses -Page 6

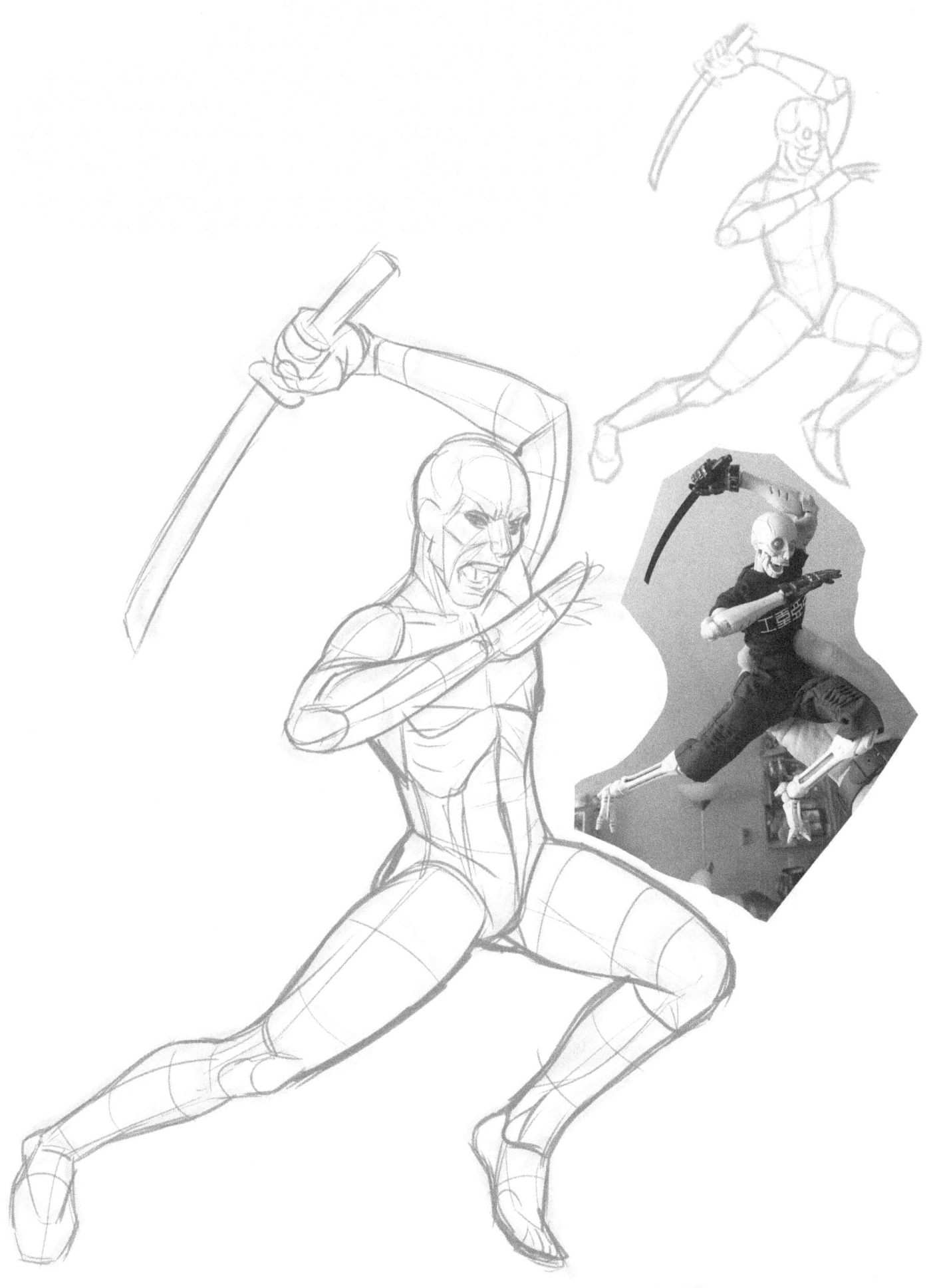

Dynamic Poses -Page 7

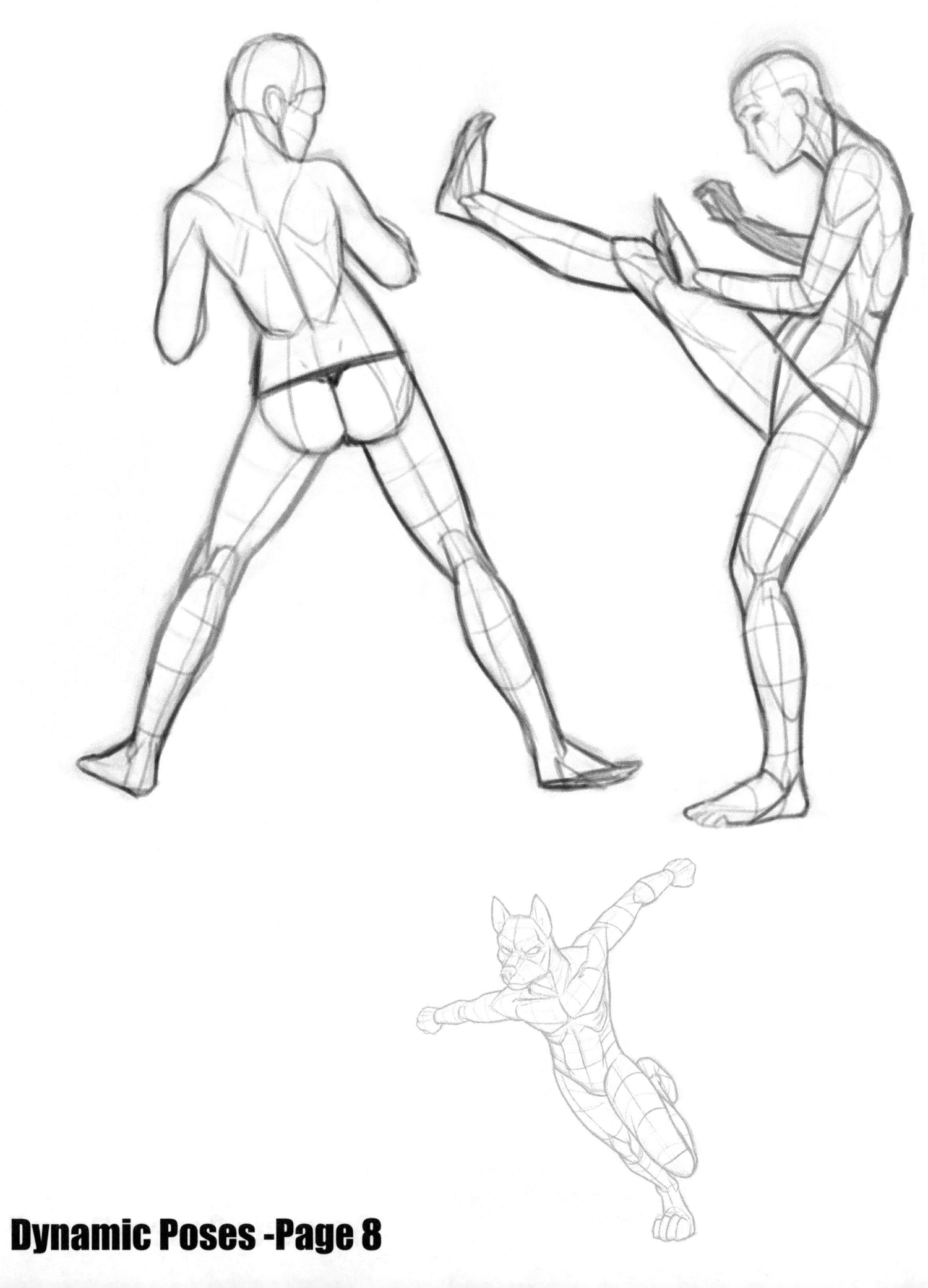

Dynamic Poses -Page 8

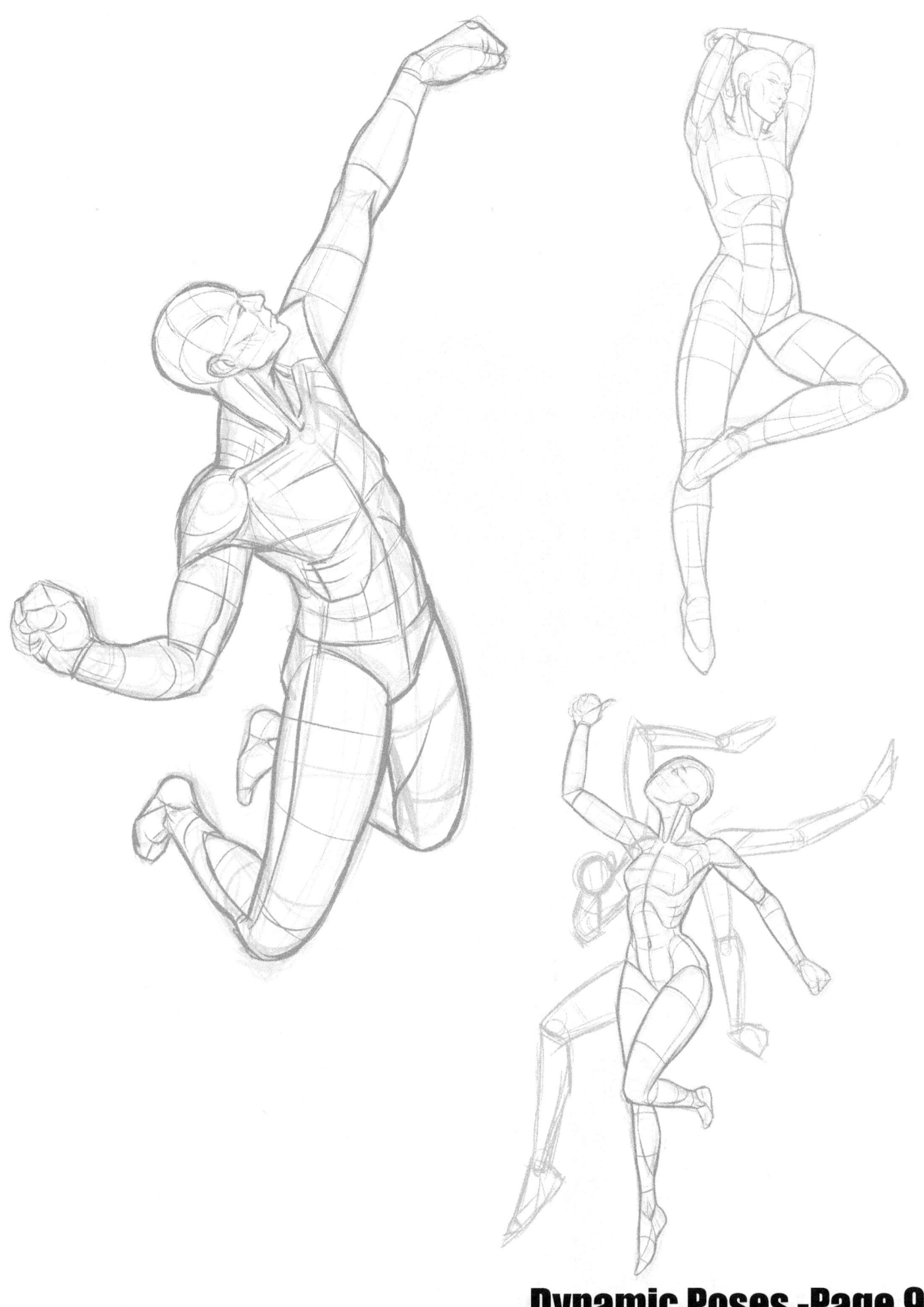

Dynamic Poses -Page 9

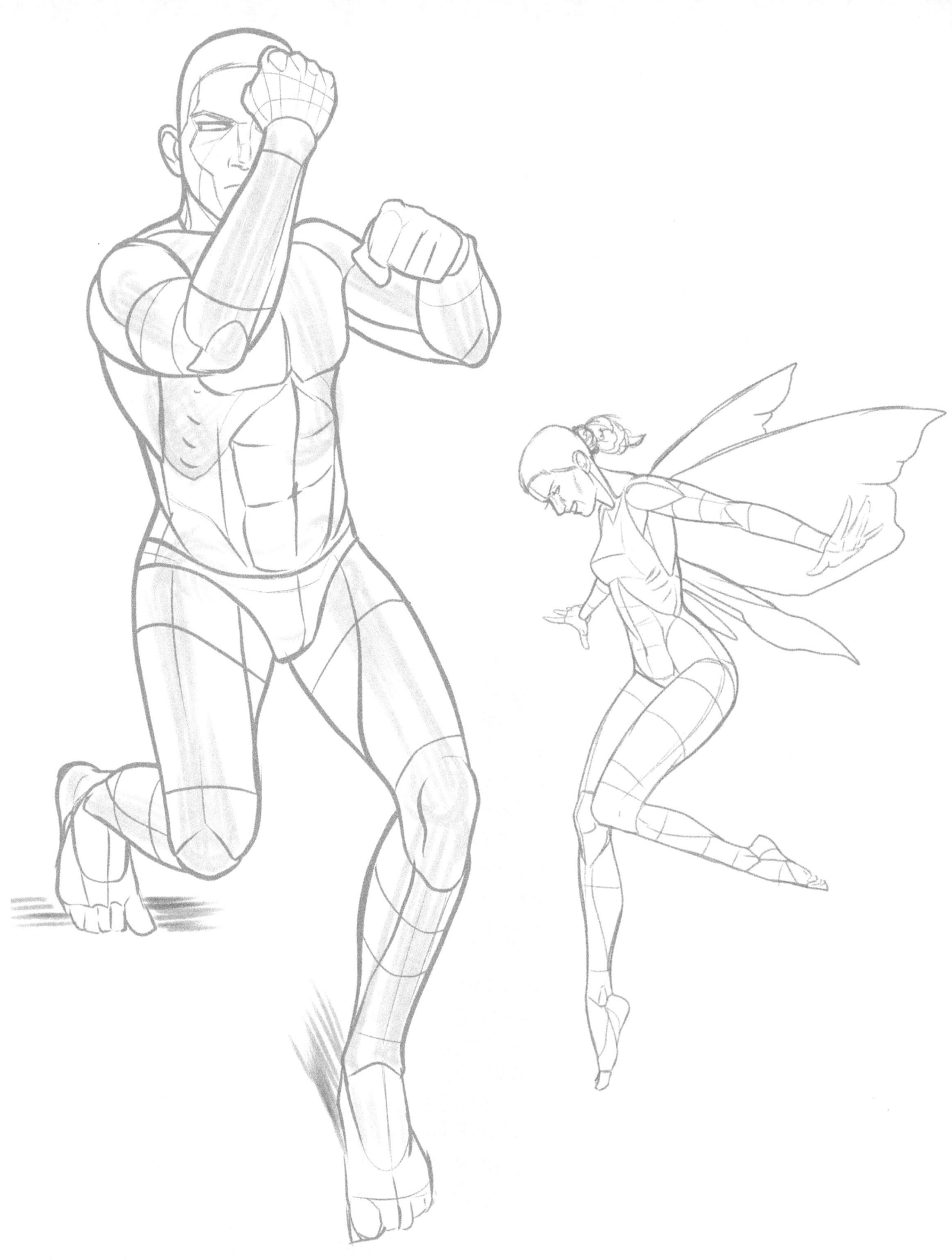

Dynamic Poses -Page 10

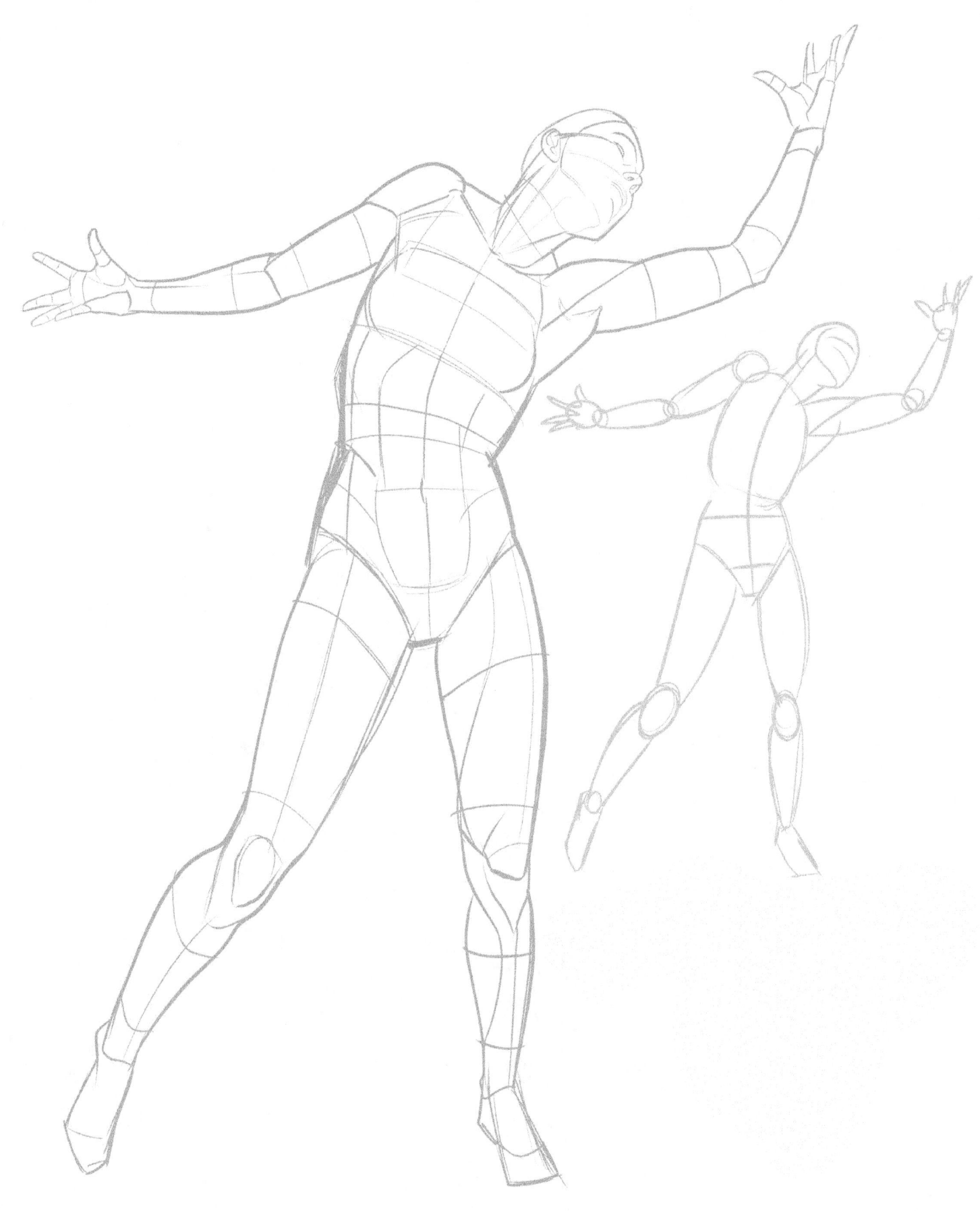

Dynamic Poses -Page 11

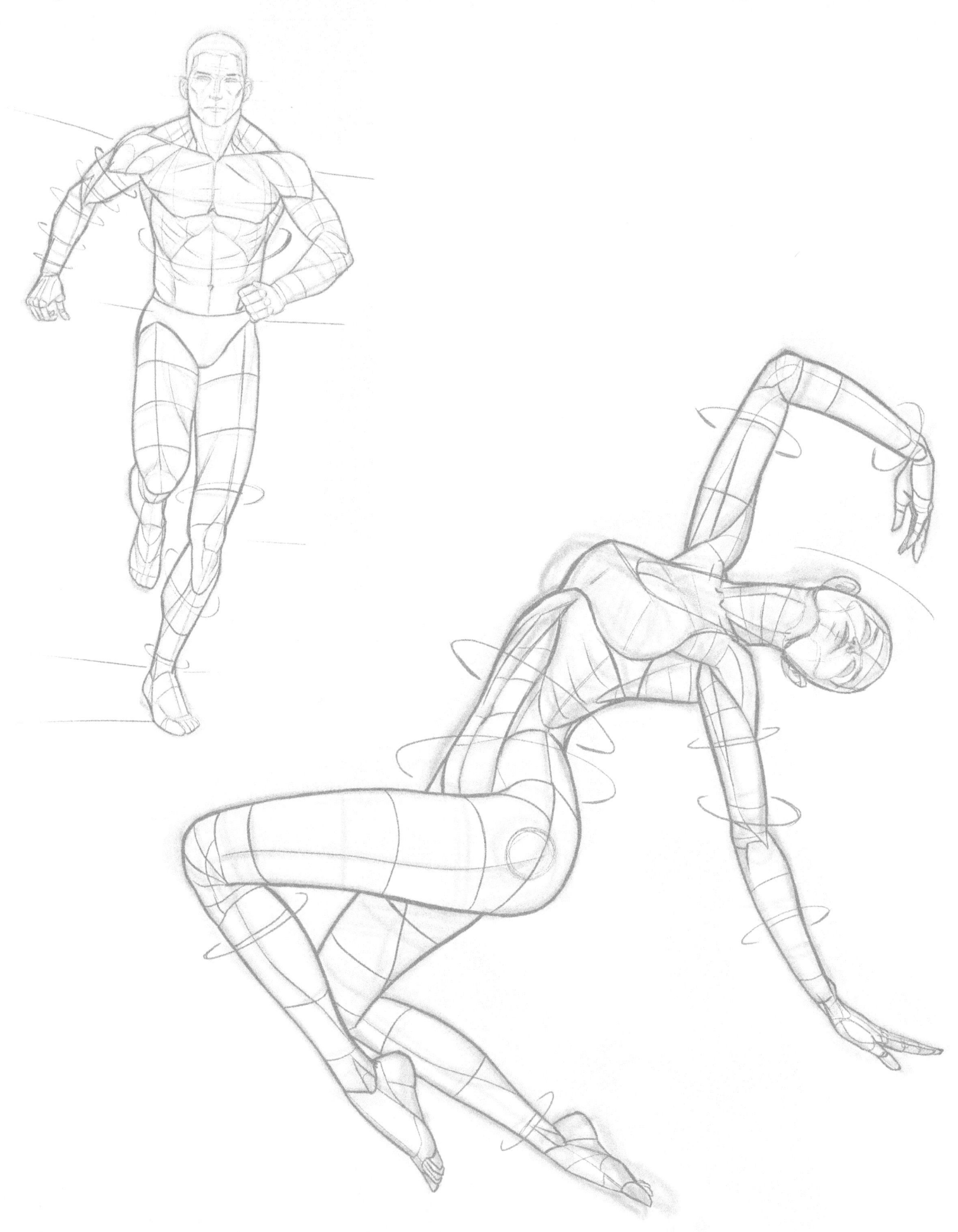

Dynamic Poses -Page 12

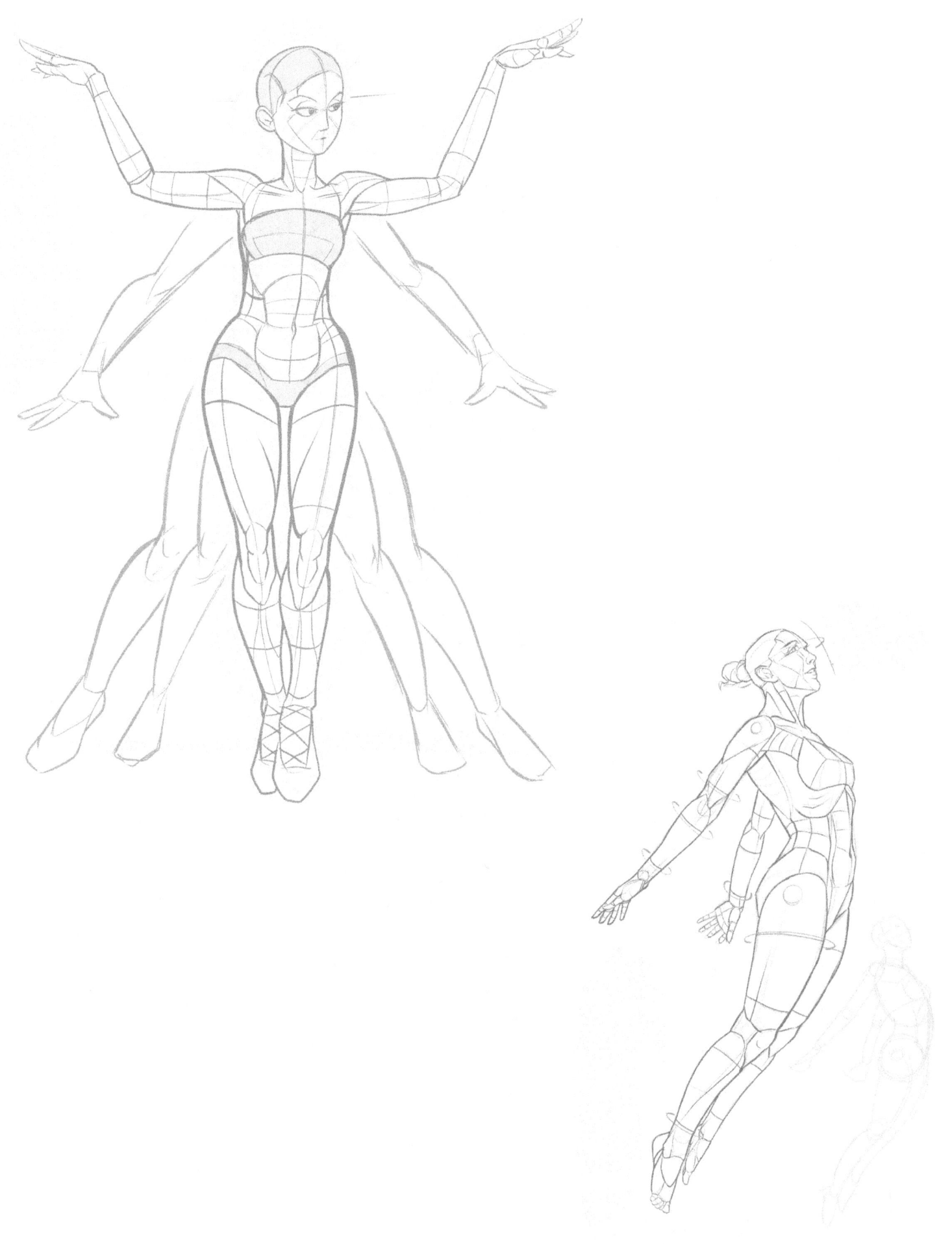

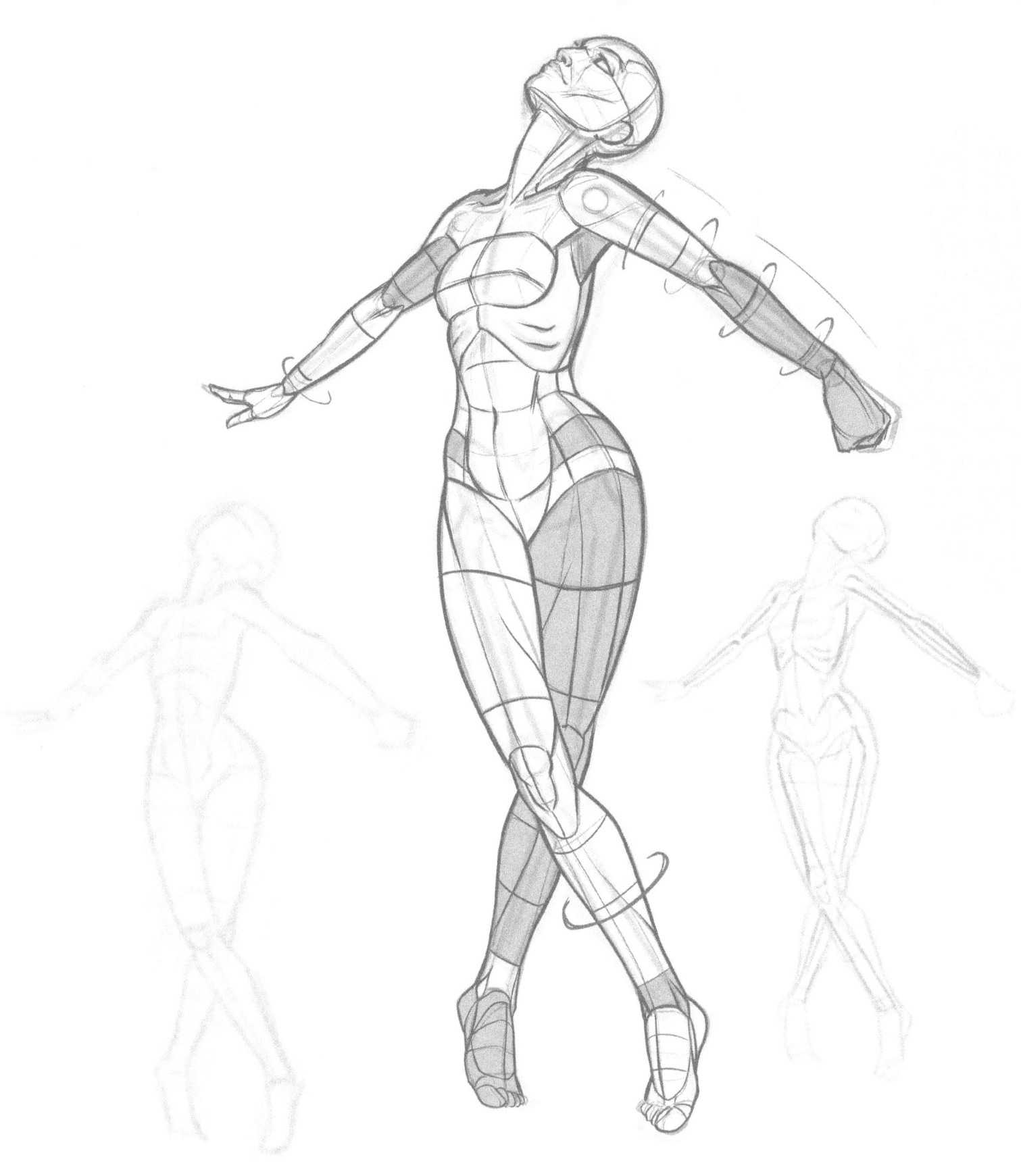

Dynamic Poses -Page 14

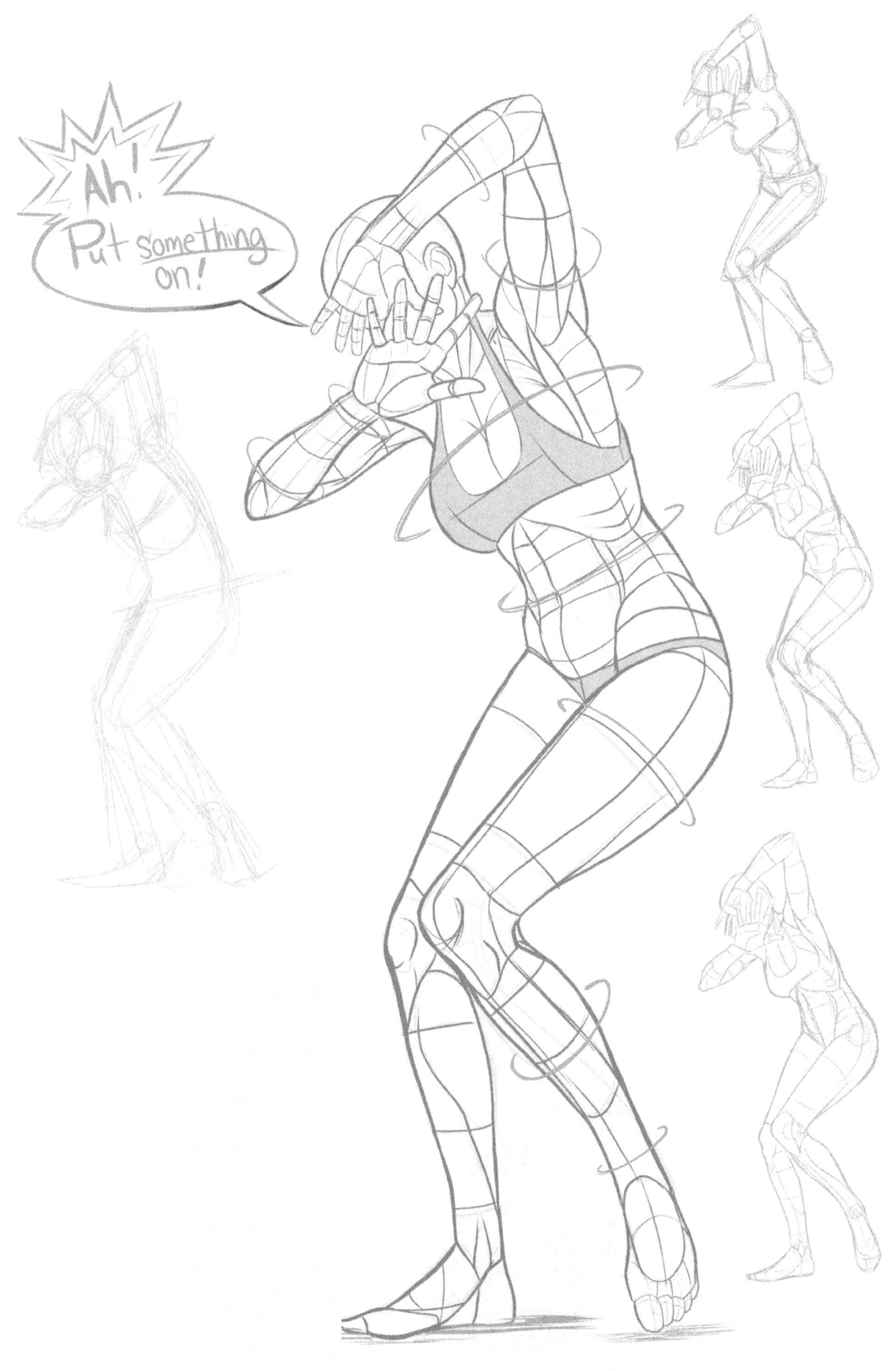

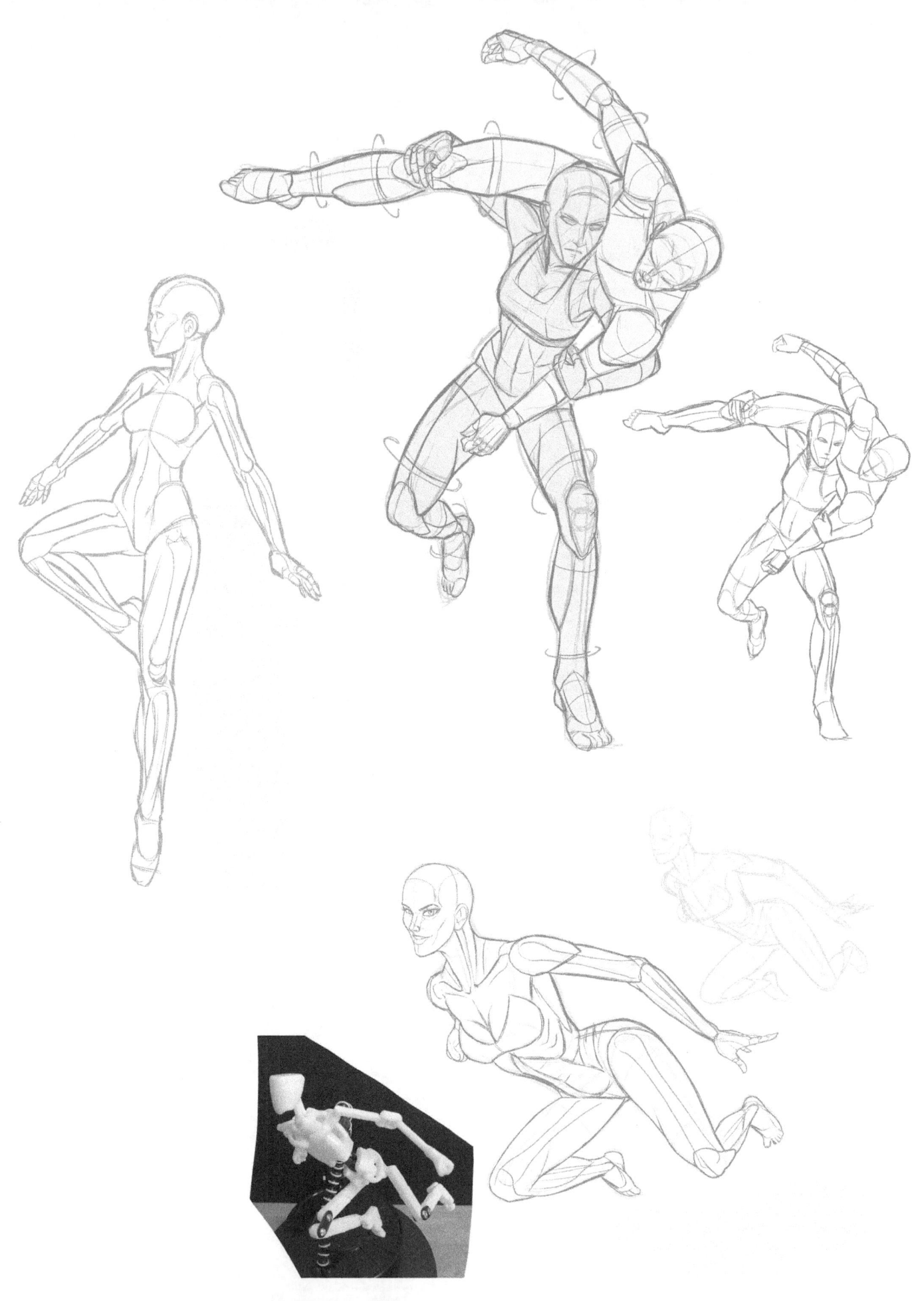

Dynamic Poses -Page 16

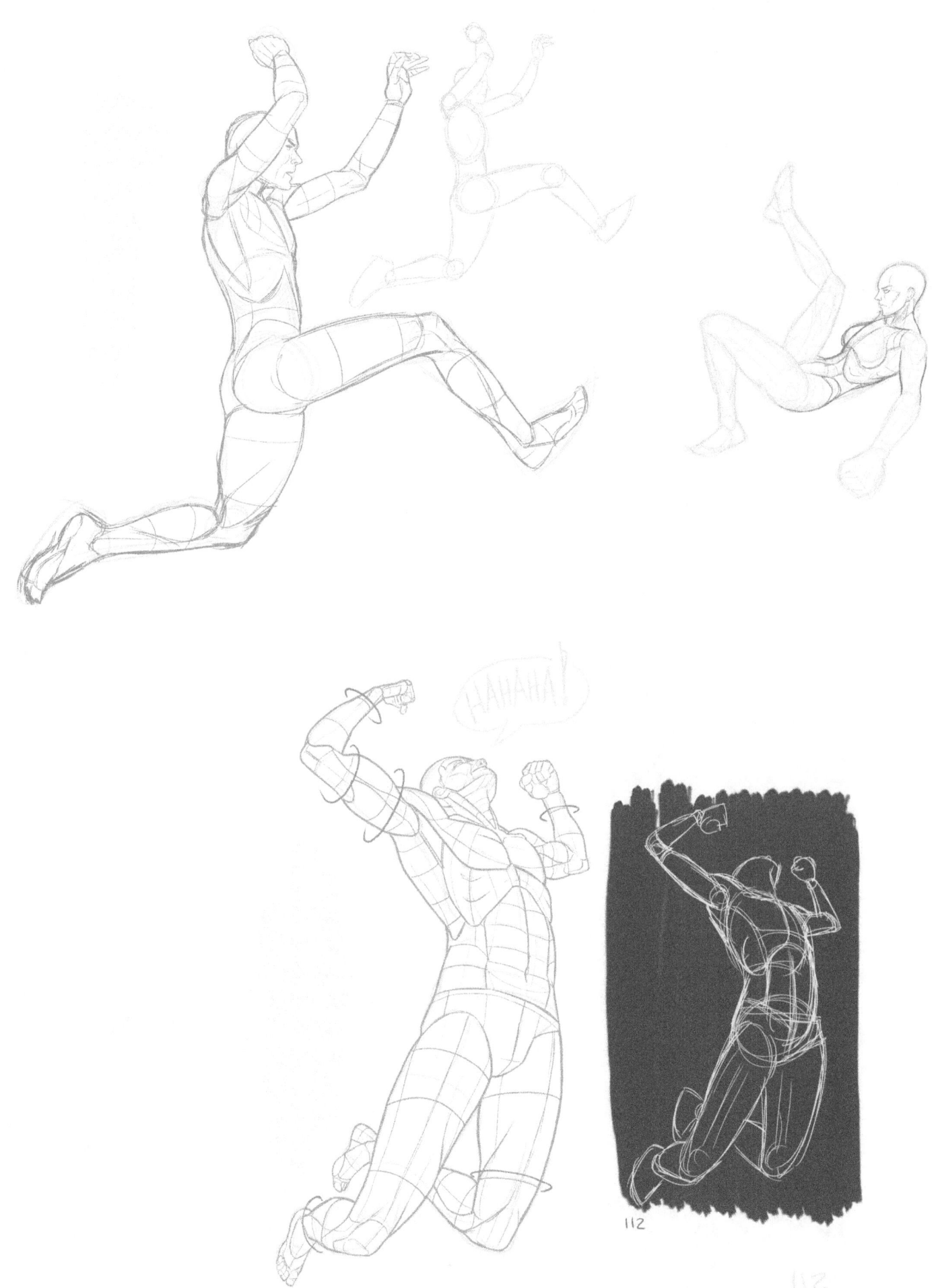

HAHAHA!

112

Dynamic Poses -Page 17

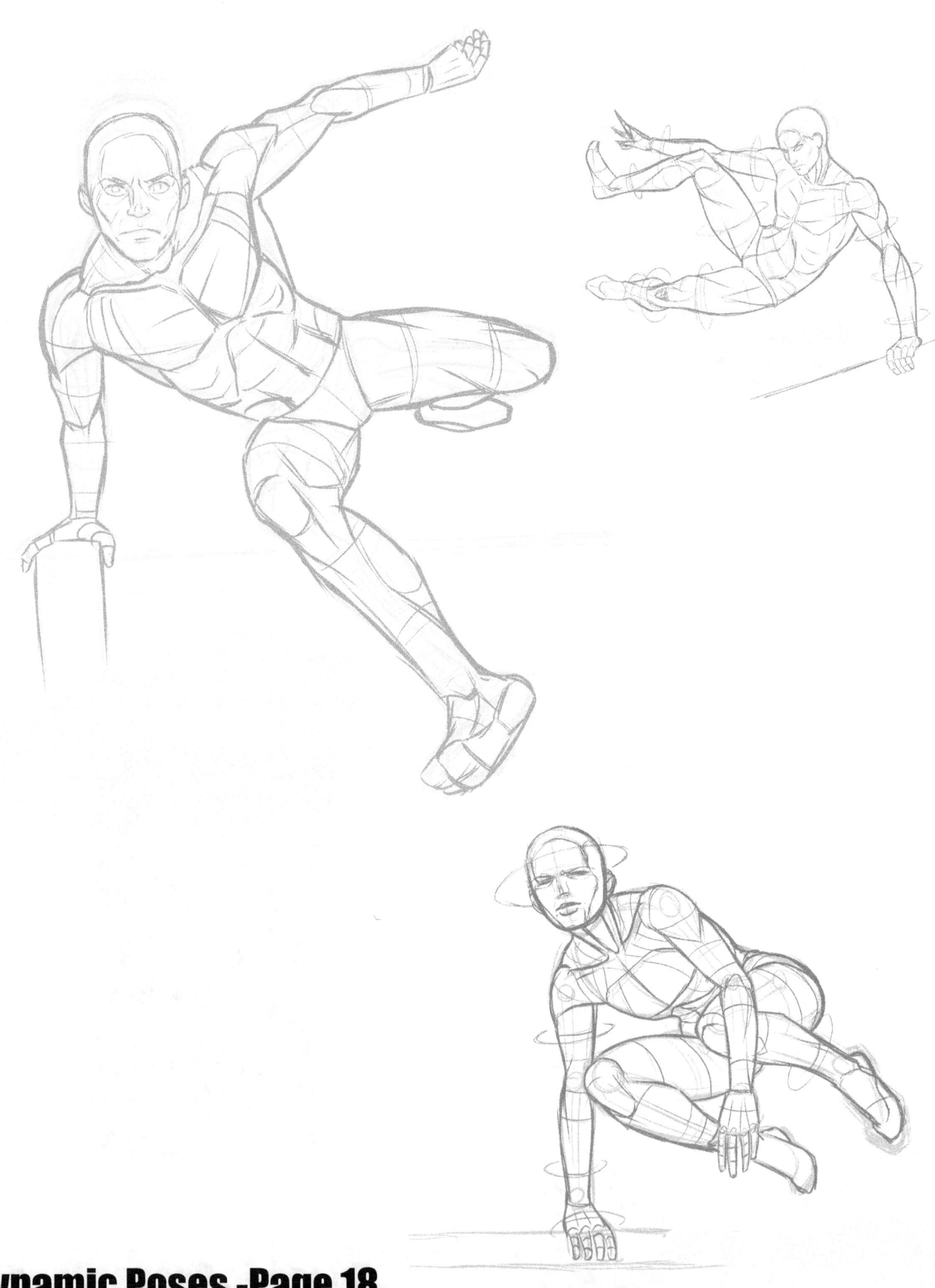

Dynamic Poses -Page 18

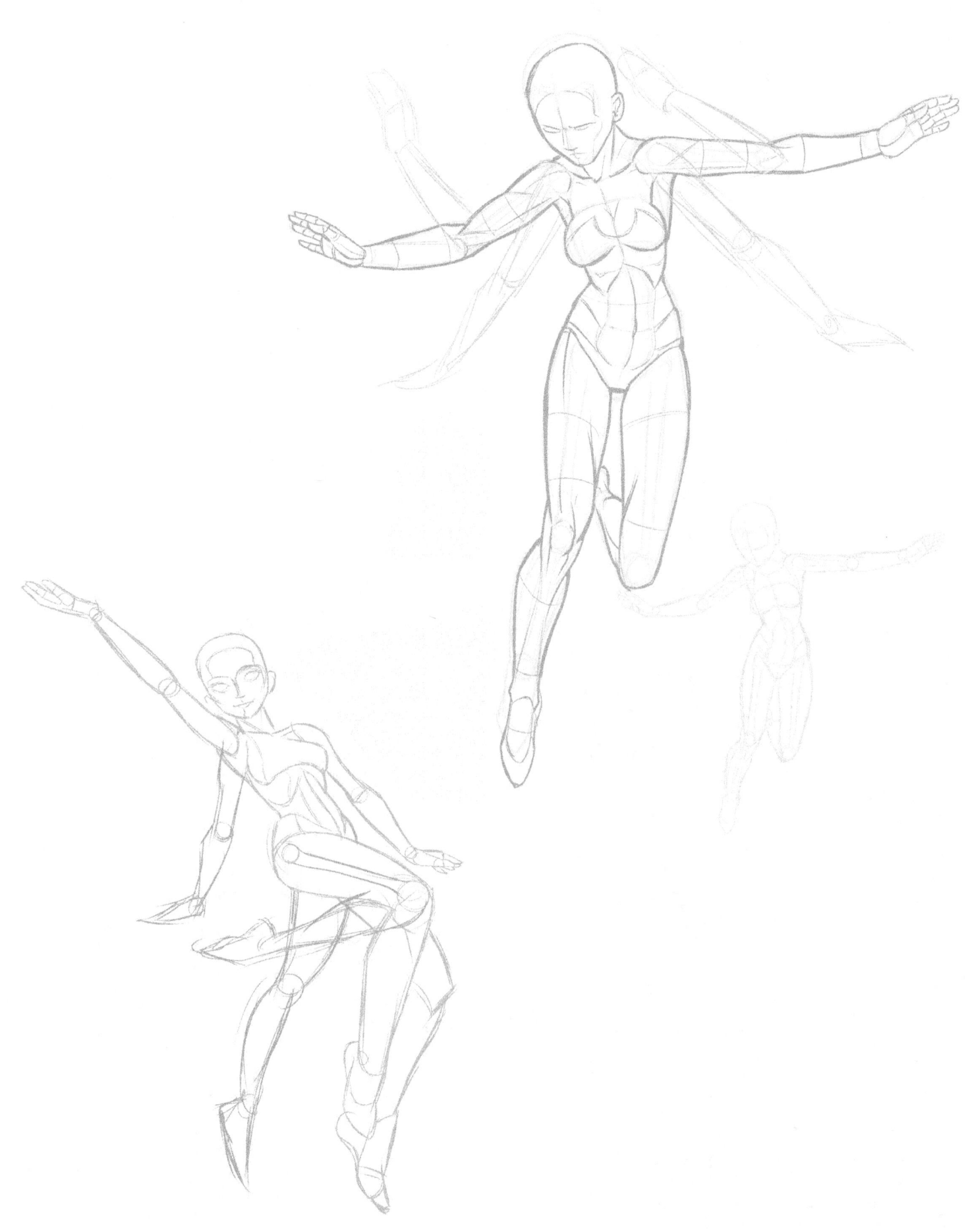

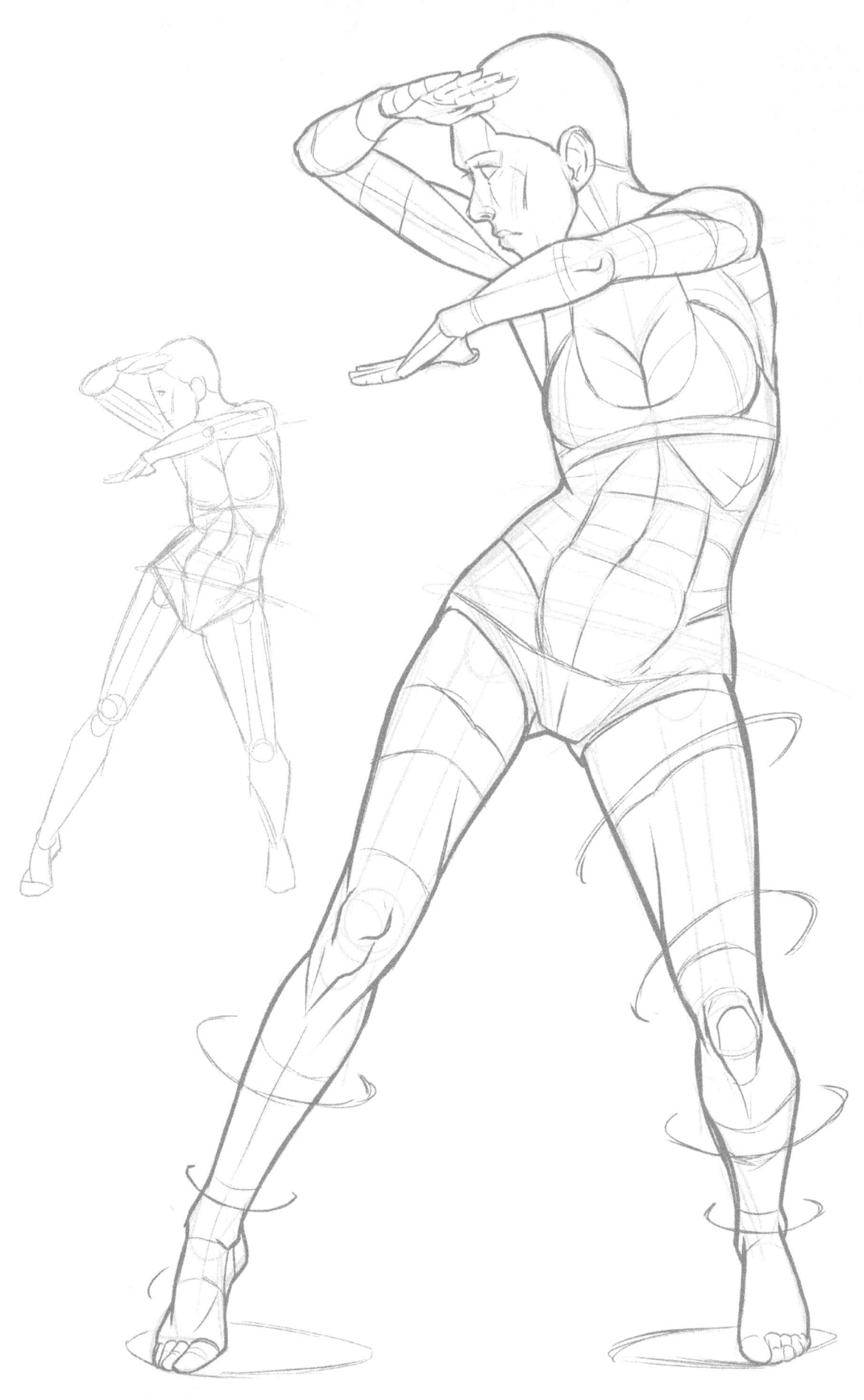

Dynamic Poses -Page 20

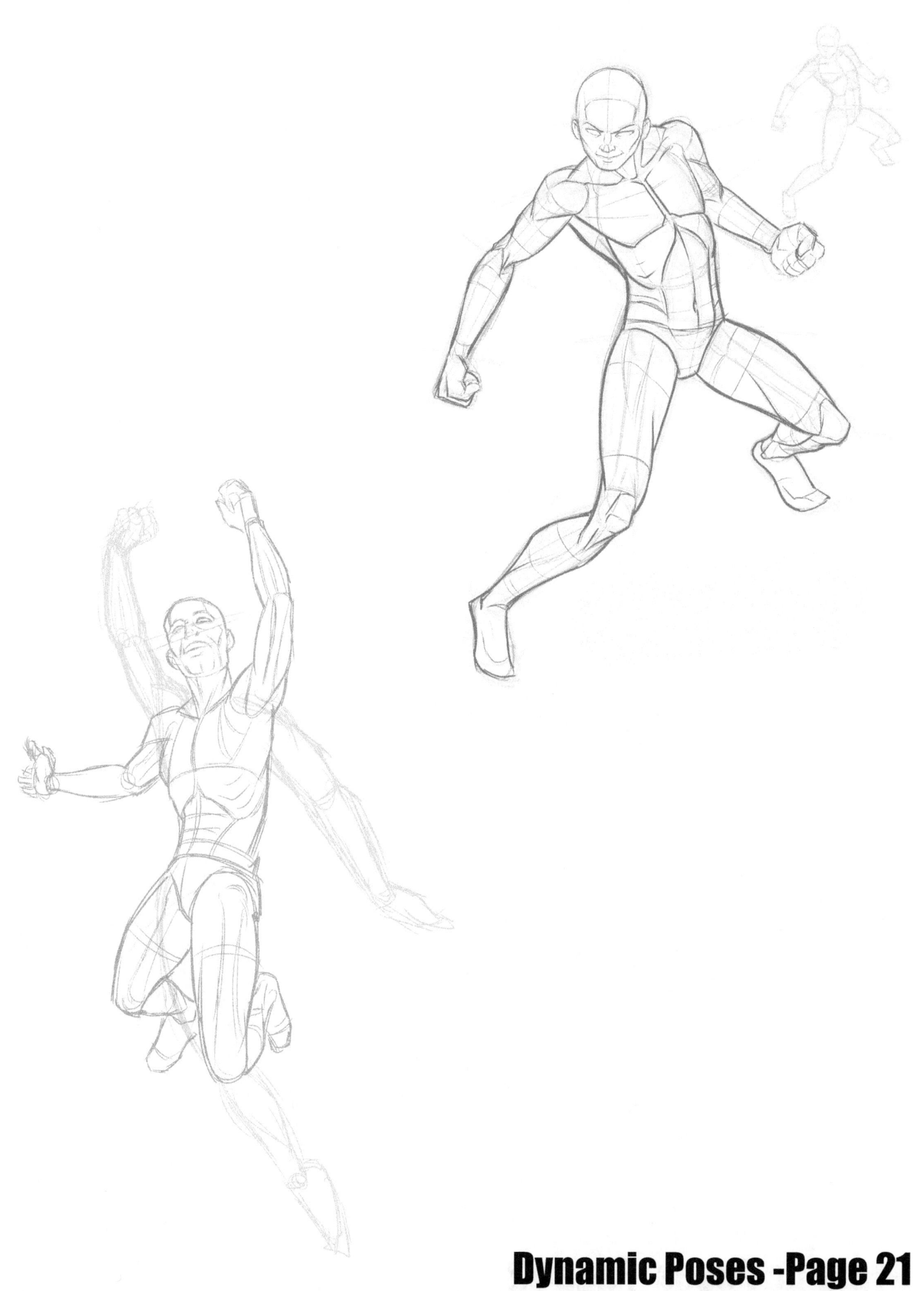

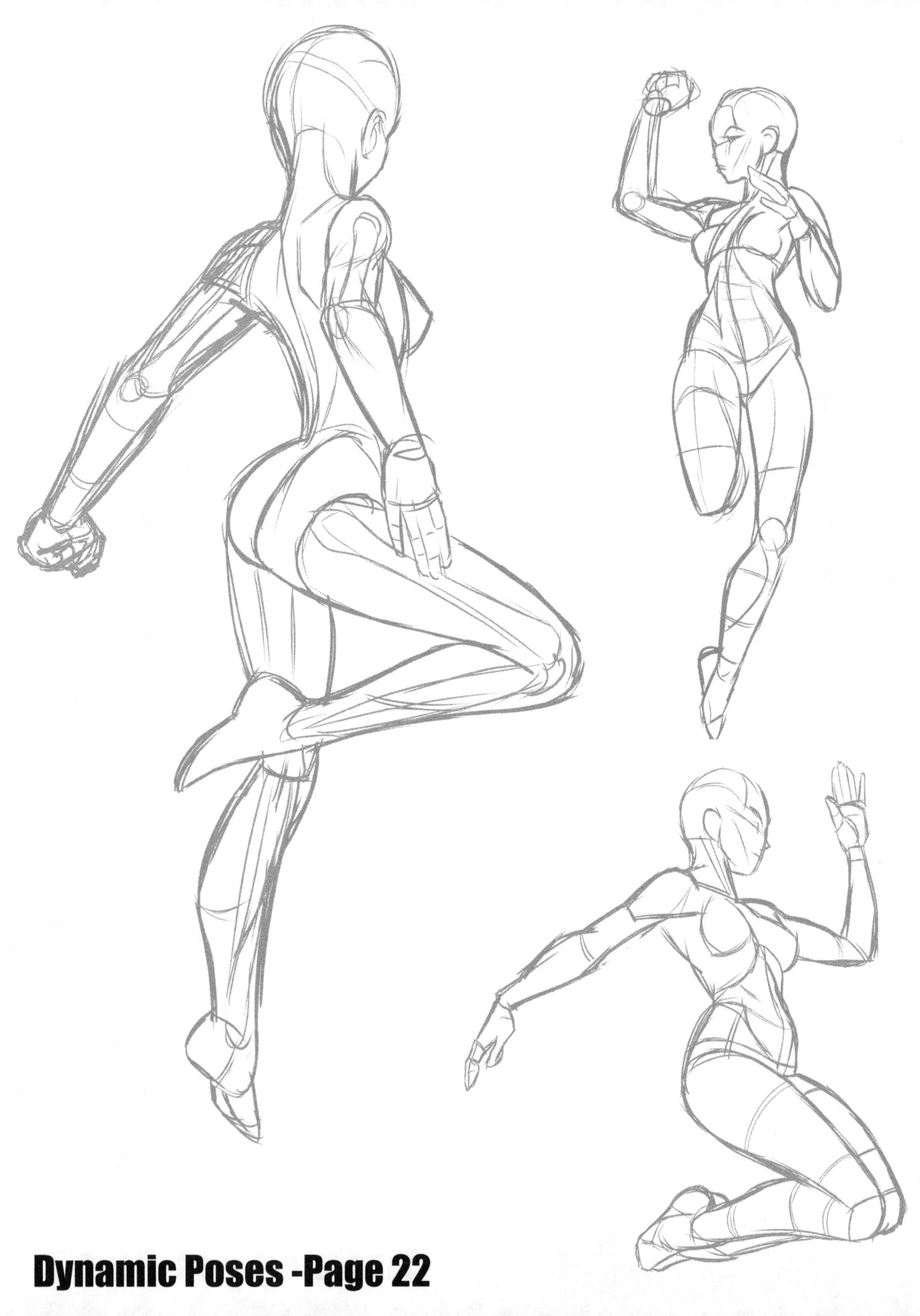

Dynamic Poses -Page 22

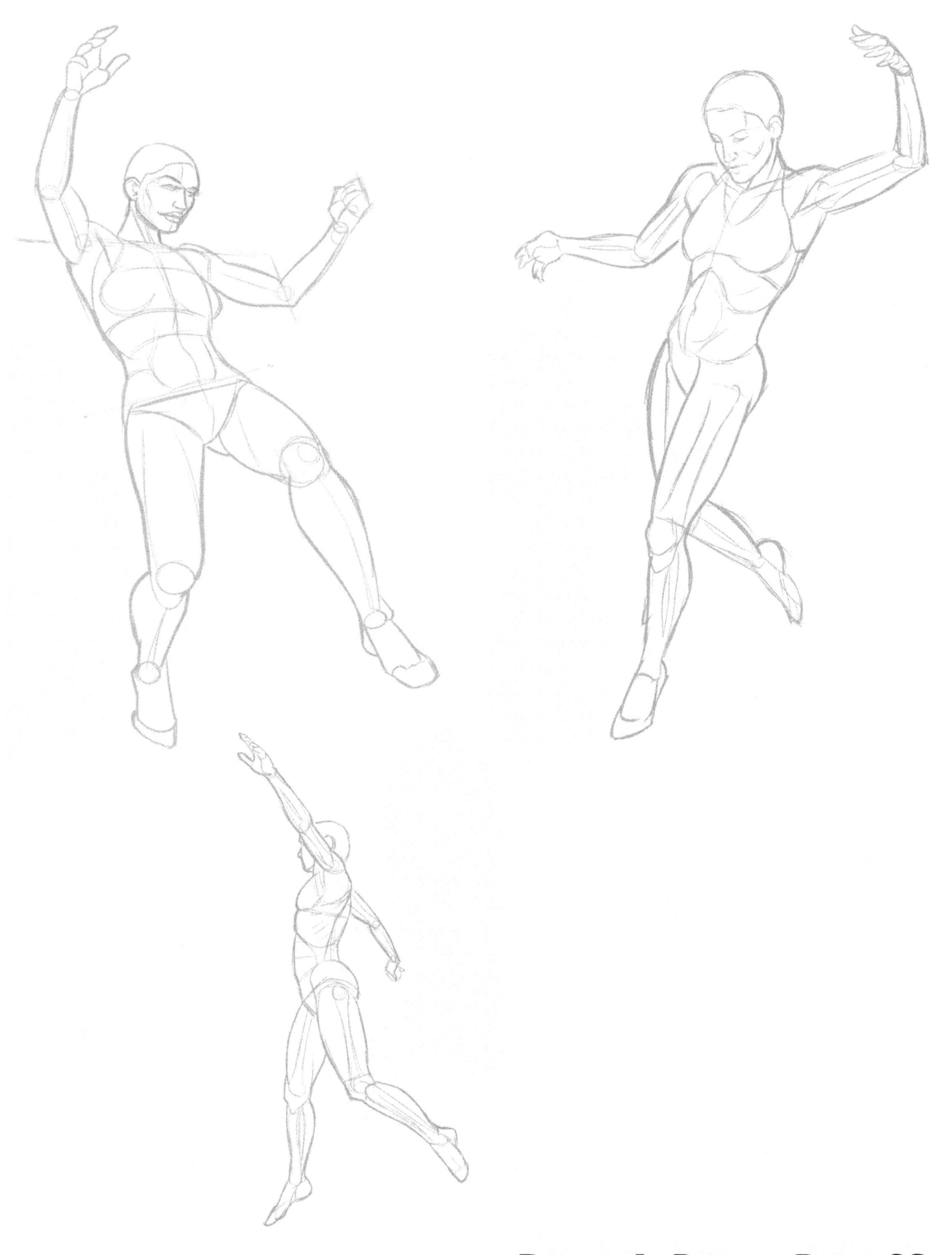

Dynamic Poses -Page 23

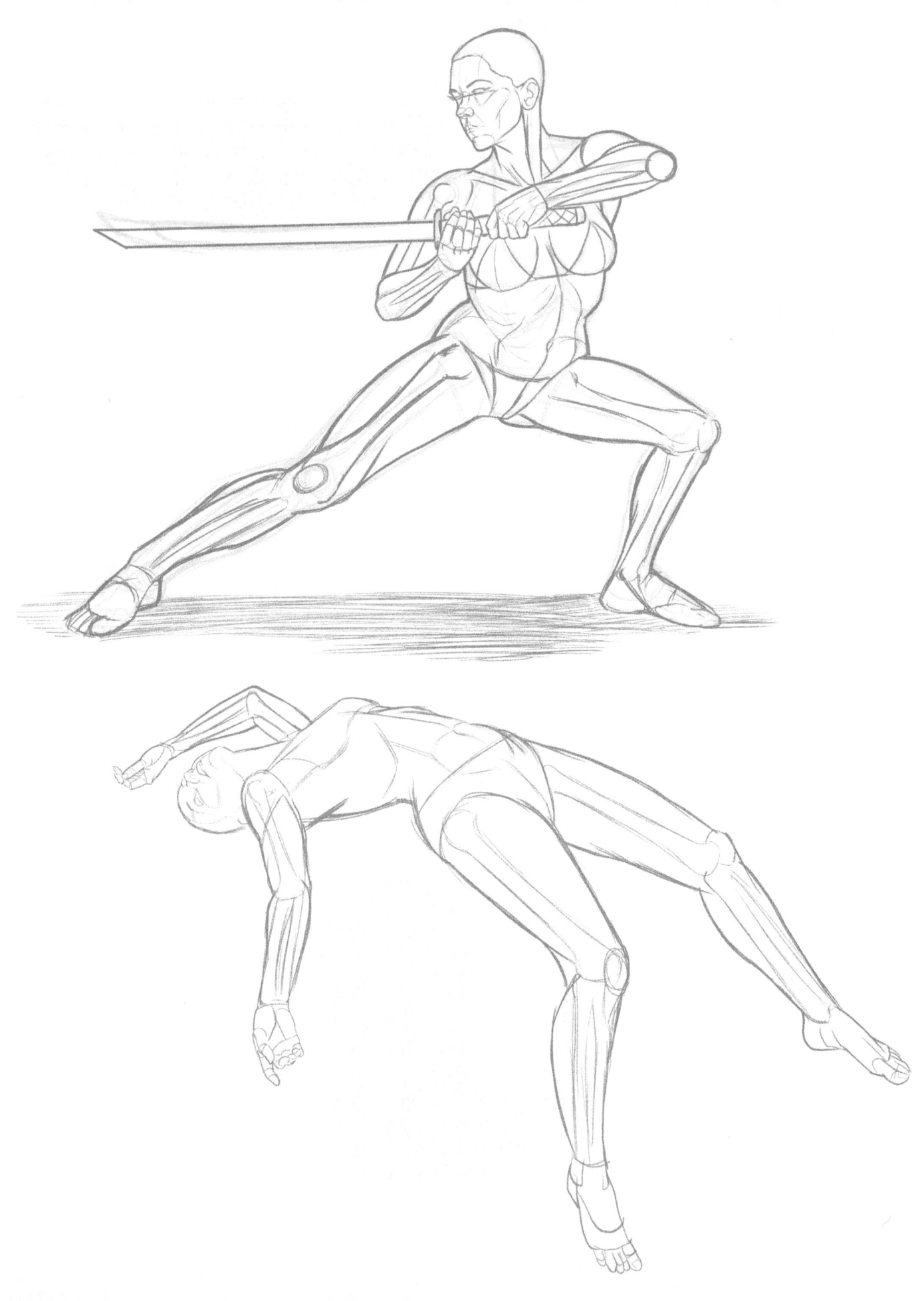

Dynamic Poses -Page 24

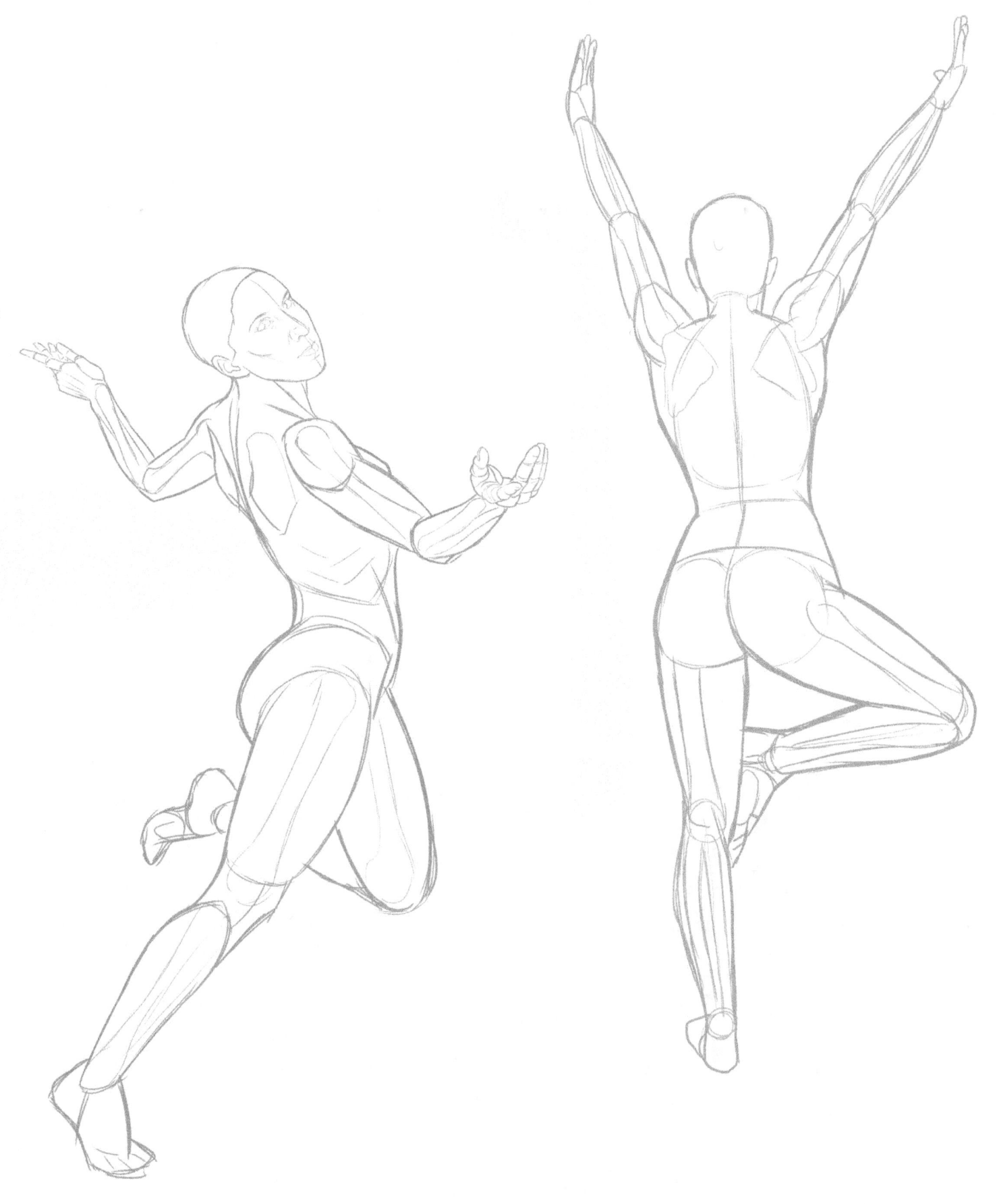

Dynamic Poses -Page 25

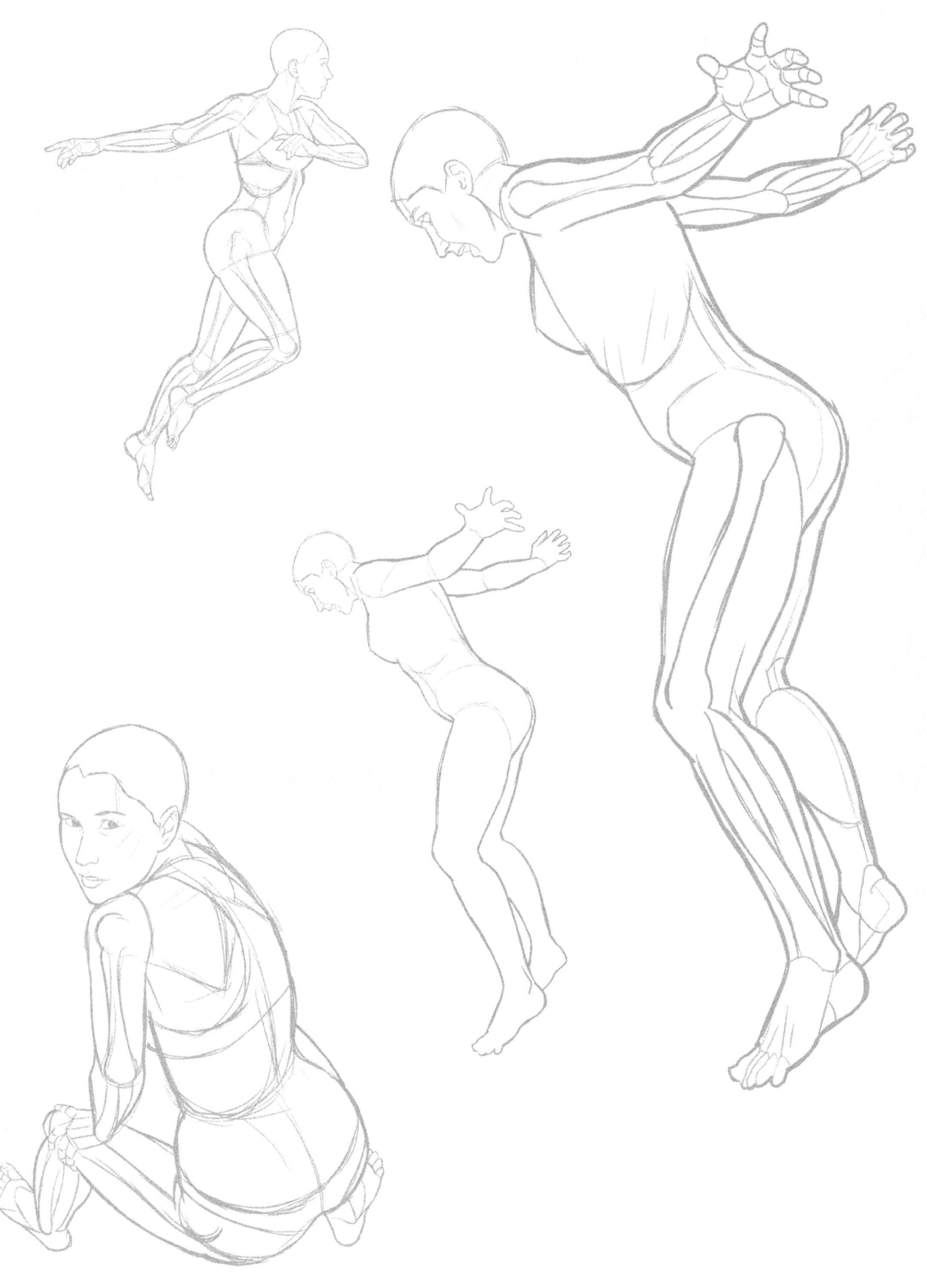

Dynamic Poses -Page 26

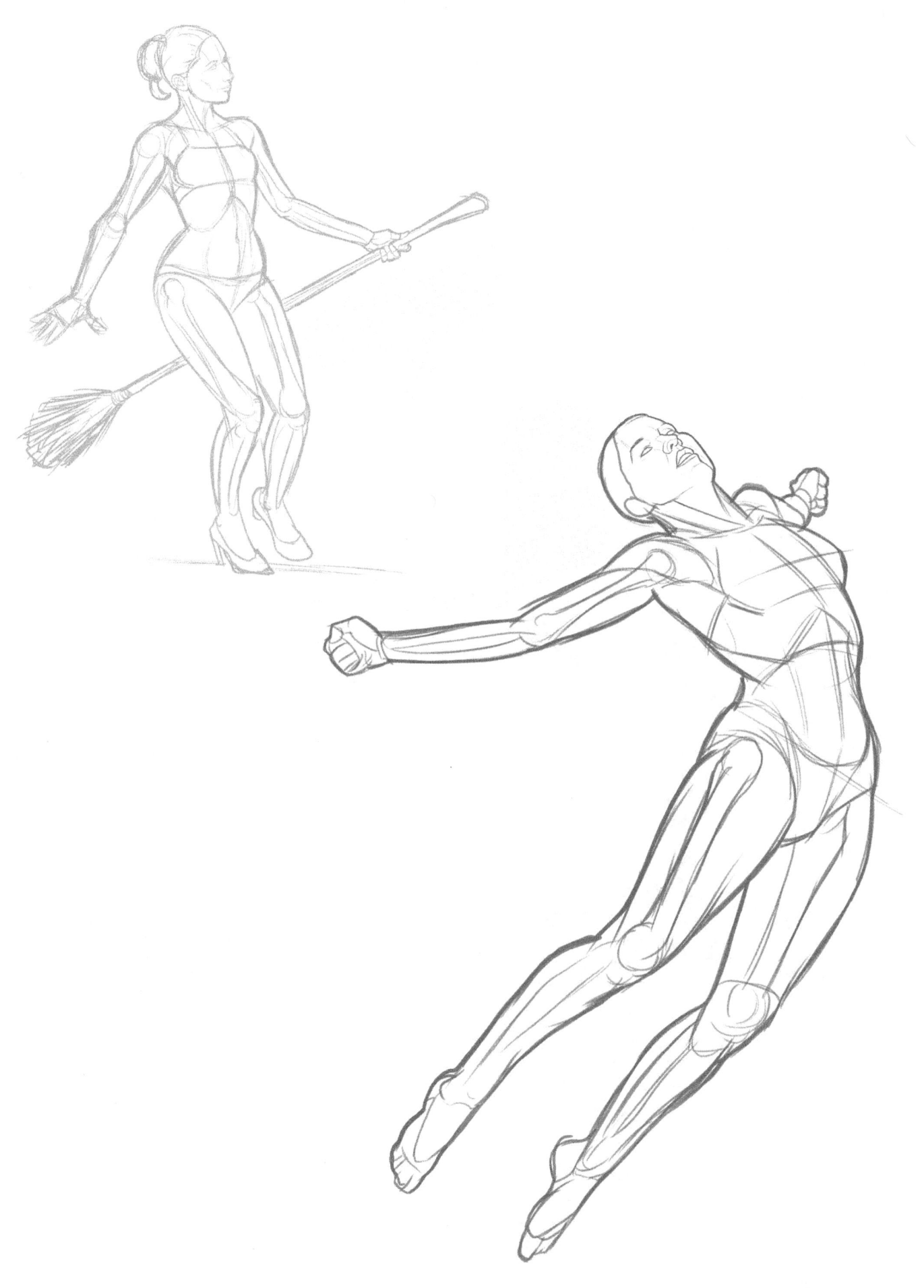

Dynamic Poses -Page 27

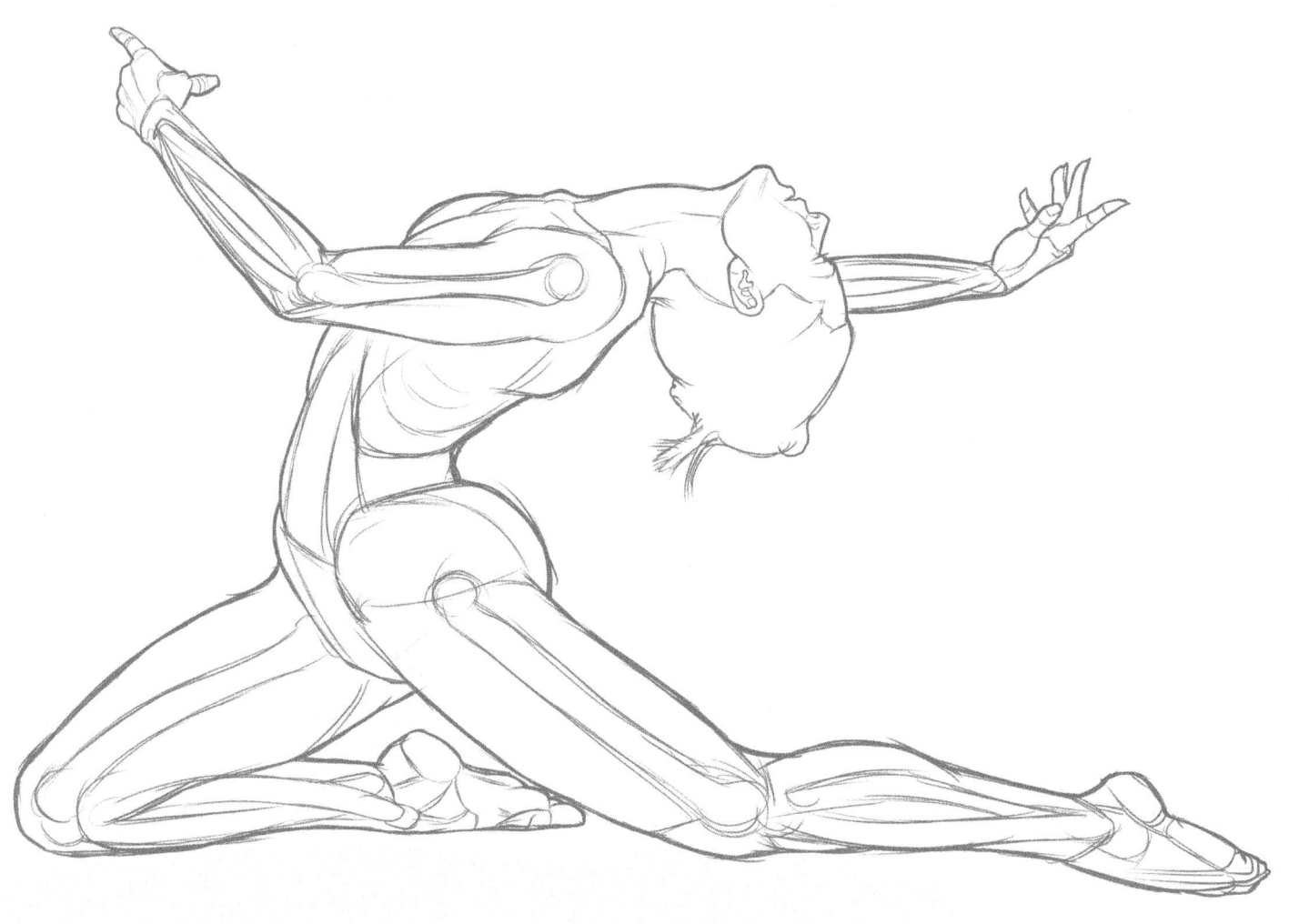

Dynamic Poses -Page 28

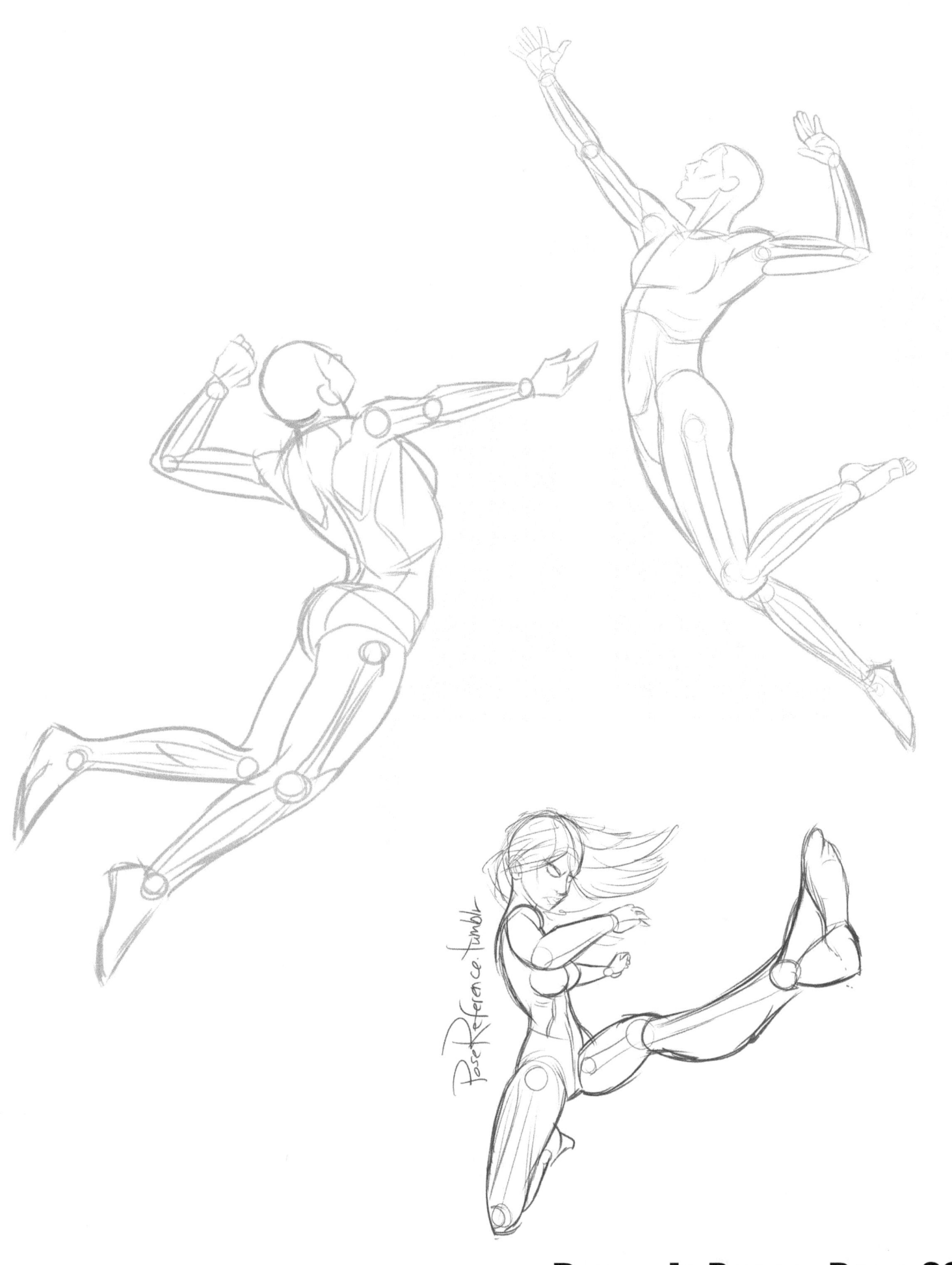

Pose Reference.Tumblr

Dynamic Poses -Page 29

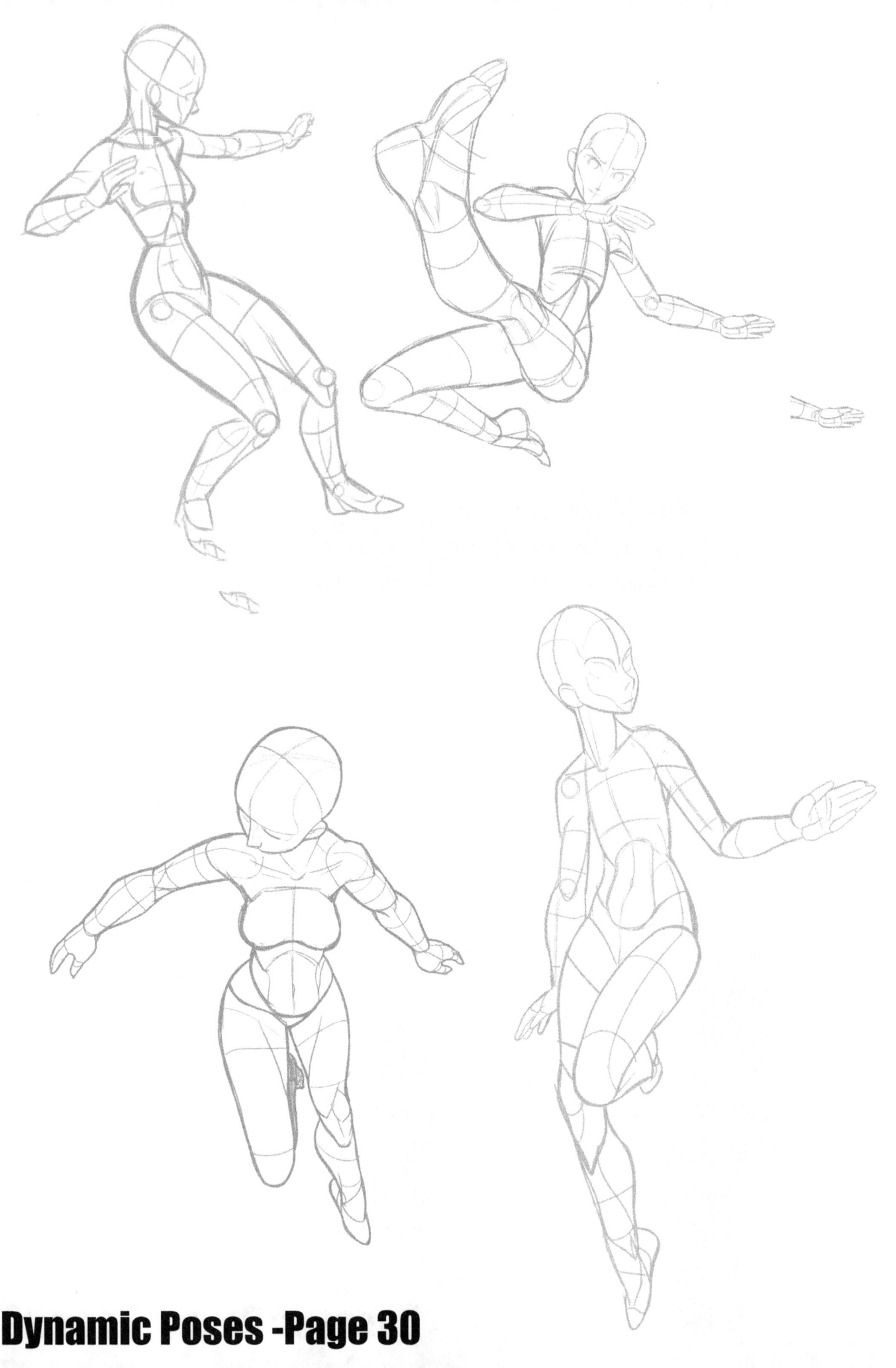

Dynamic Poses -Page 30

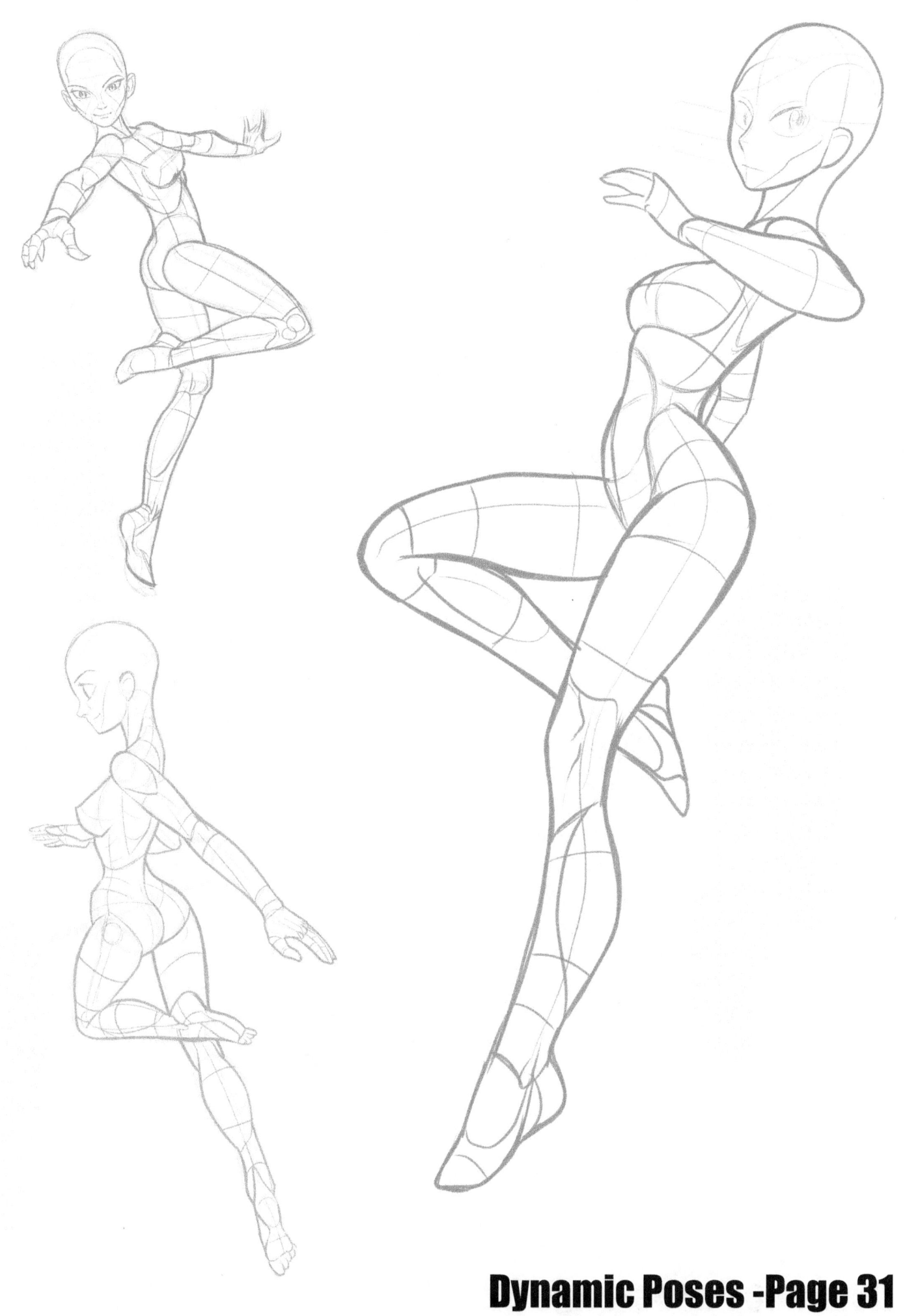

Dynamic Poses -Page 31

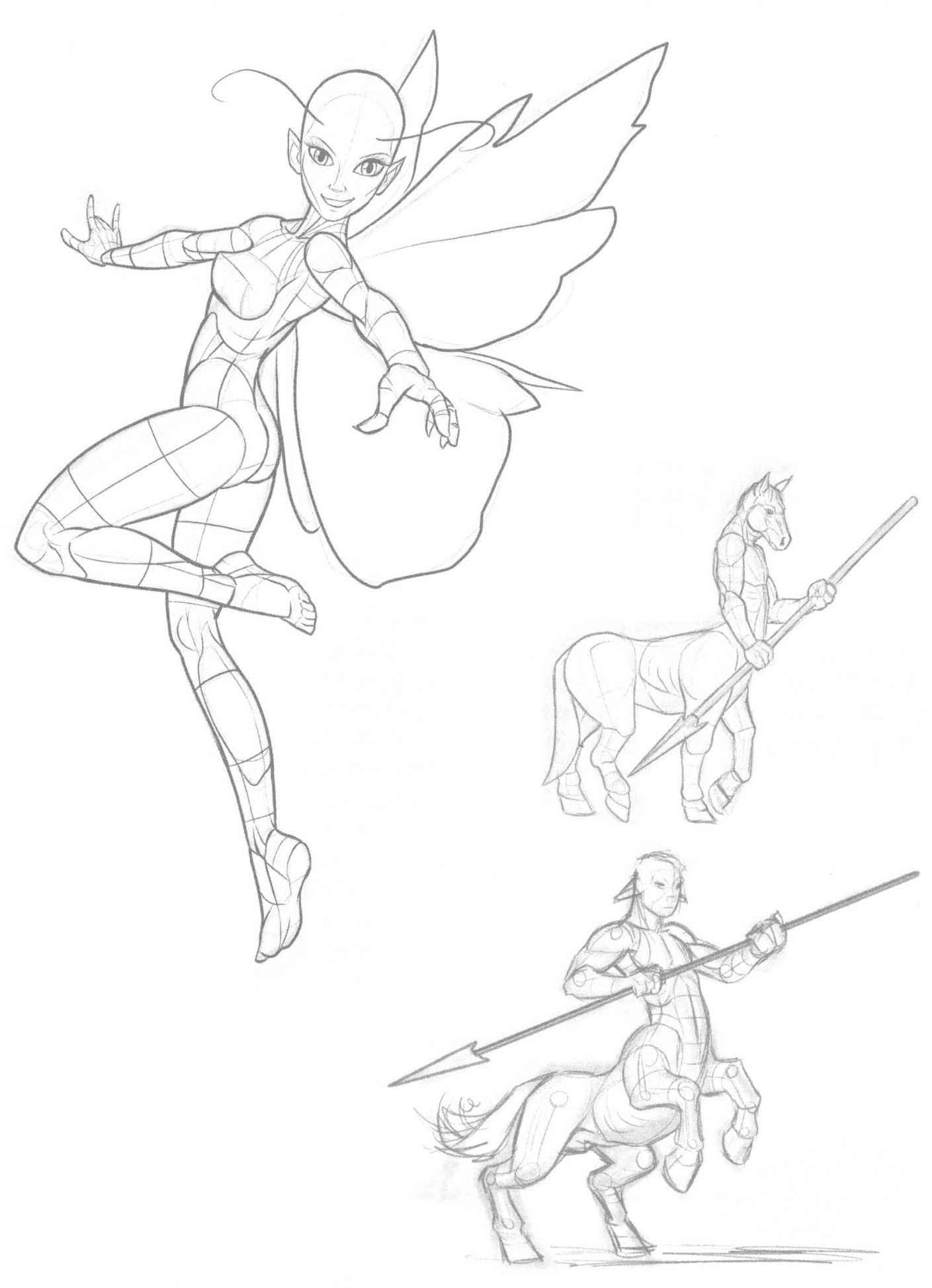

Dynamic Poses -Page 32

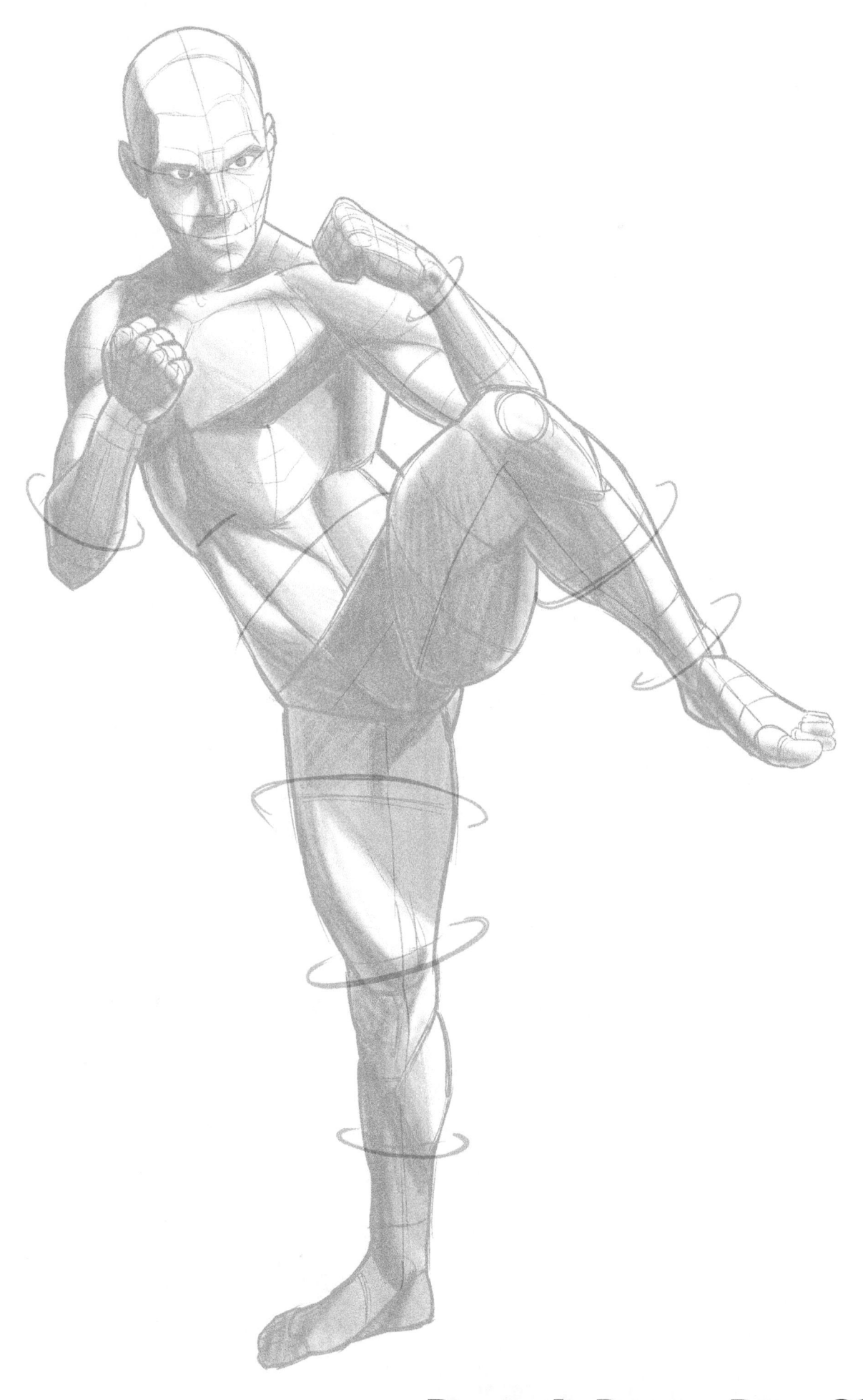

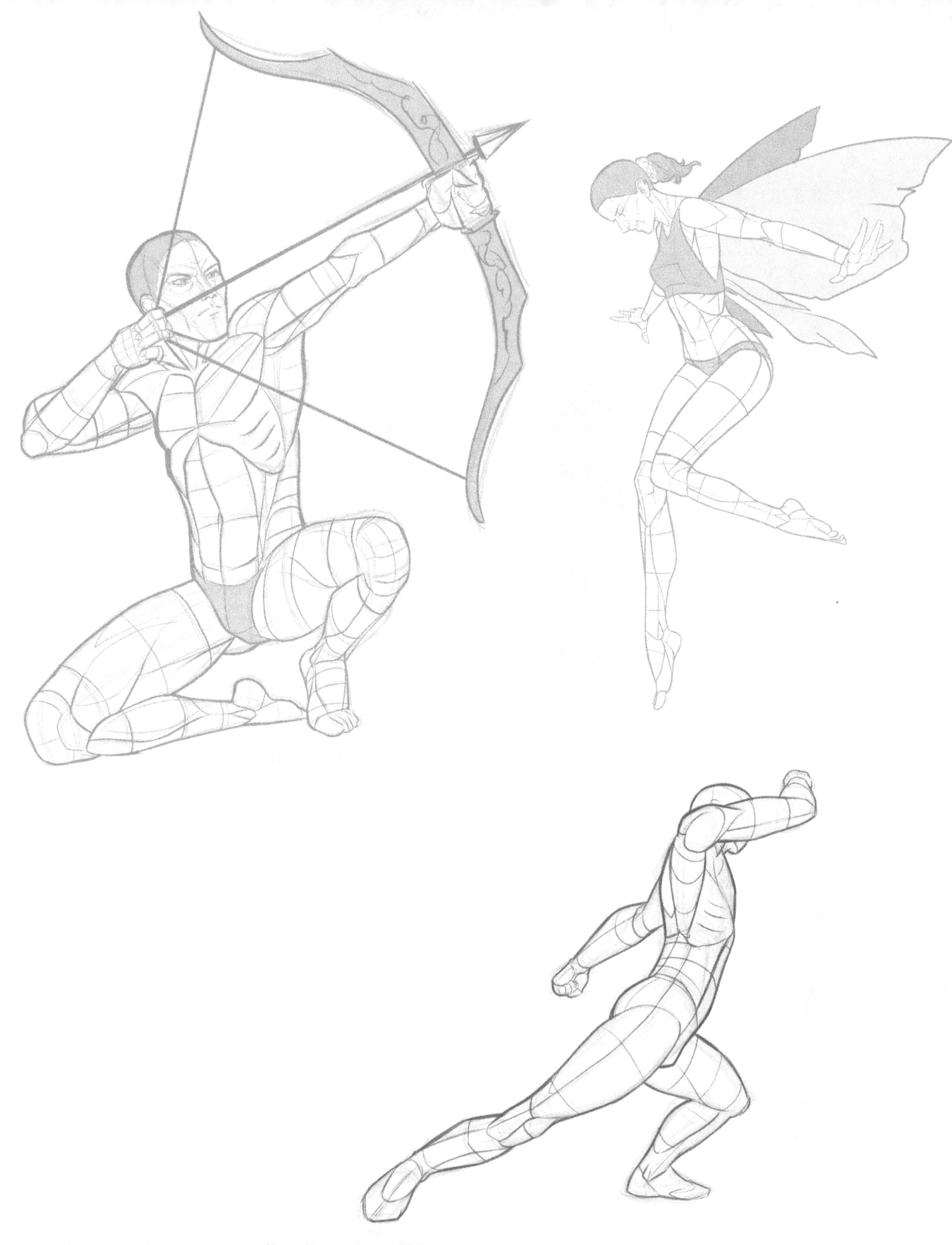

Dynamic Poses -Page 34

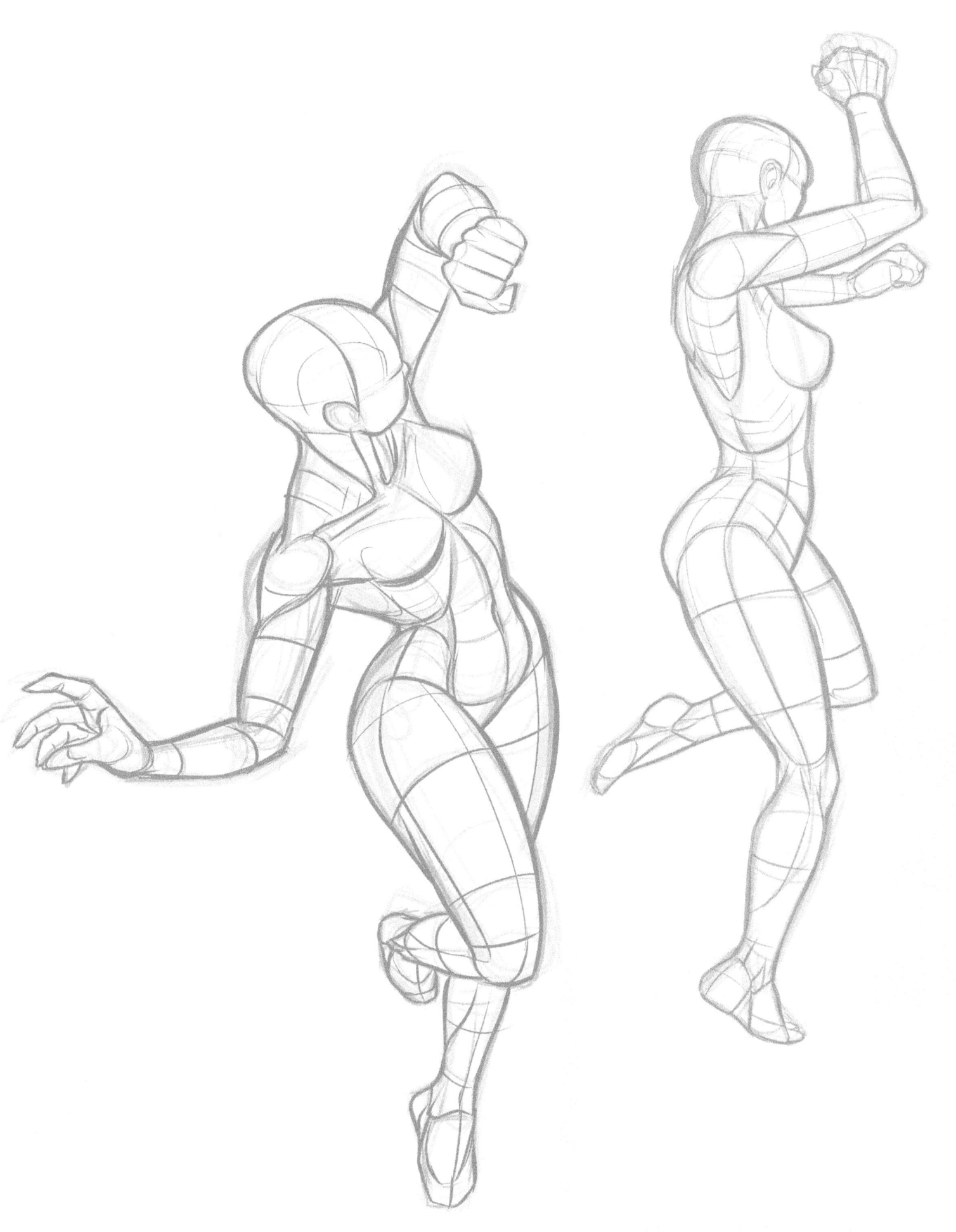

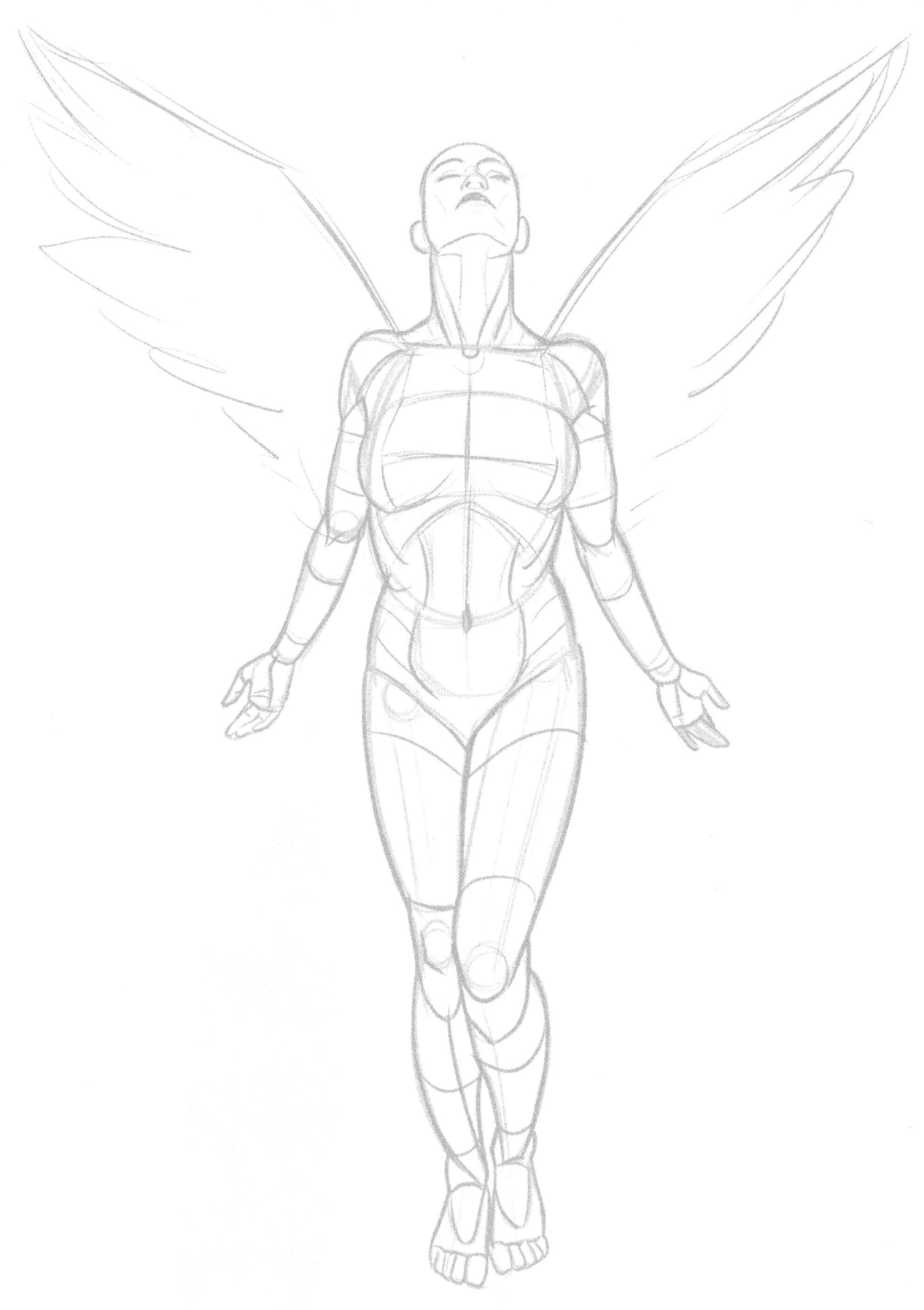

Dynamic Poses -Page 36

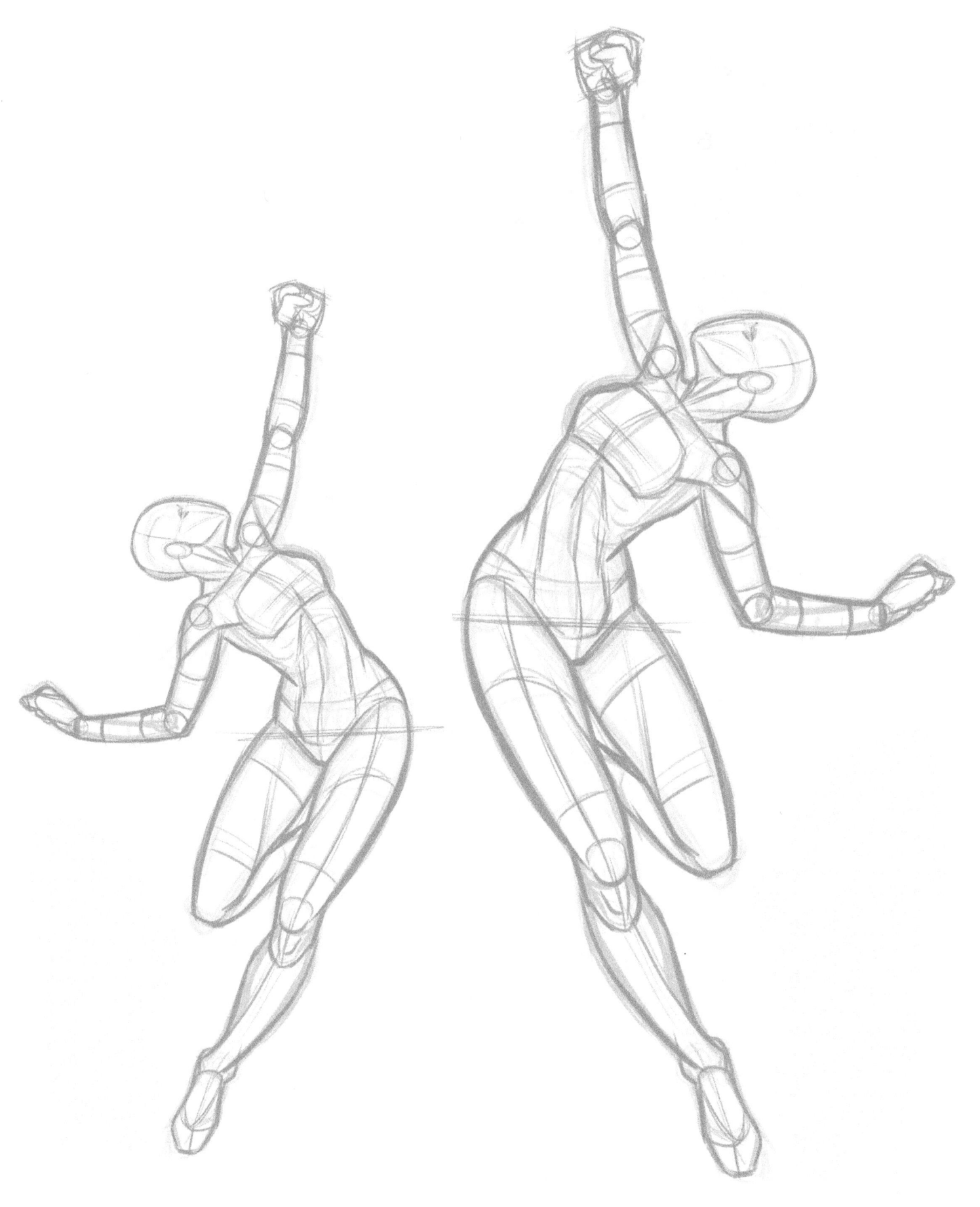

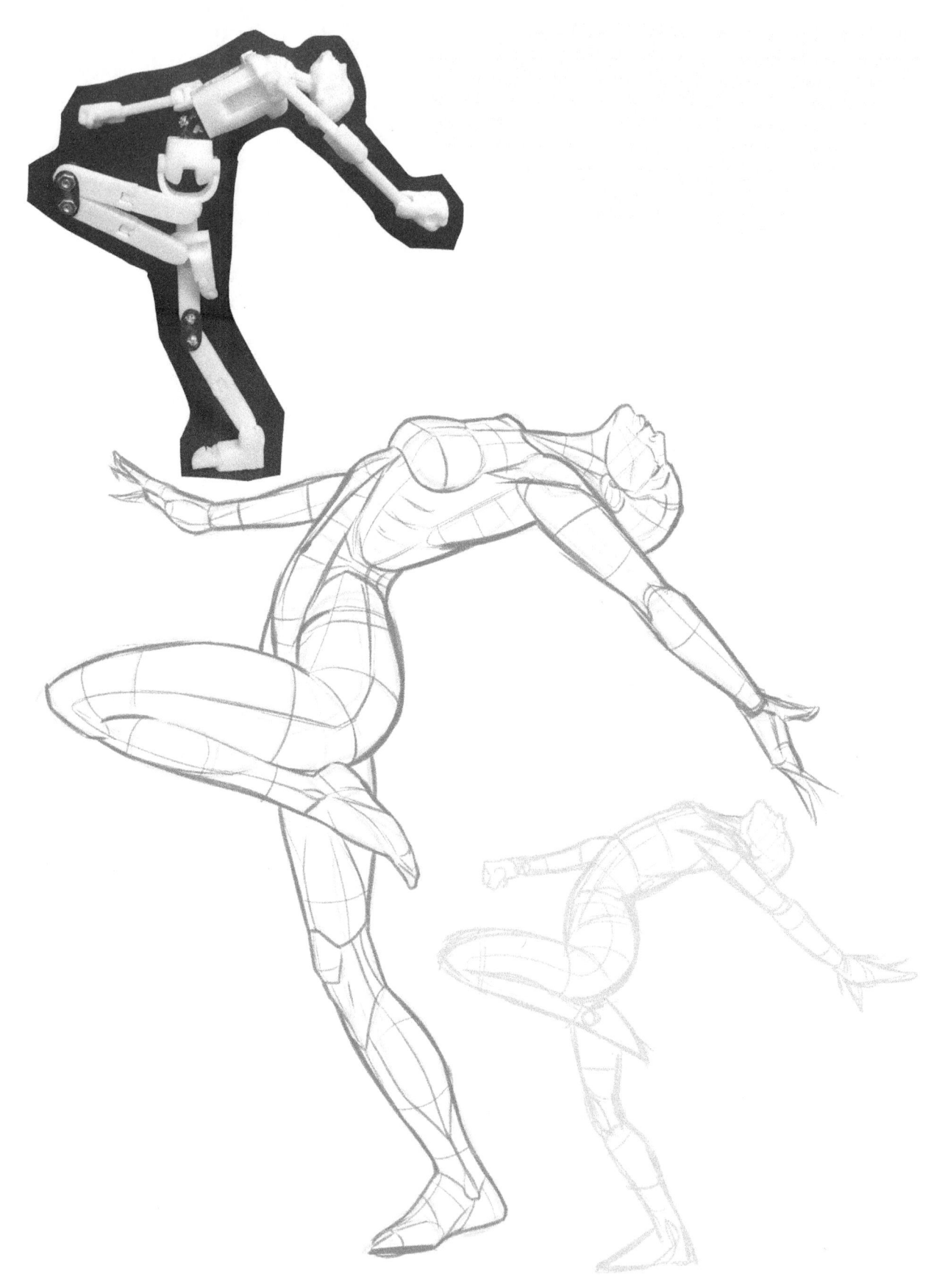

Dynamic Poses -Page 38

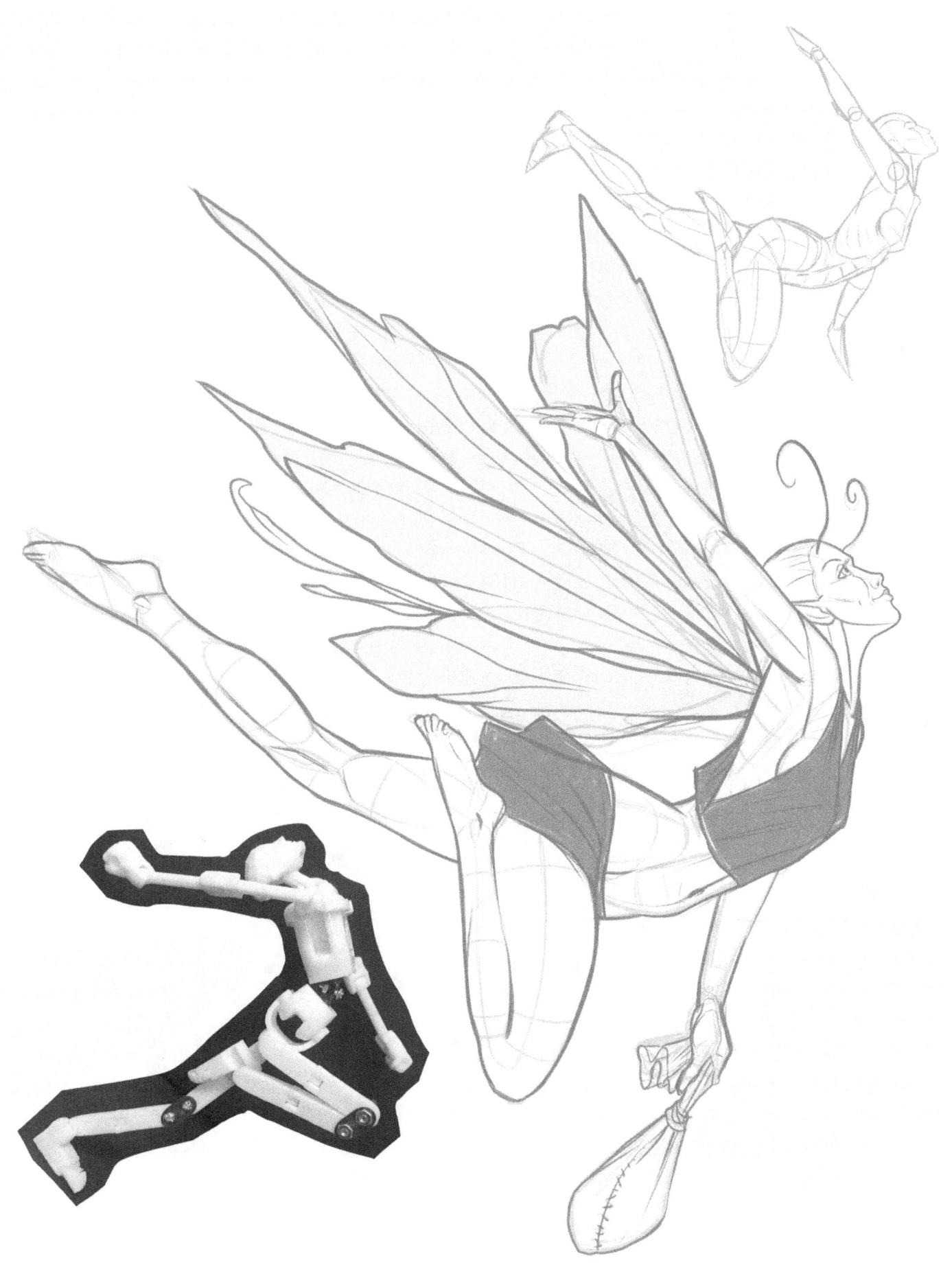

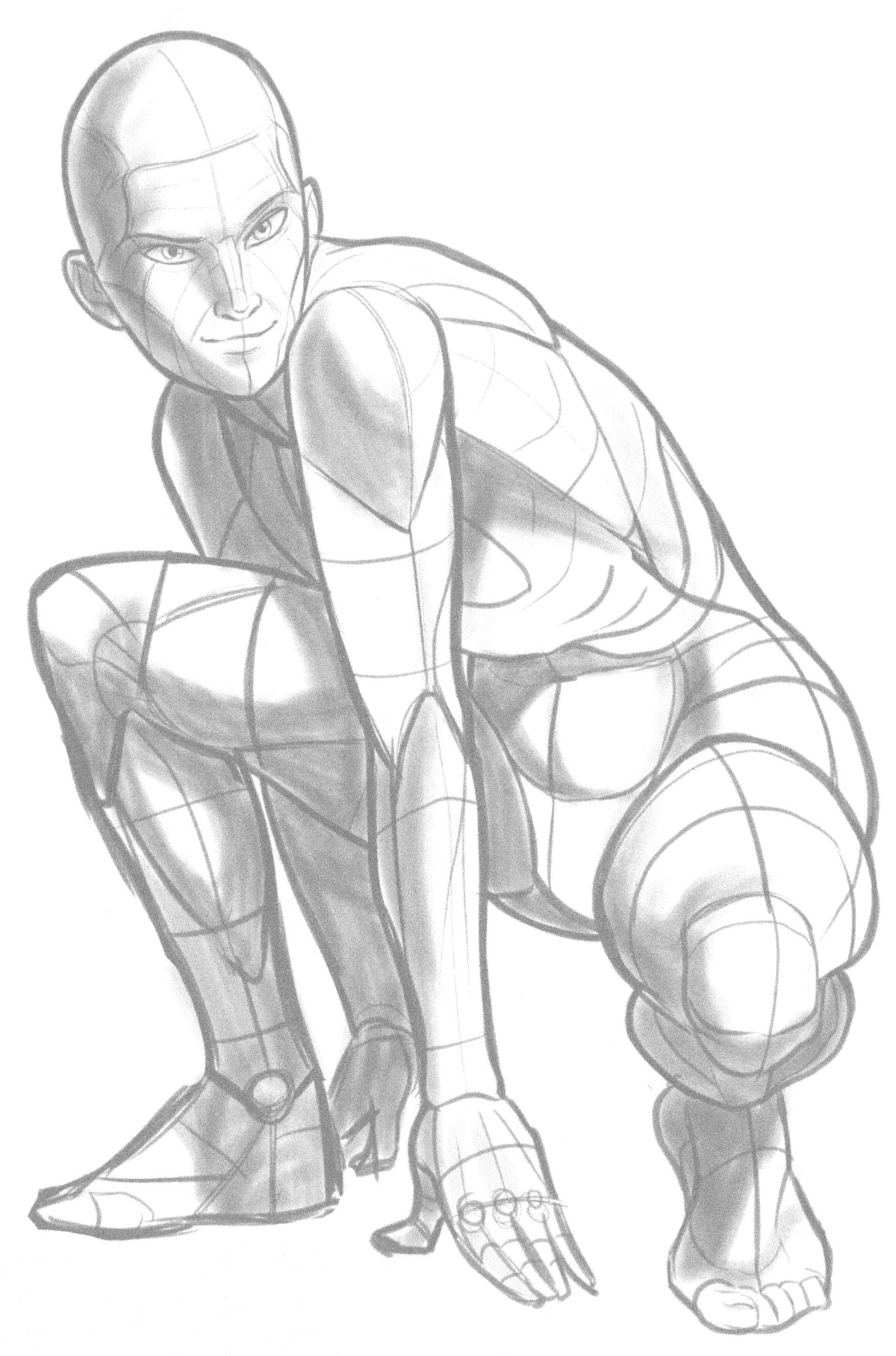

Dynamic Poses -Page 40

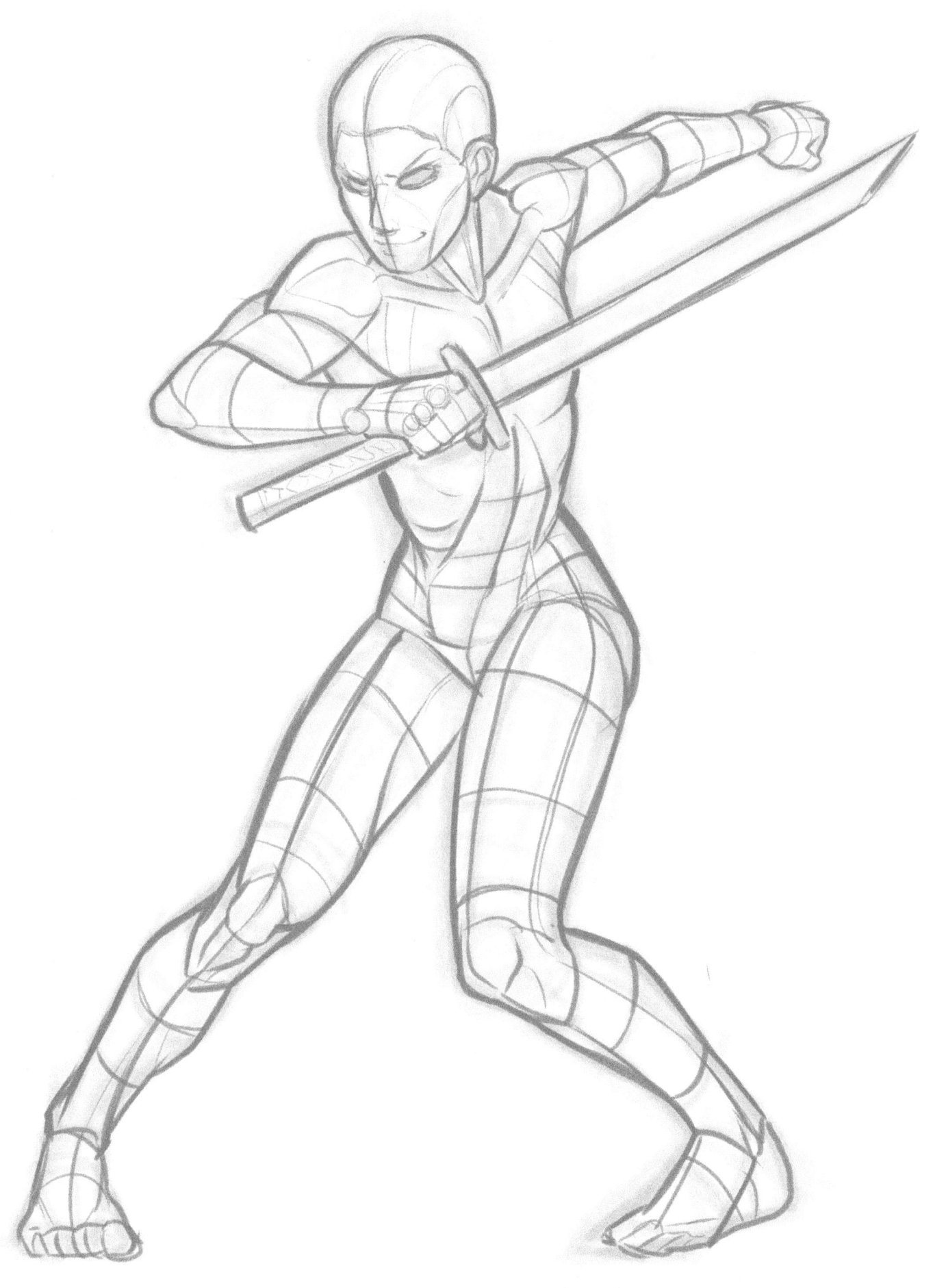

Dynamic Poses -Page 41

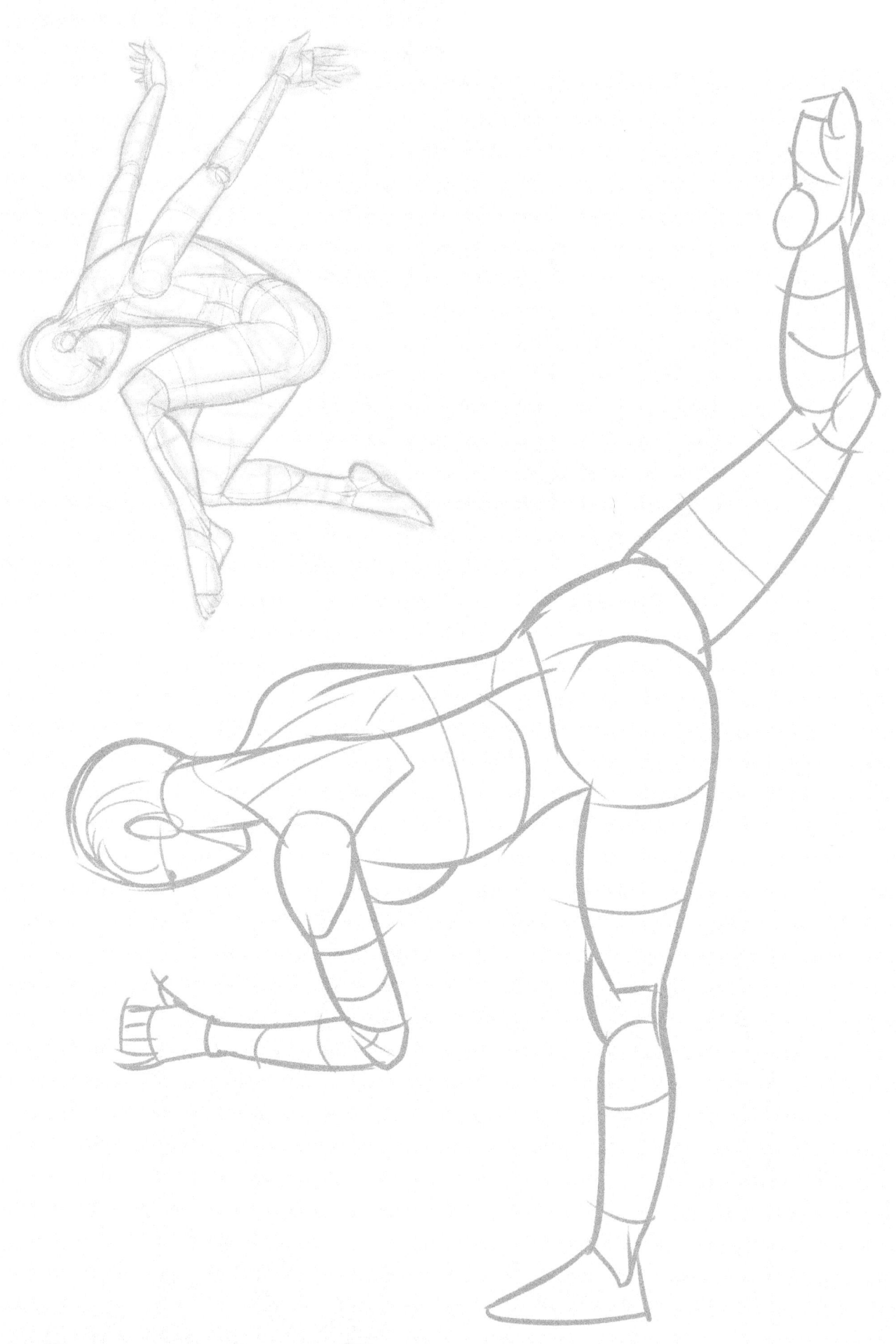

Dynamic Poses -Page 42

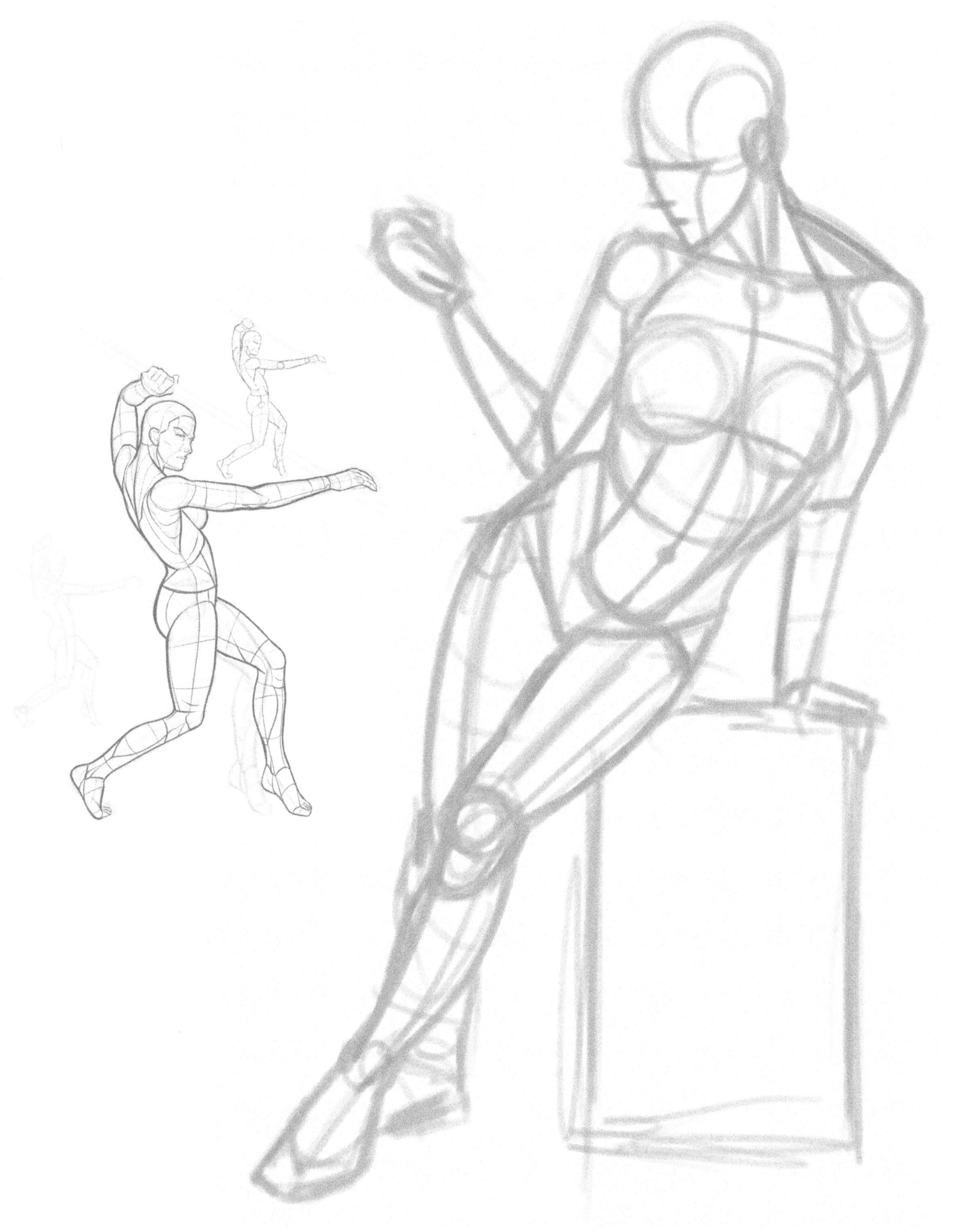

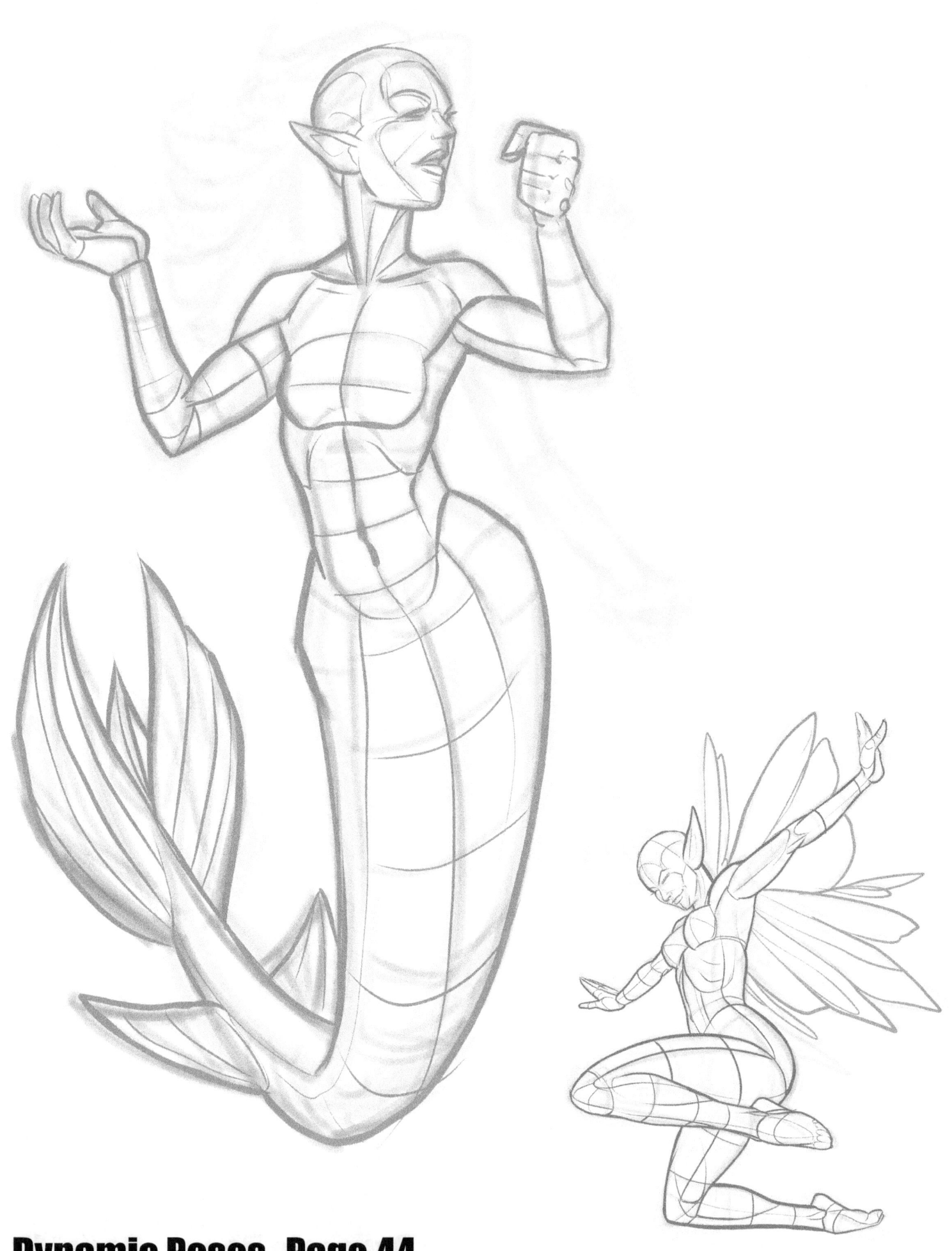

Dynamic Poses -Page 44

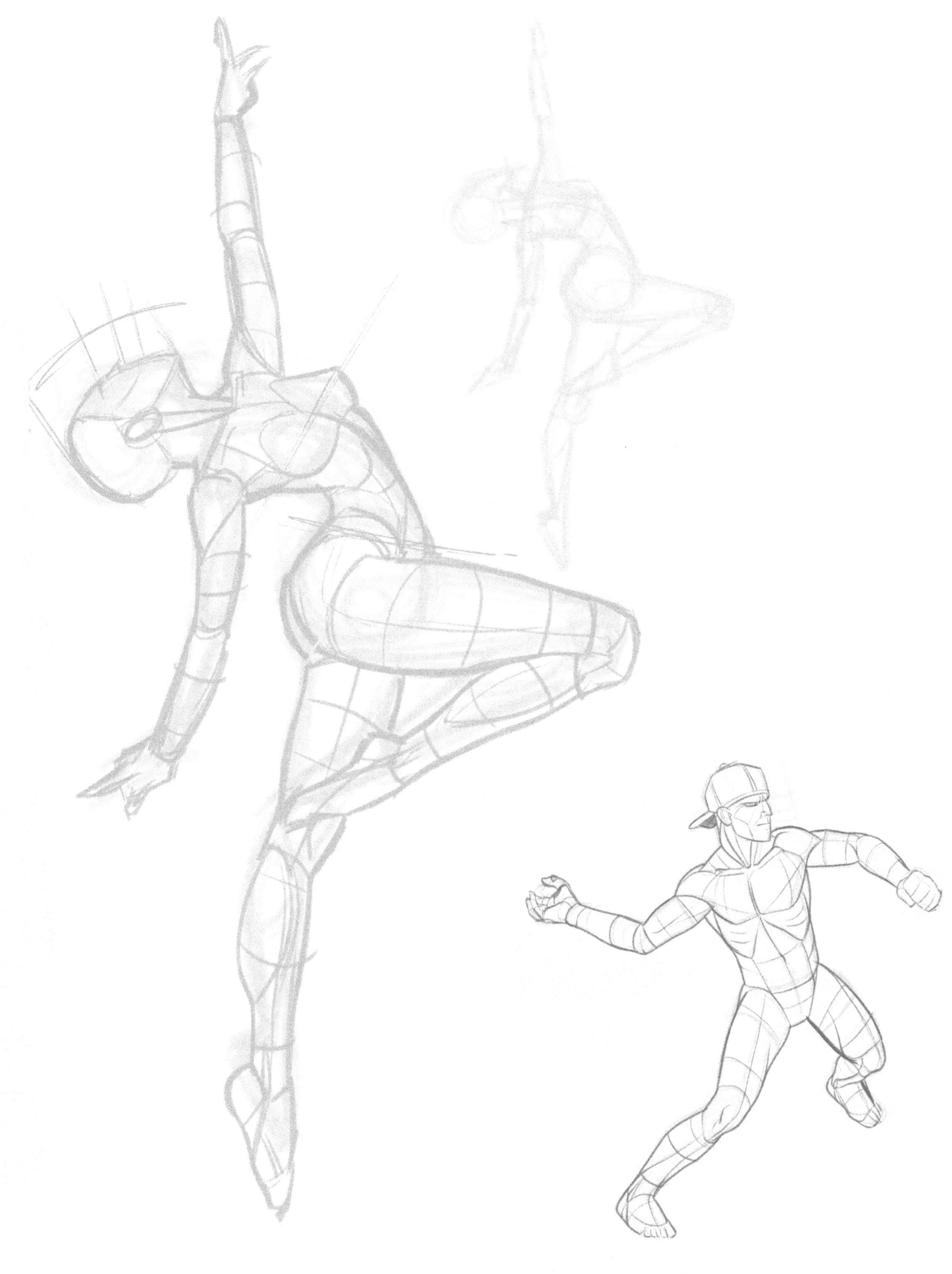

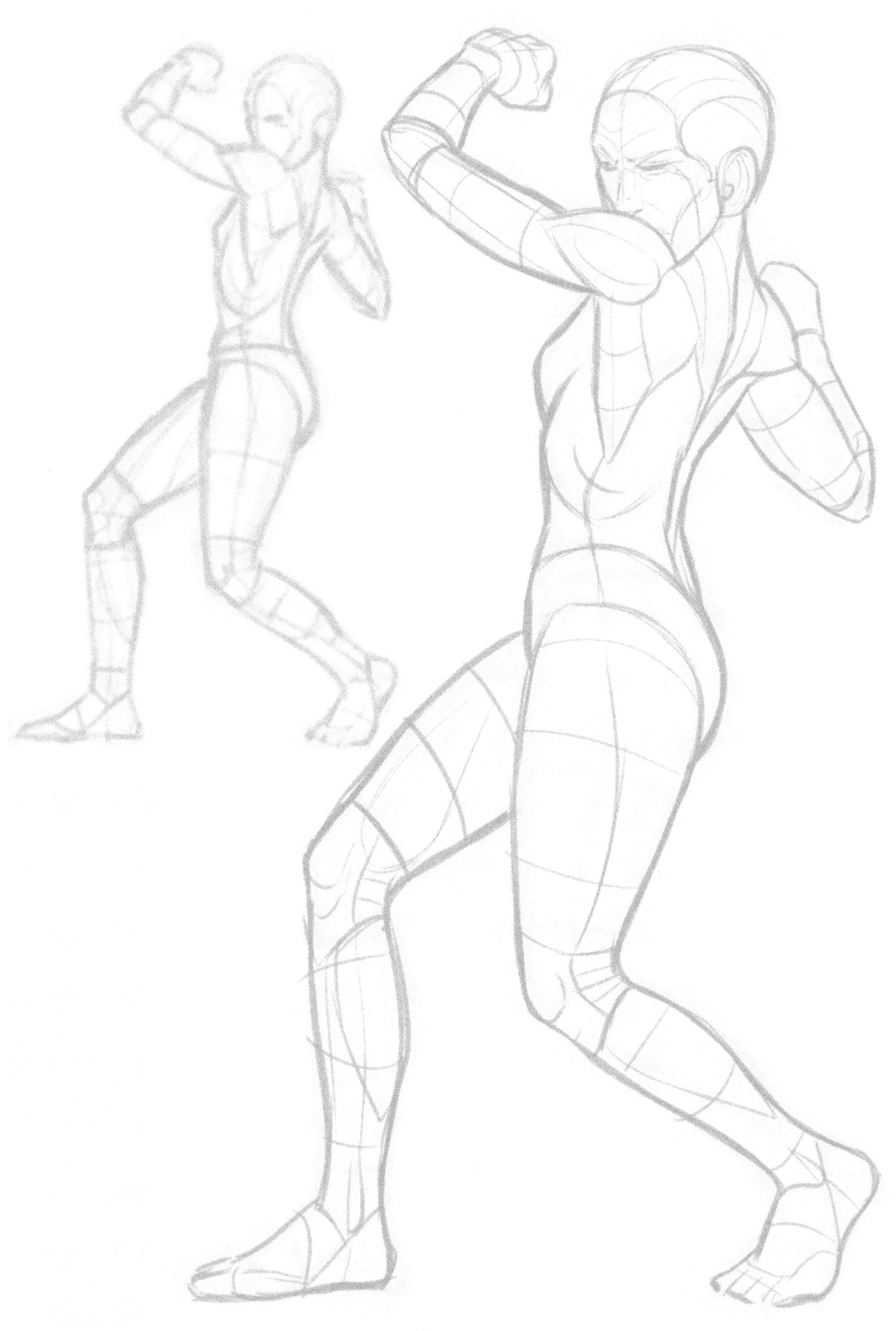

Dynamic Poses -Page 46

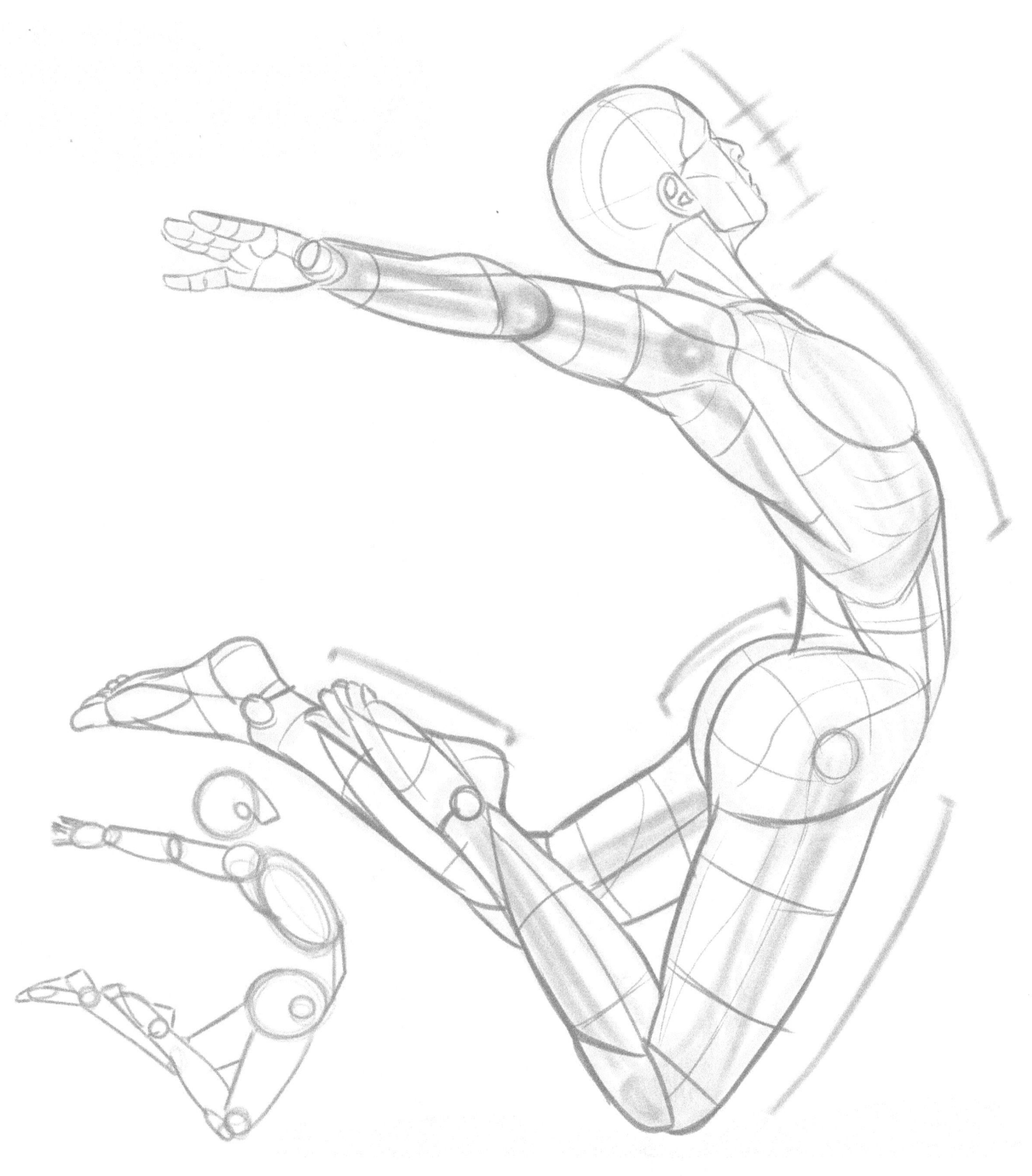

Dynamic Poses -Page 47

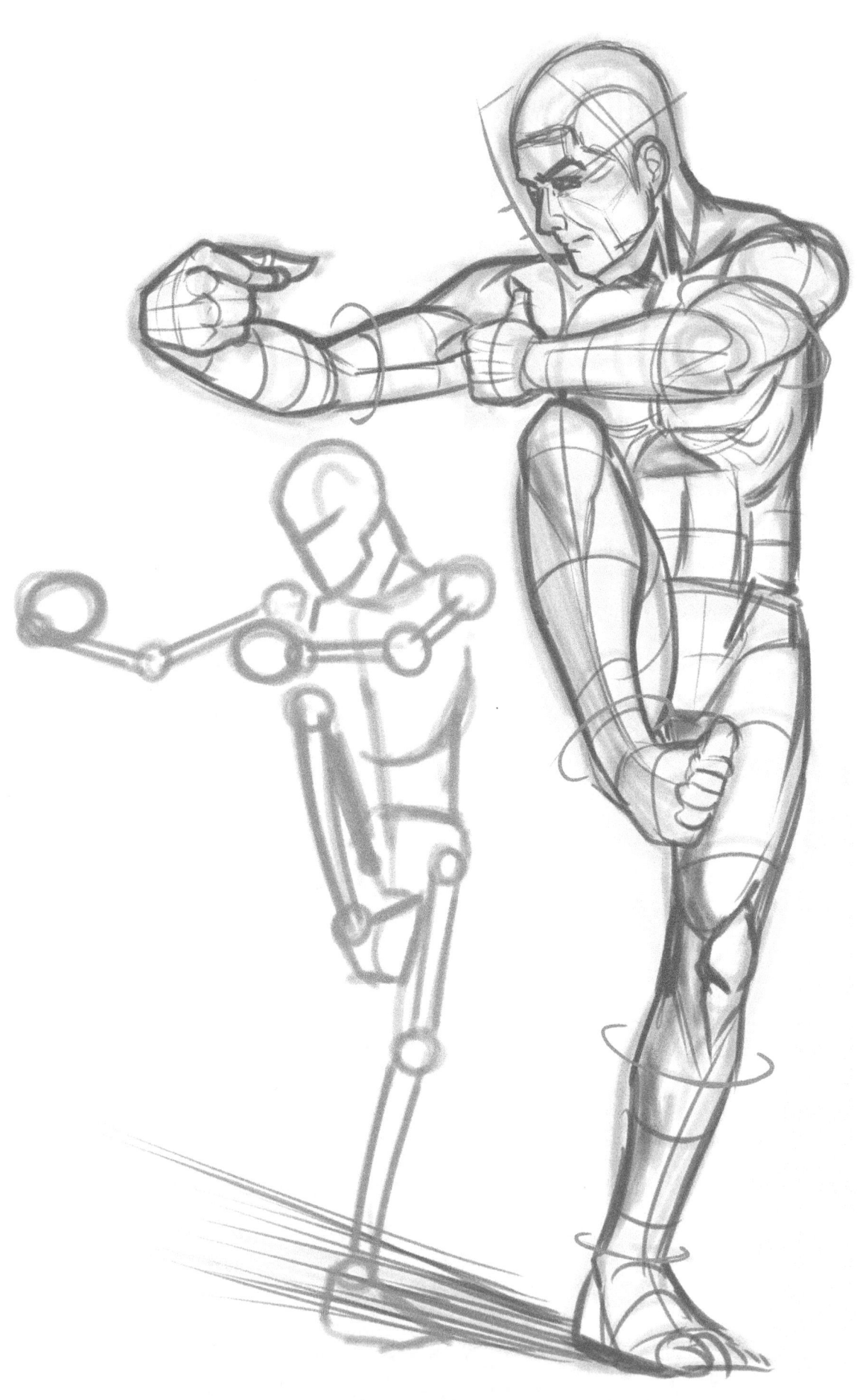

Dynamic Poses -Page 48

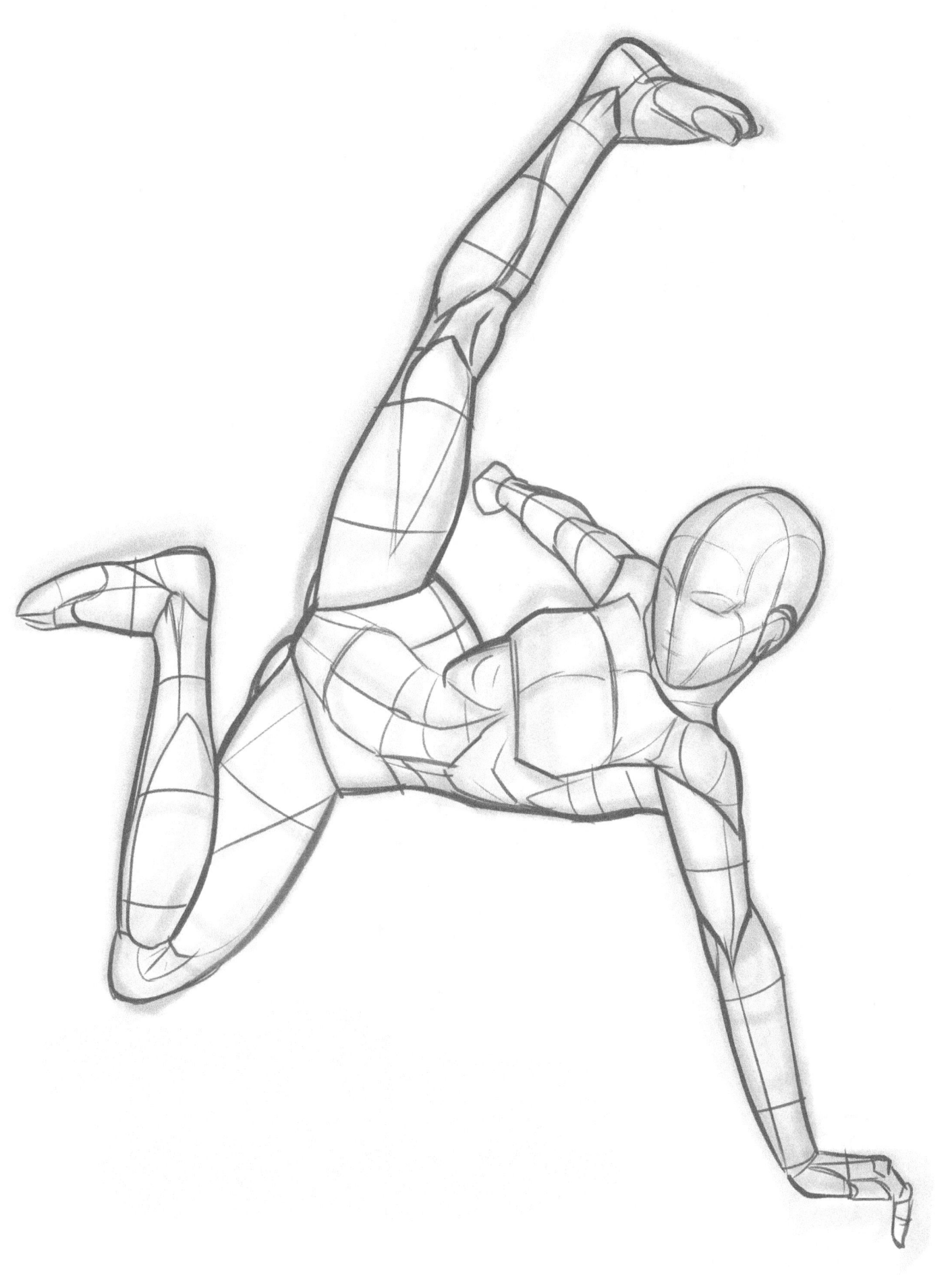

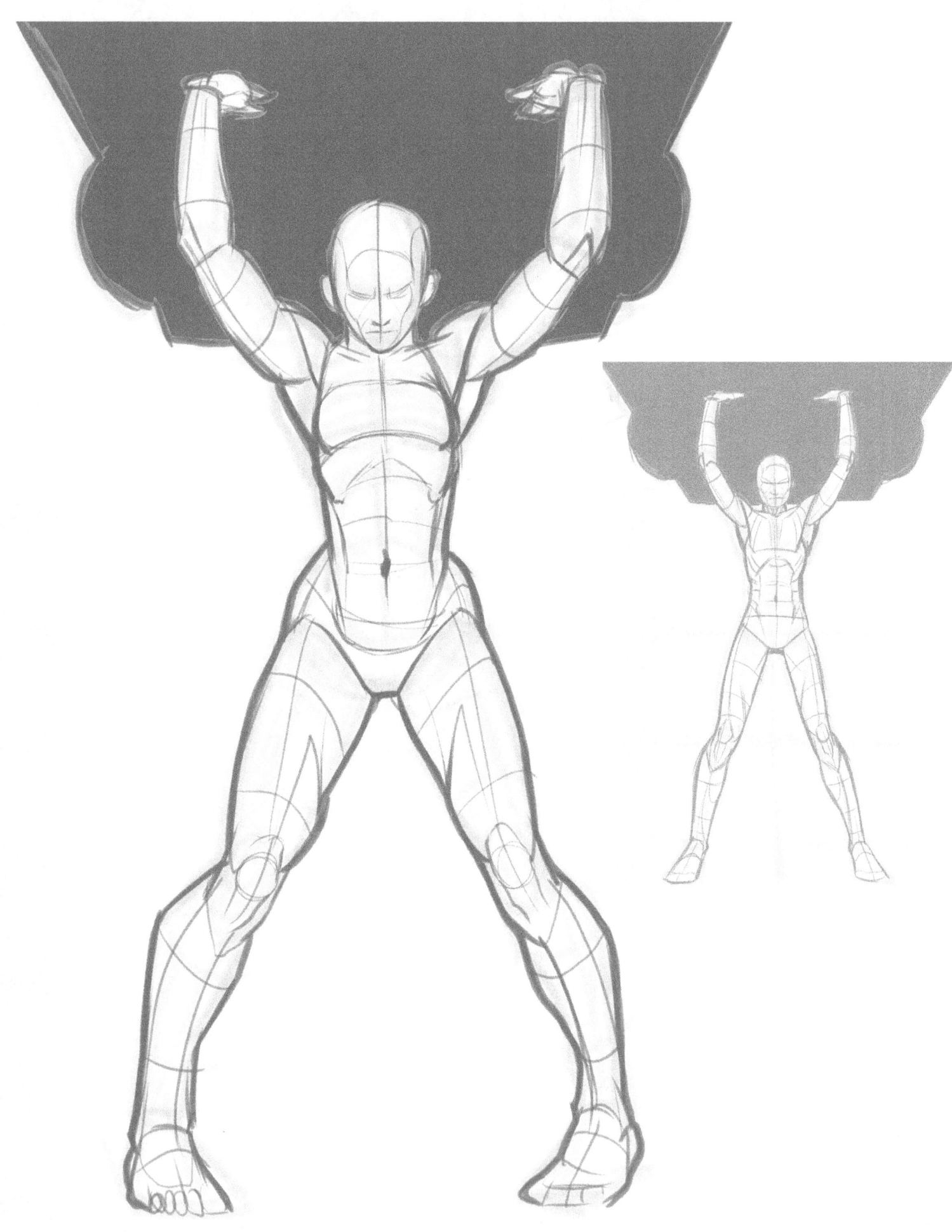

Dynamic Poses -Page 50

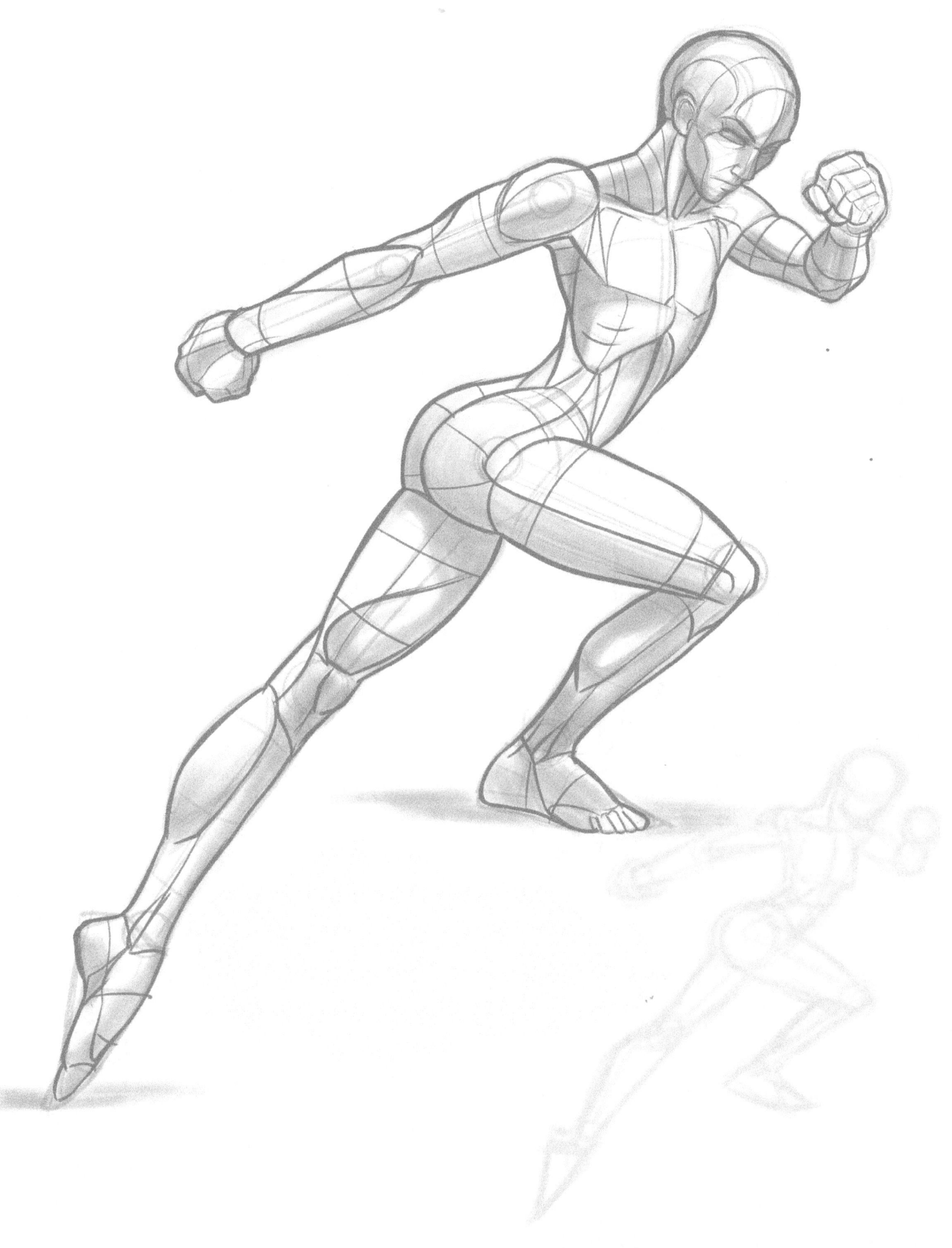

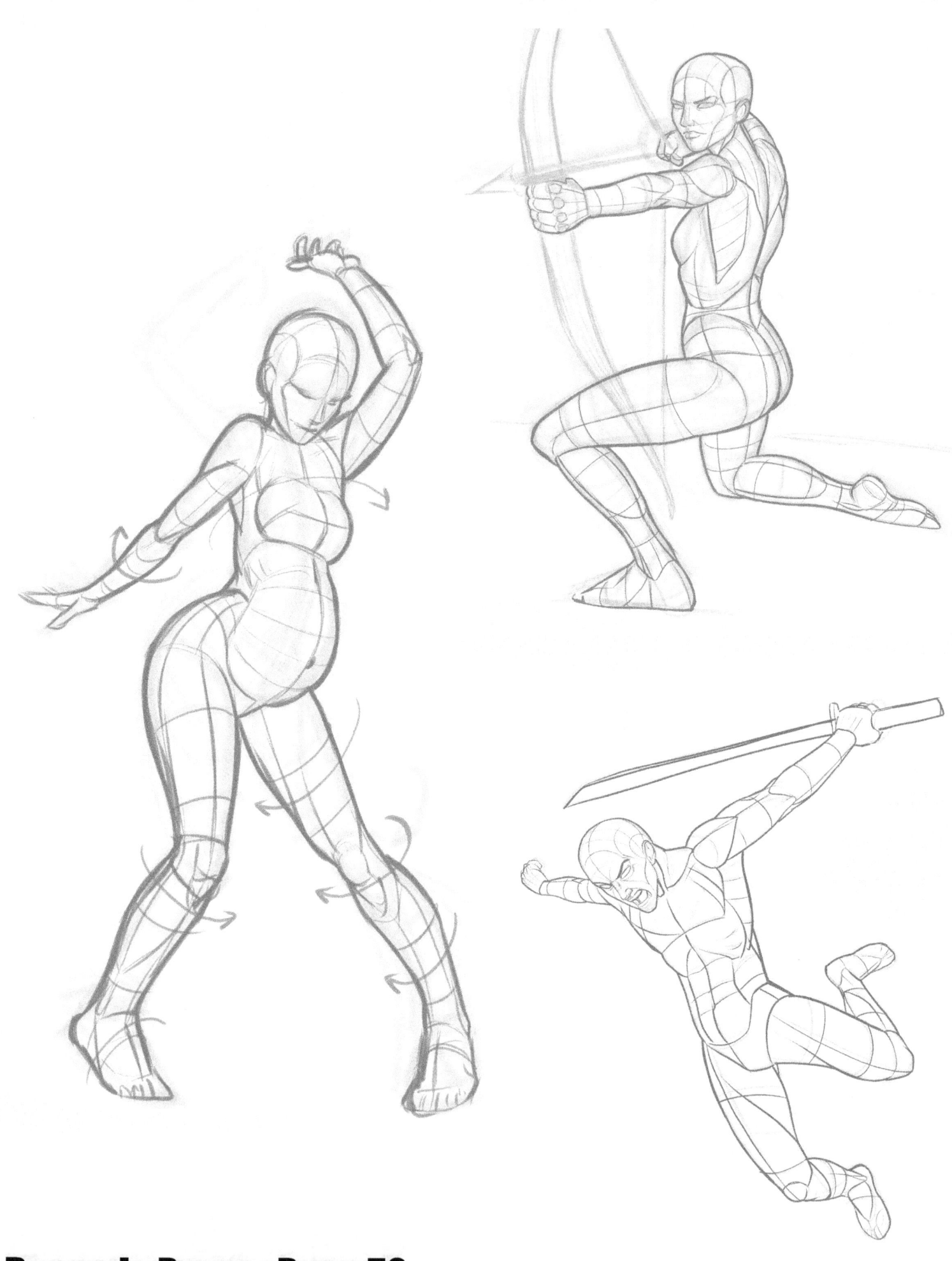

Dynamic Poses -Page 52

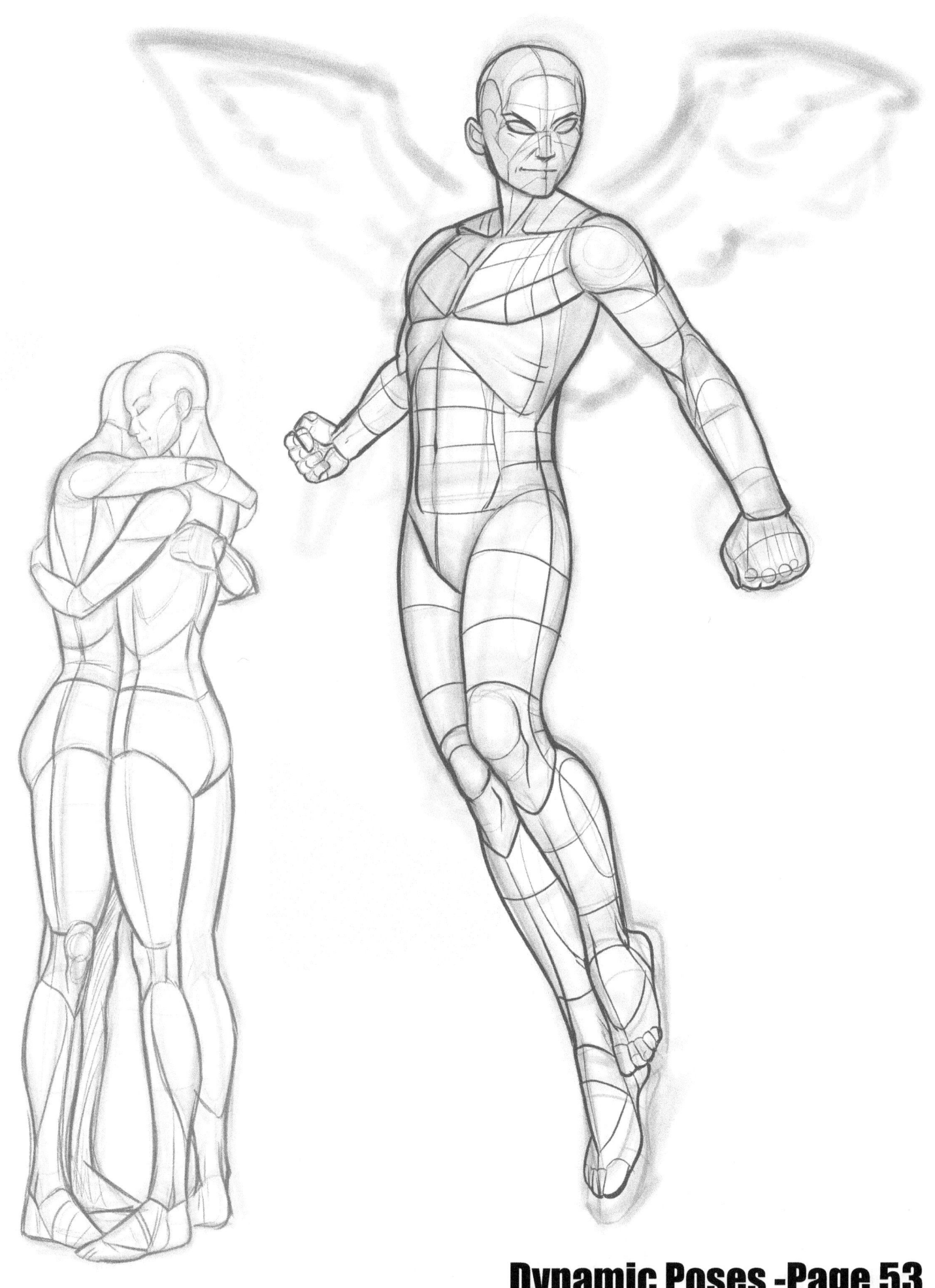

Dynamic Poses -Page 53

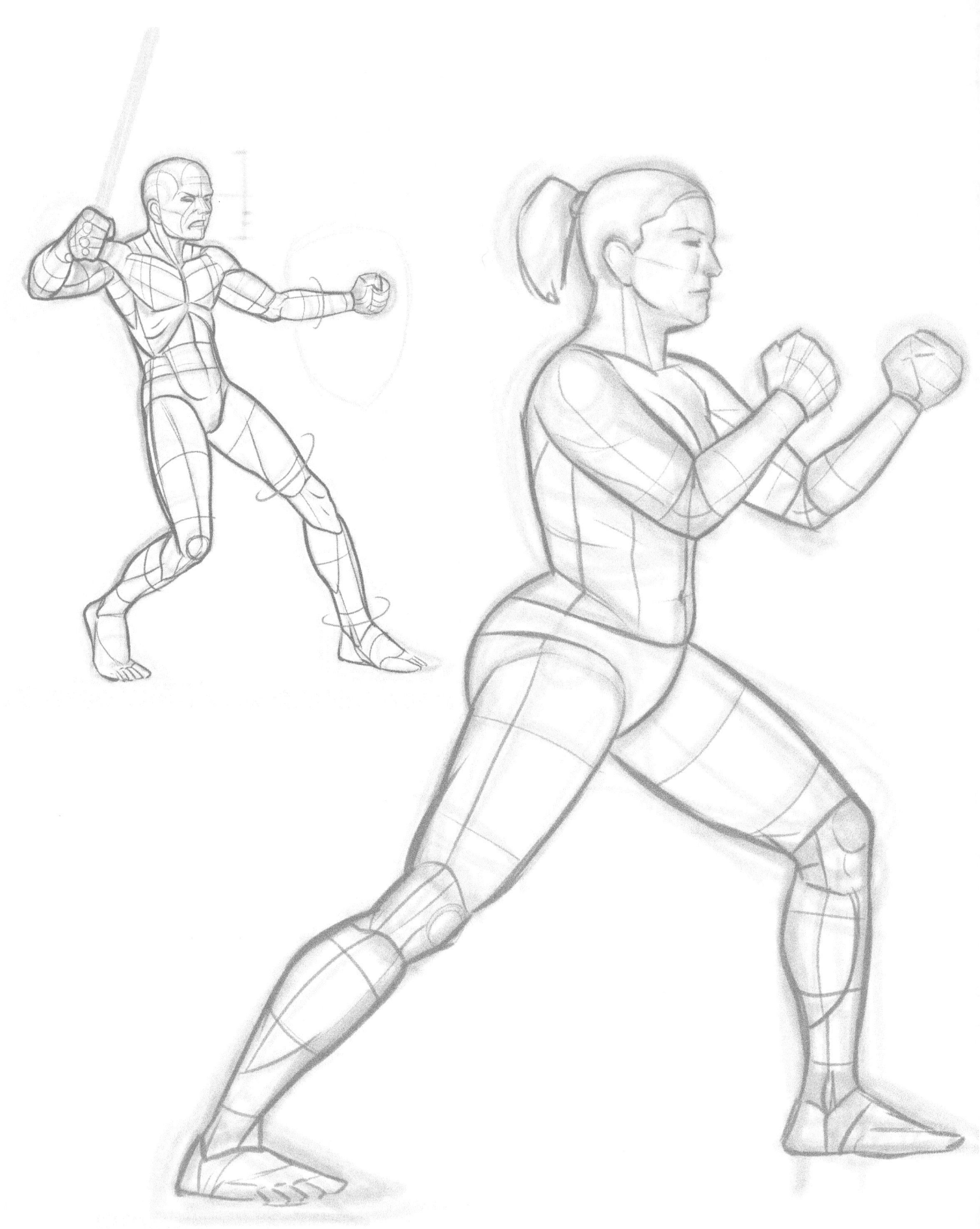

Dynamic Poses -Page 54

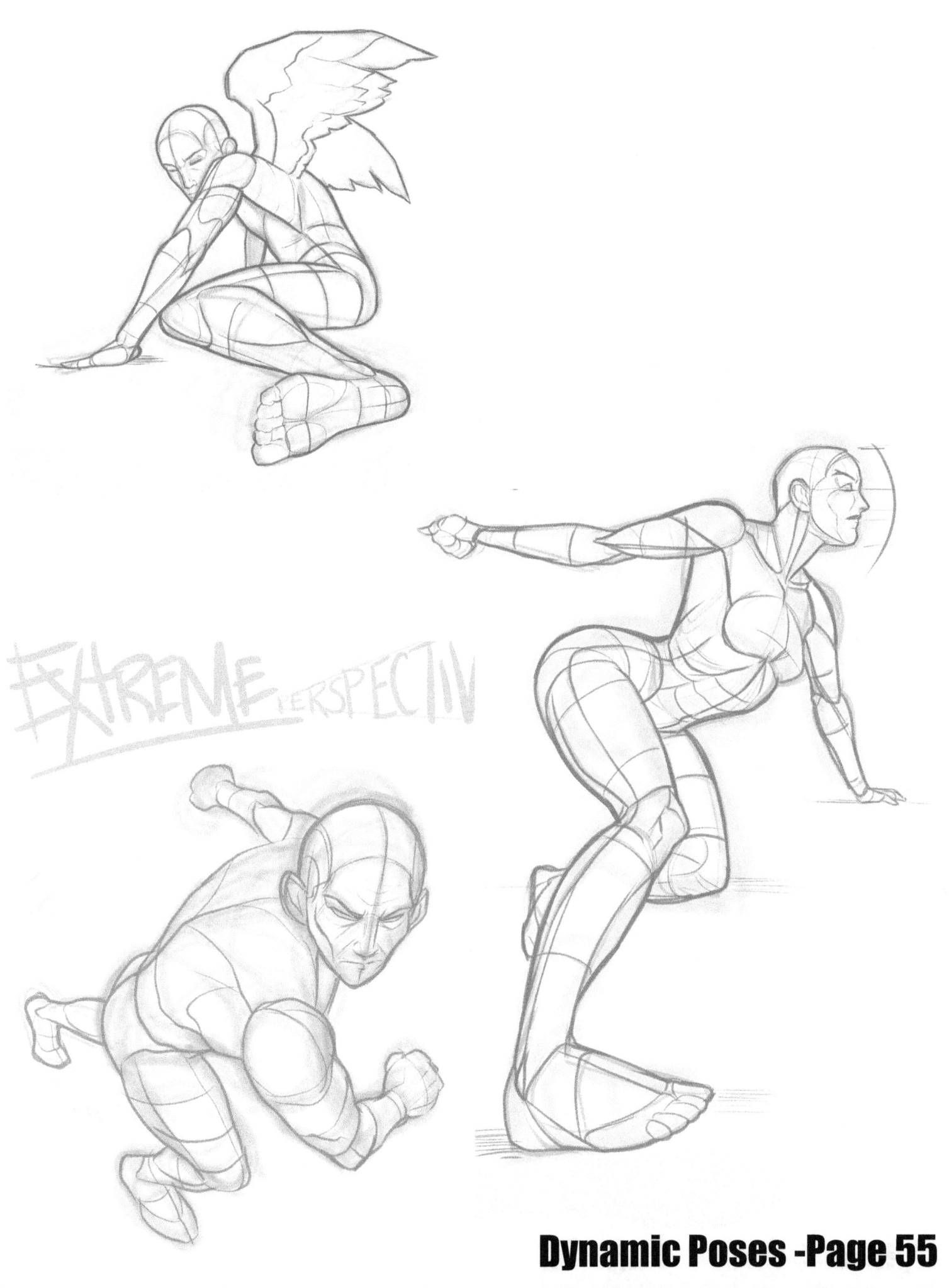

EXTREME PERSPECTIV

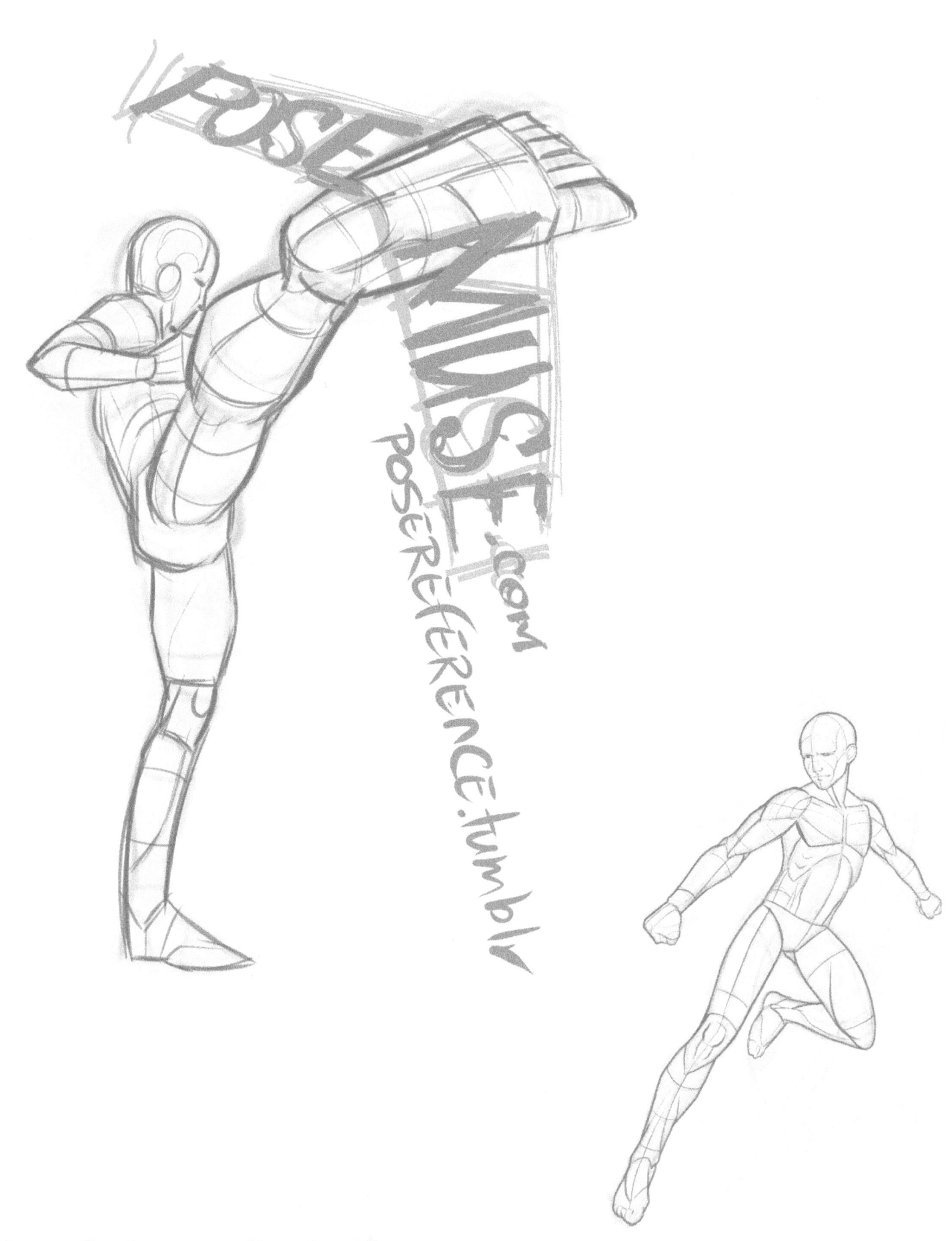

Dynamic Poses -Page 56

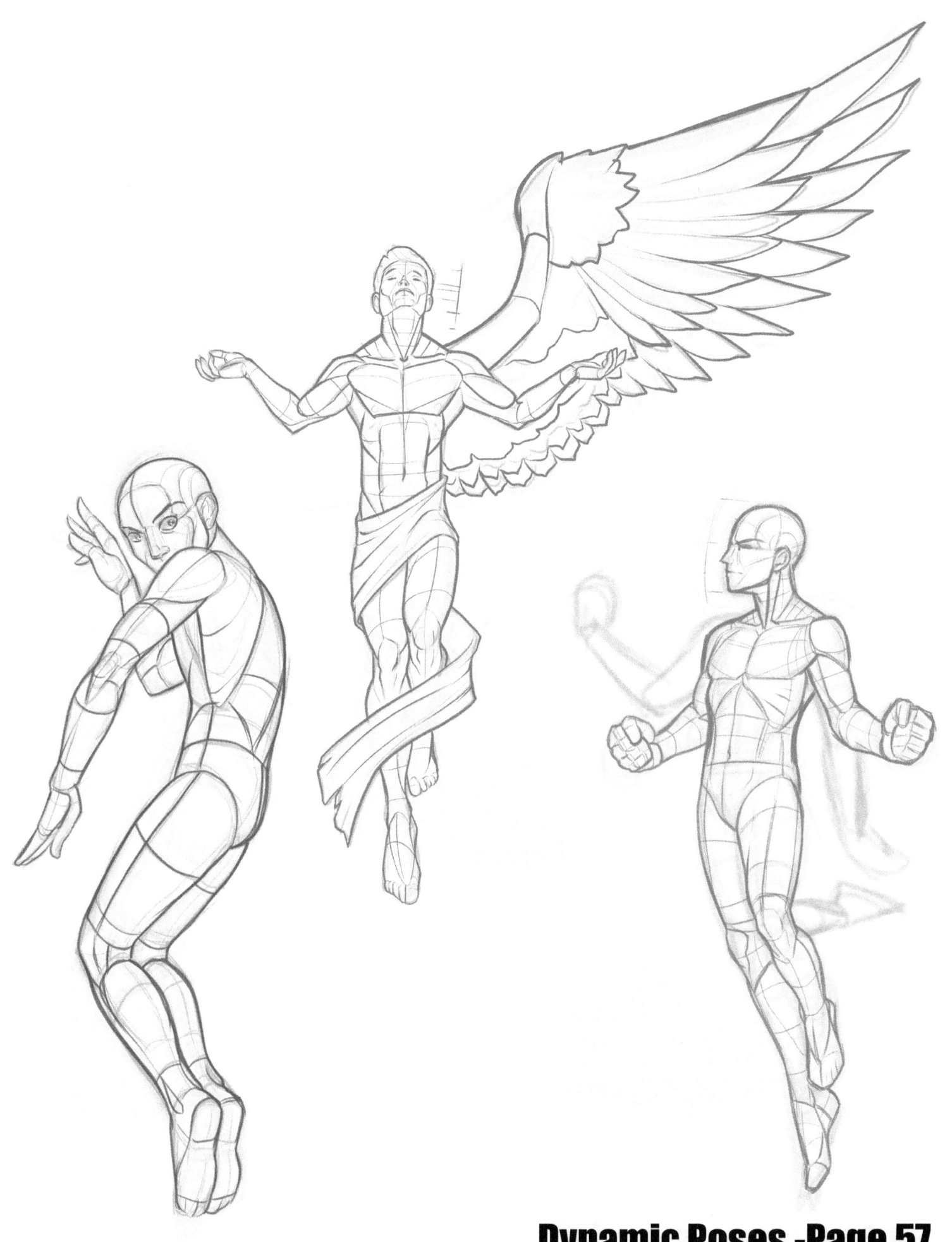

Dynamic Poses -Page 57

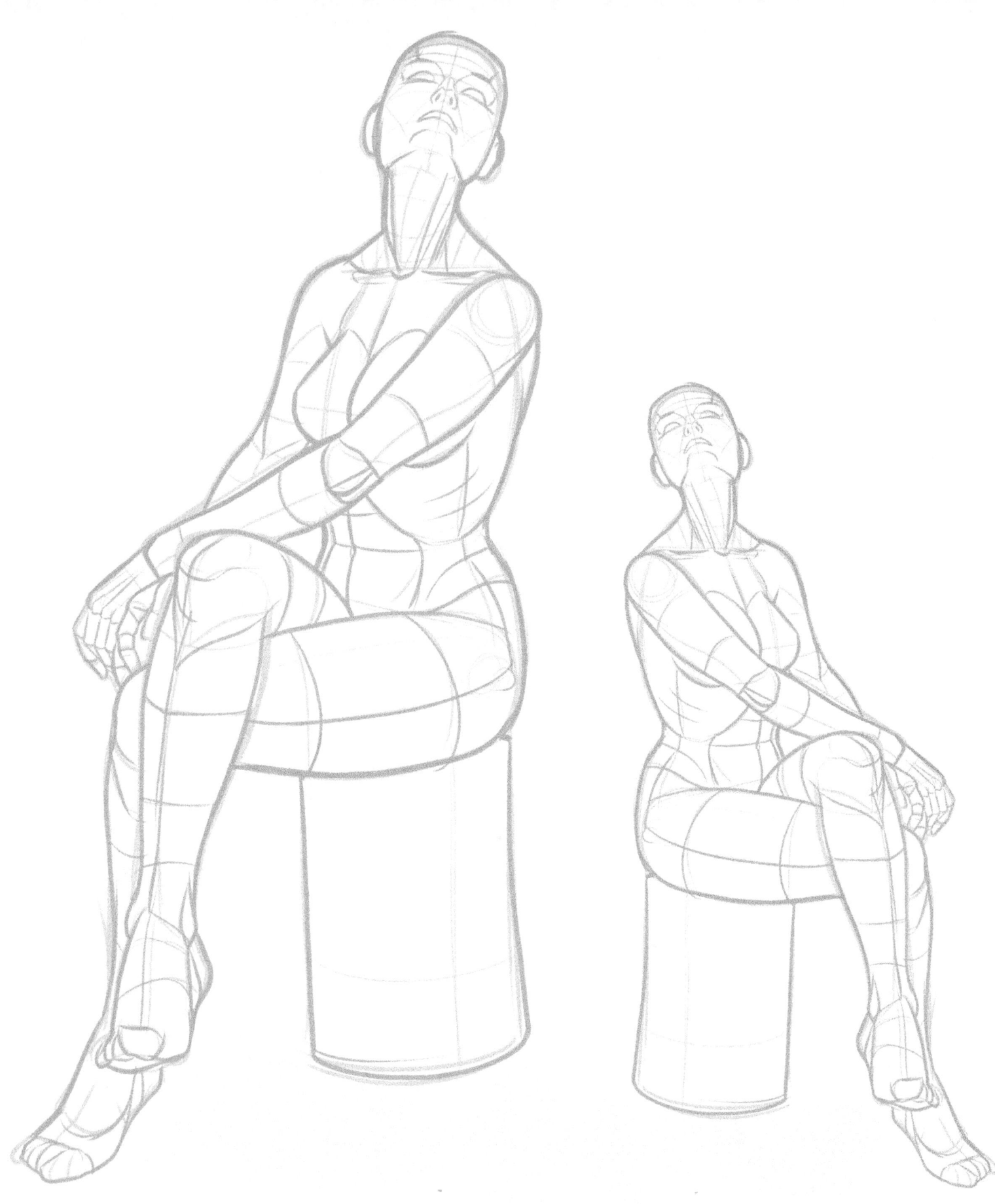

Sitting Poses -Page 58

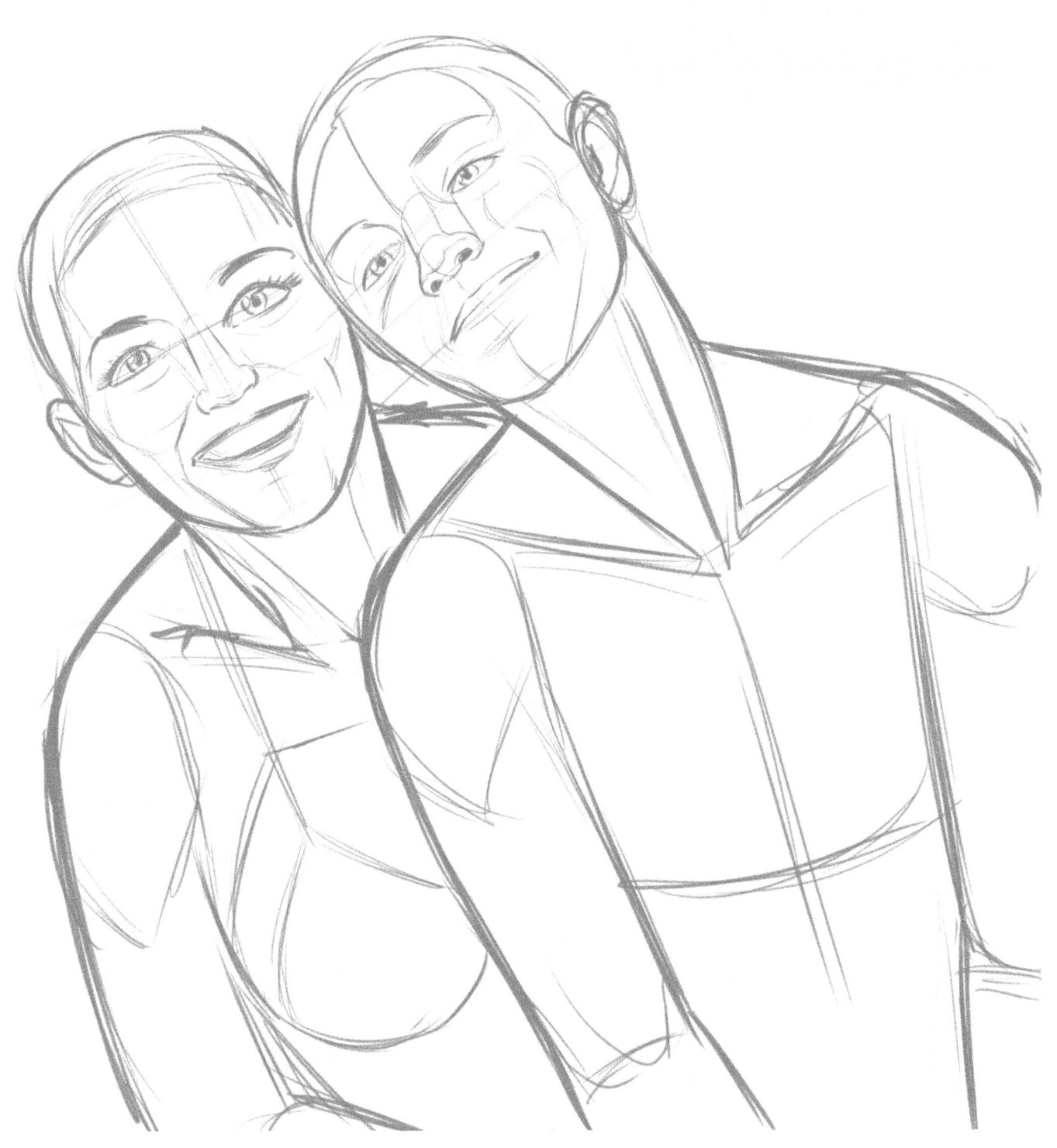

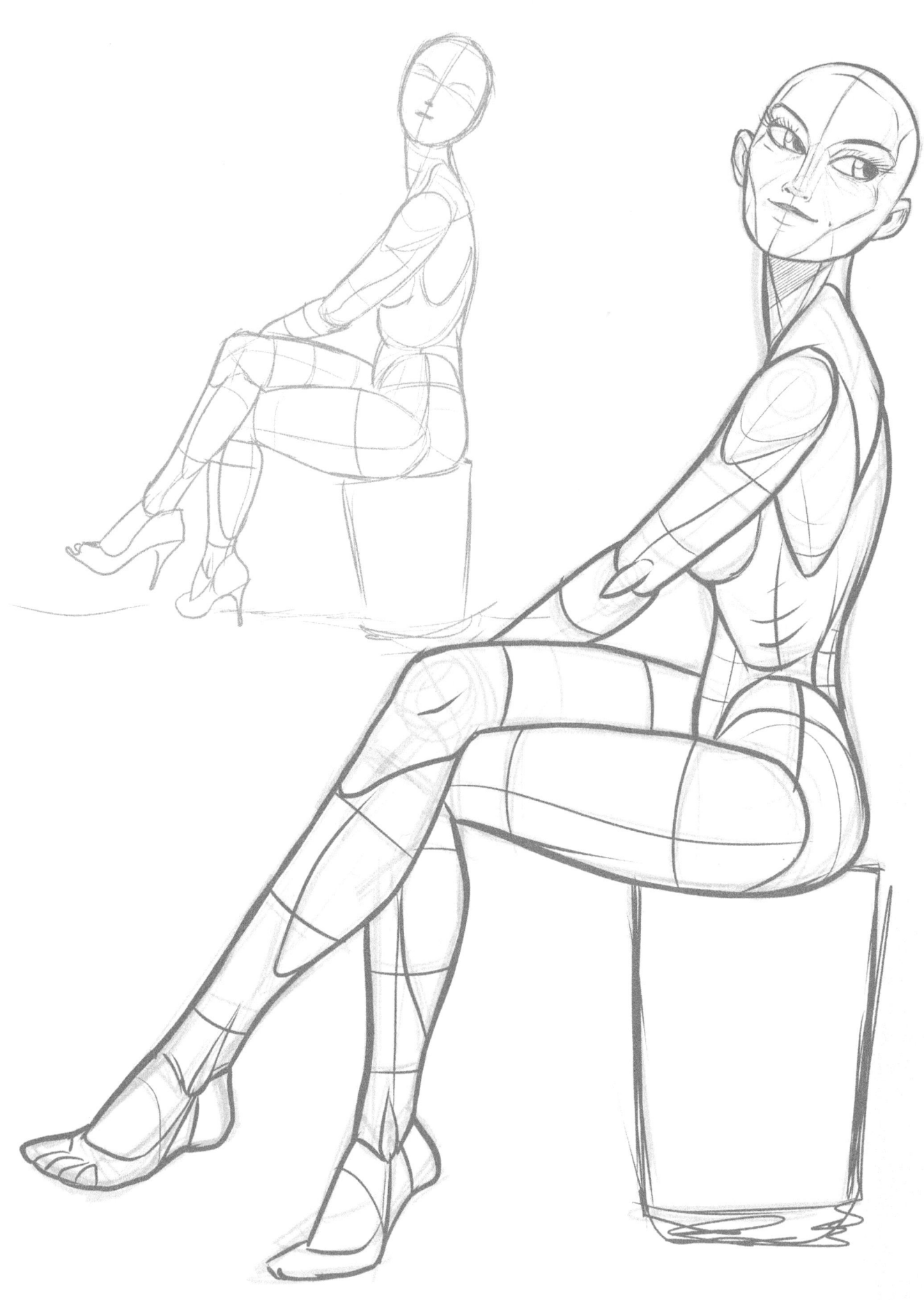

Sitting Poses -Page 60

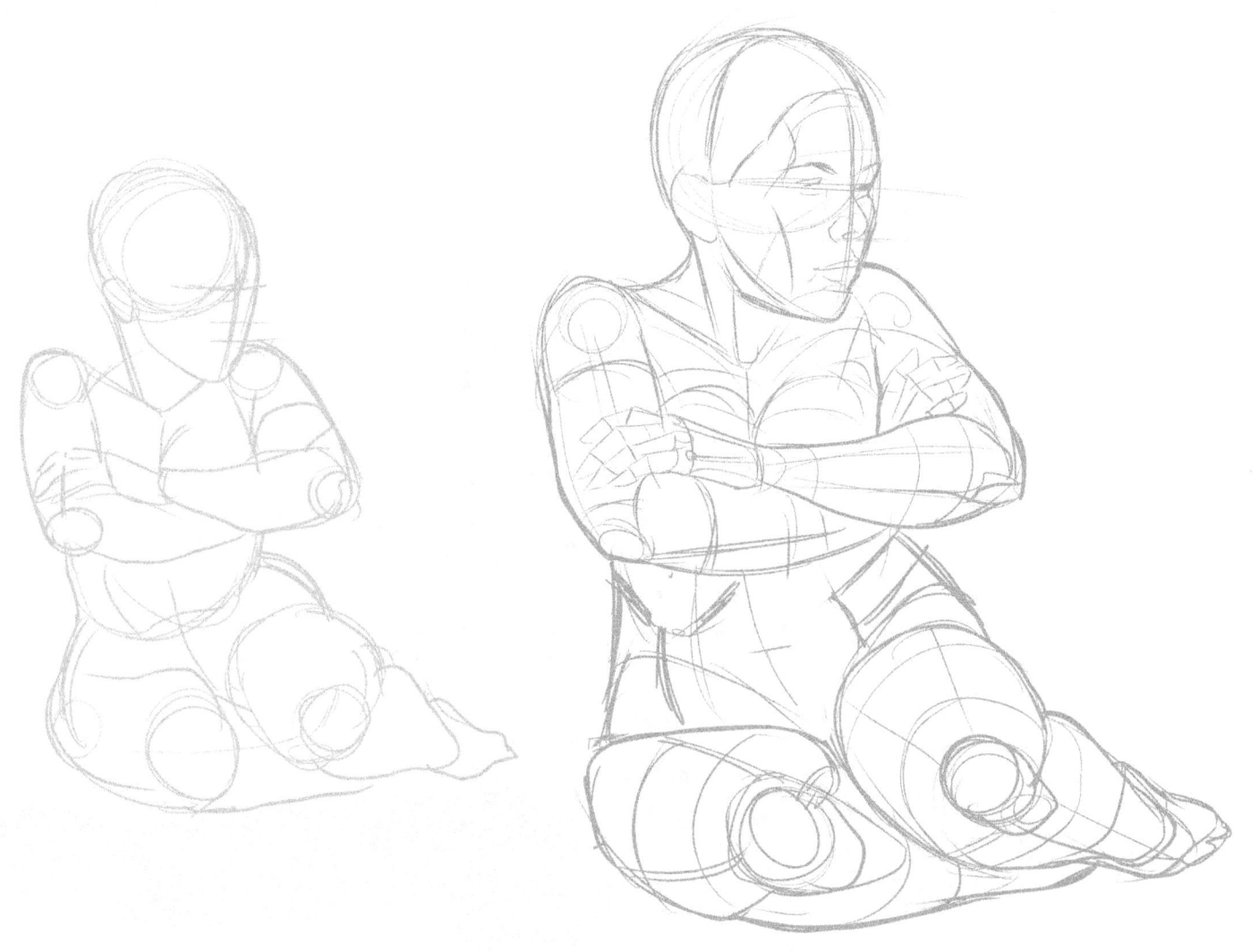

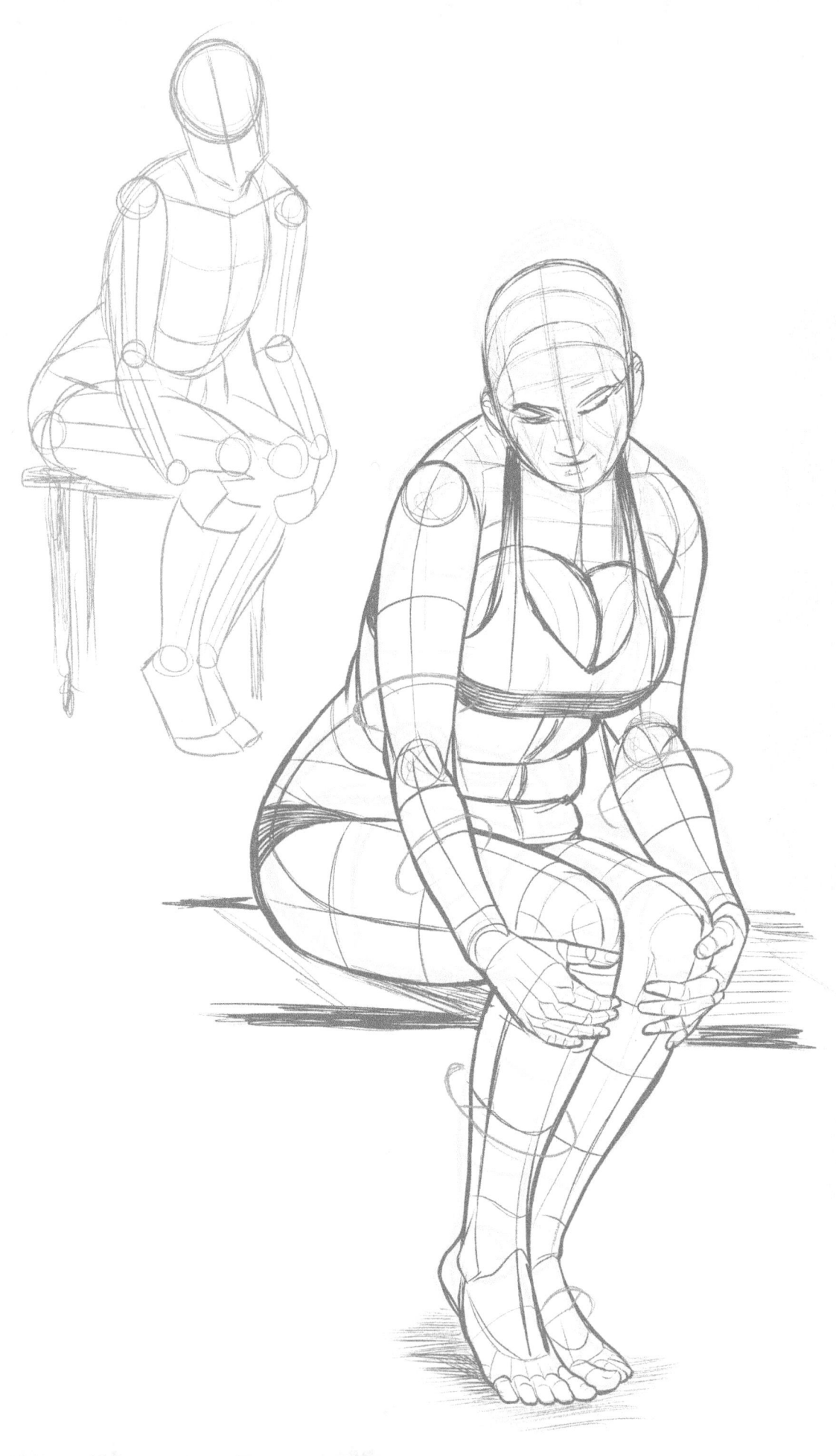

Sitting Poses -Page 62

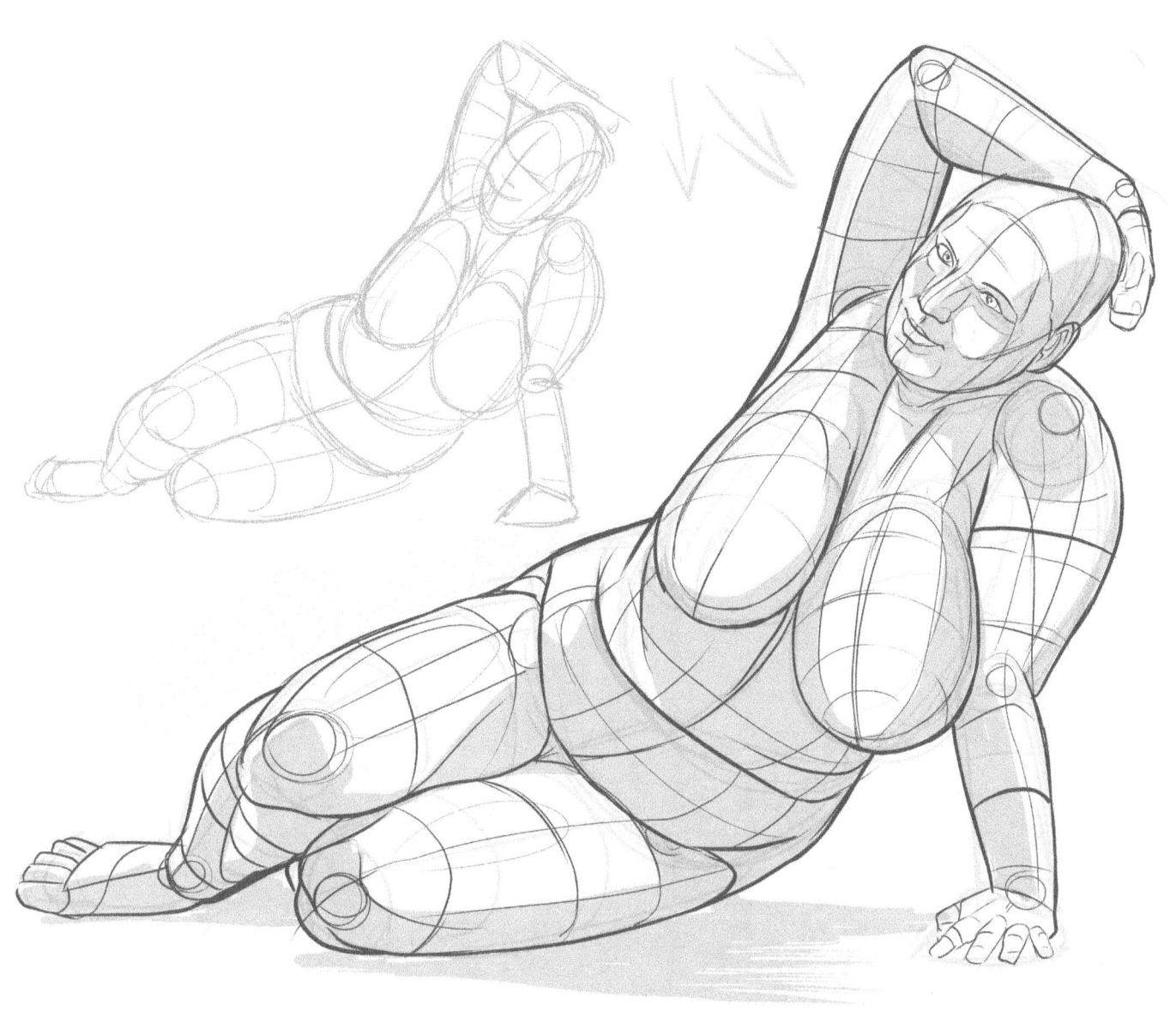

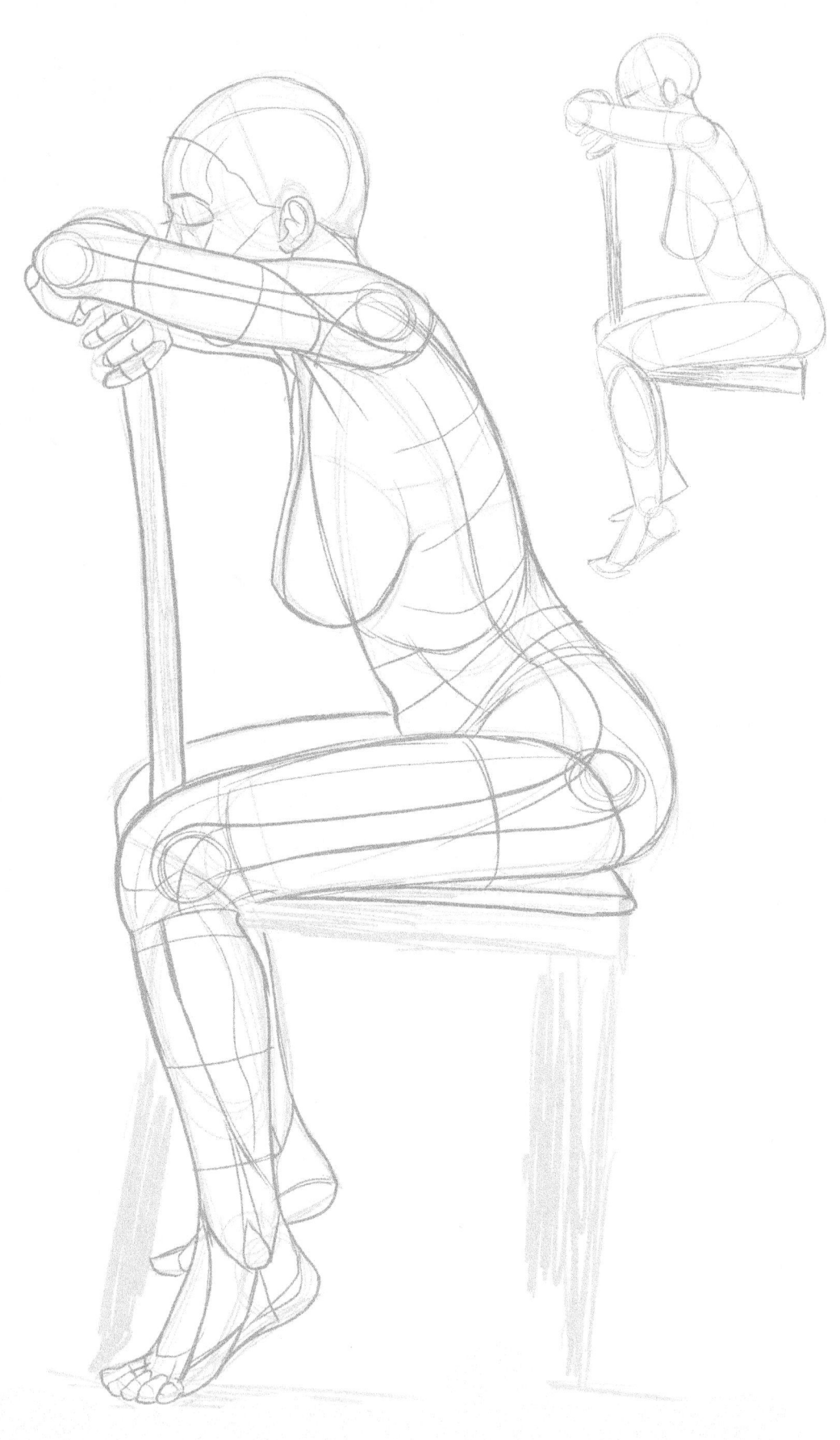

Sitting Poses -Page 64

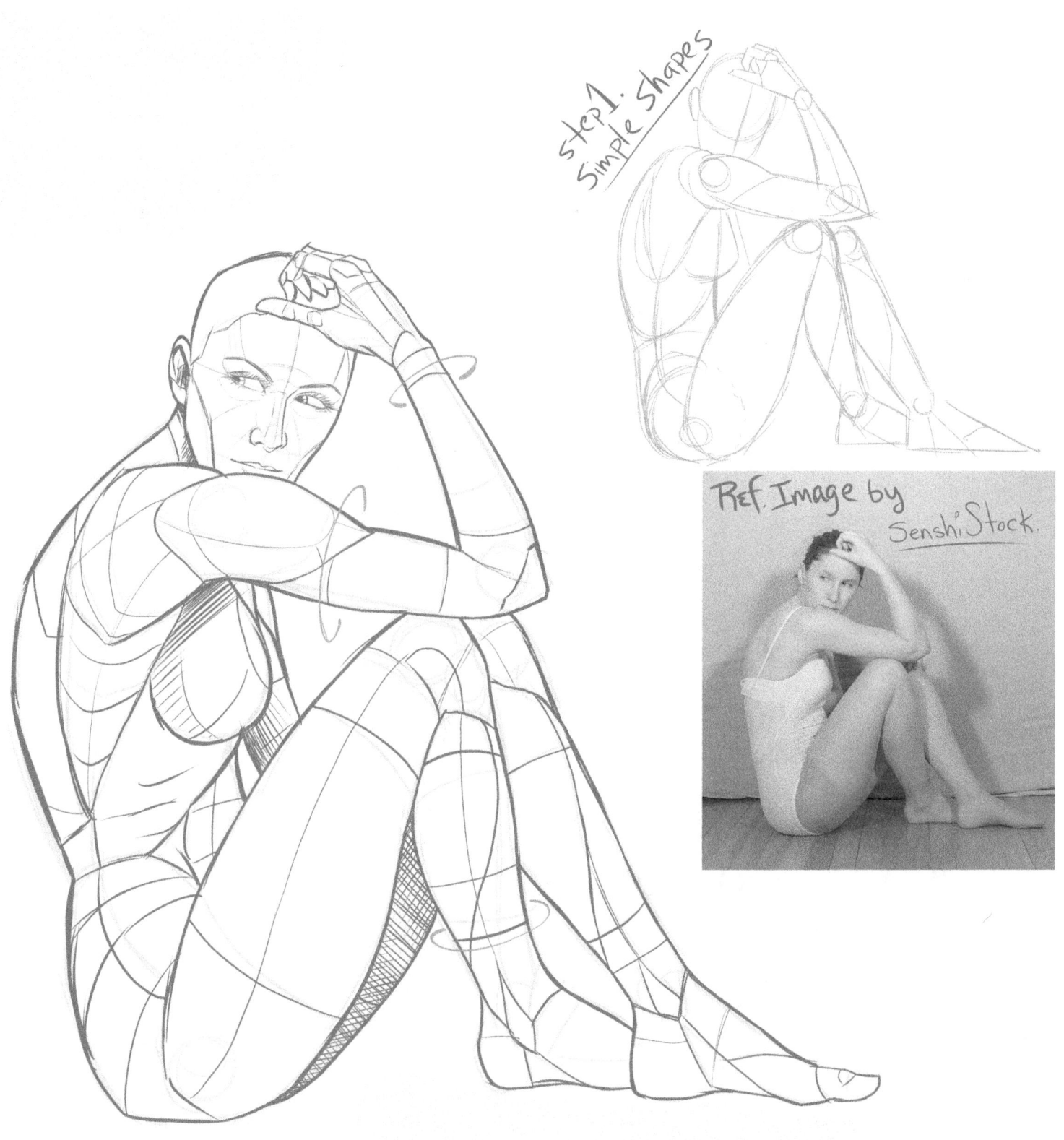

step 1. Simple shapes

Ref. Image by Senshi Stock.

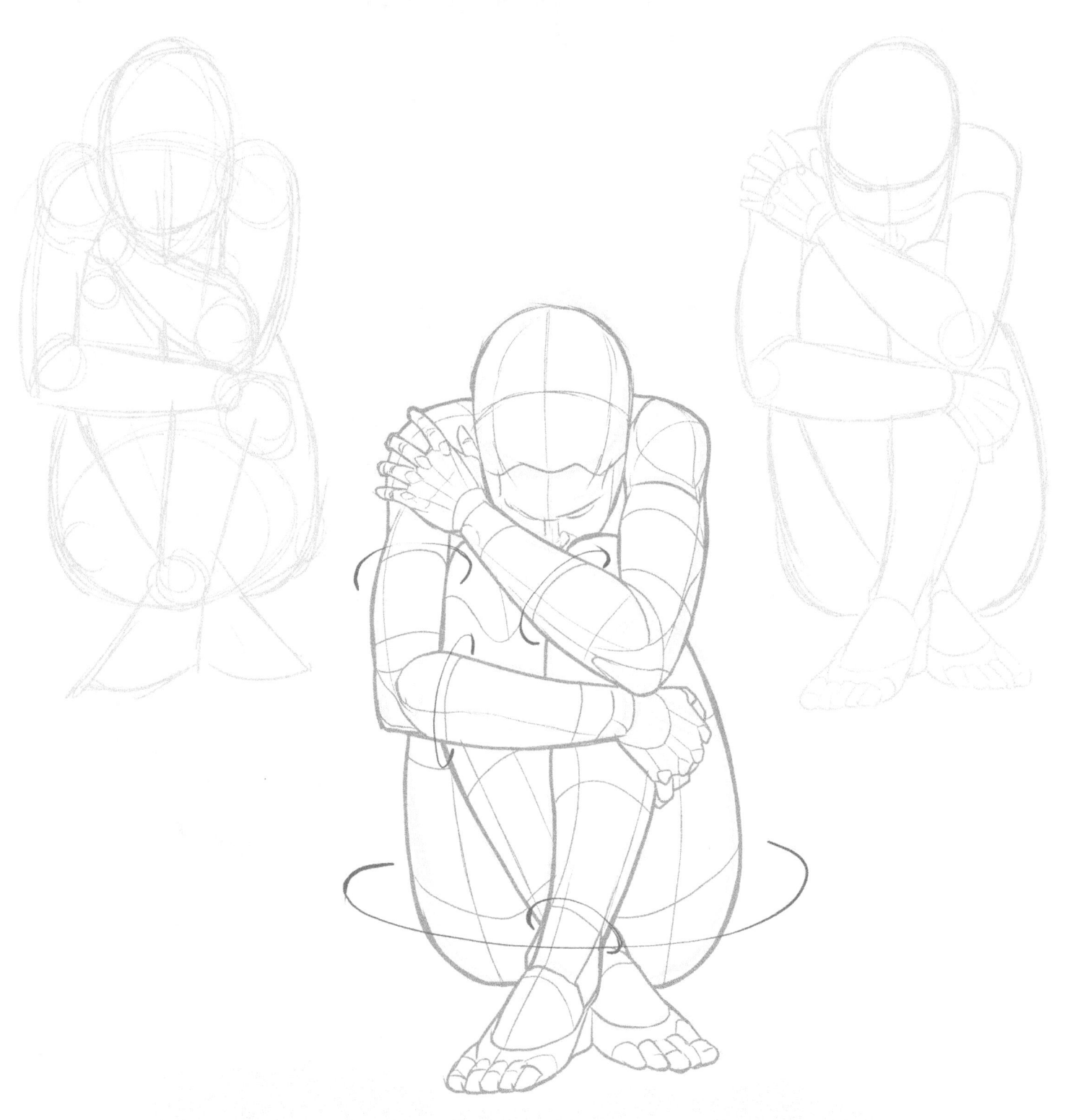

Sitting Poses -Page 66

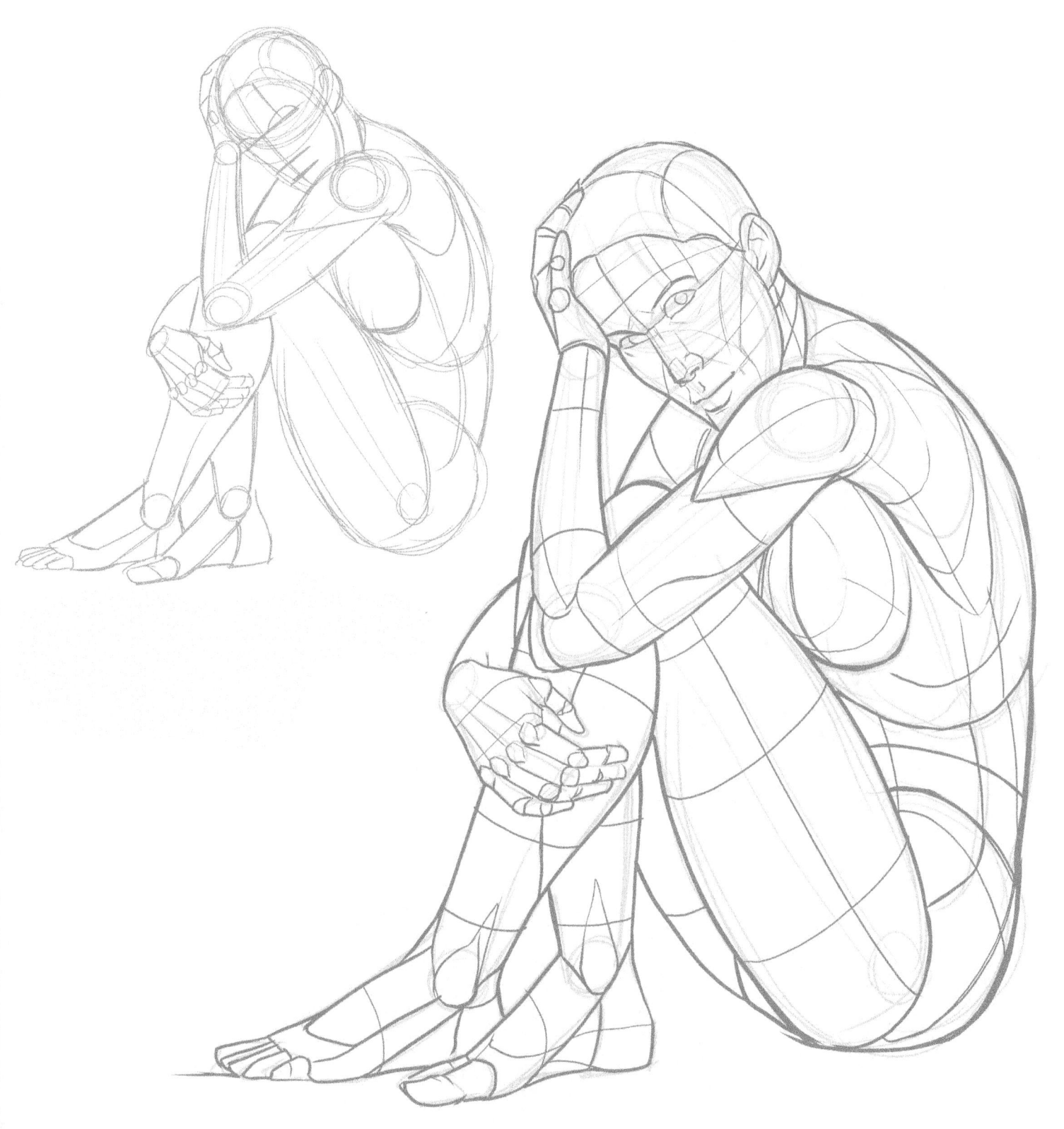

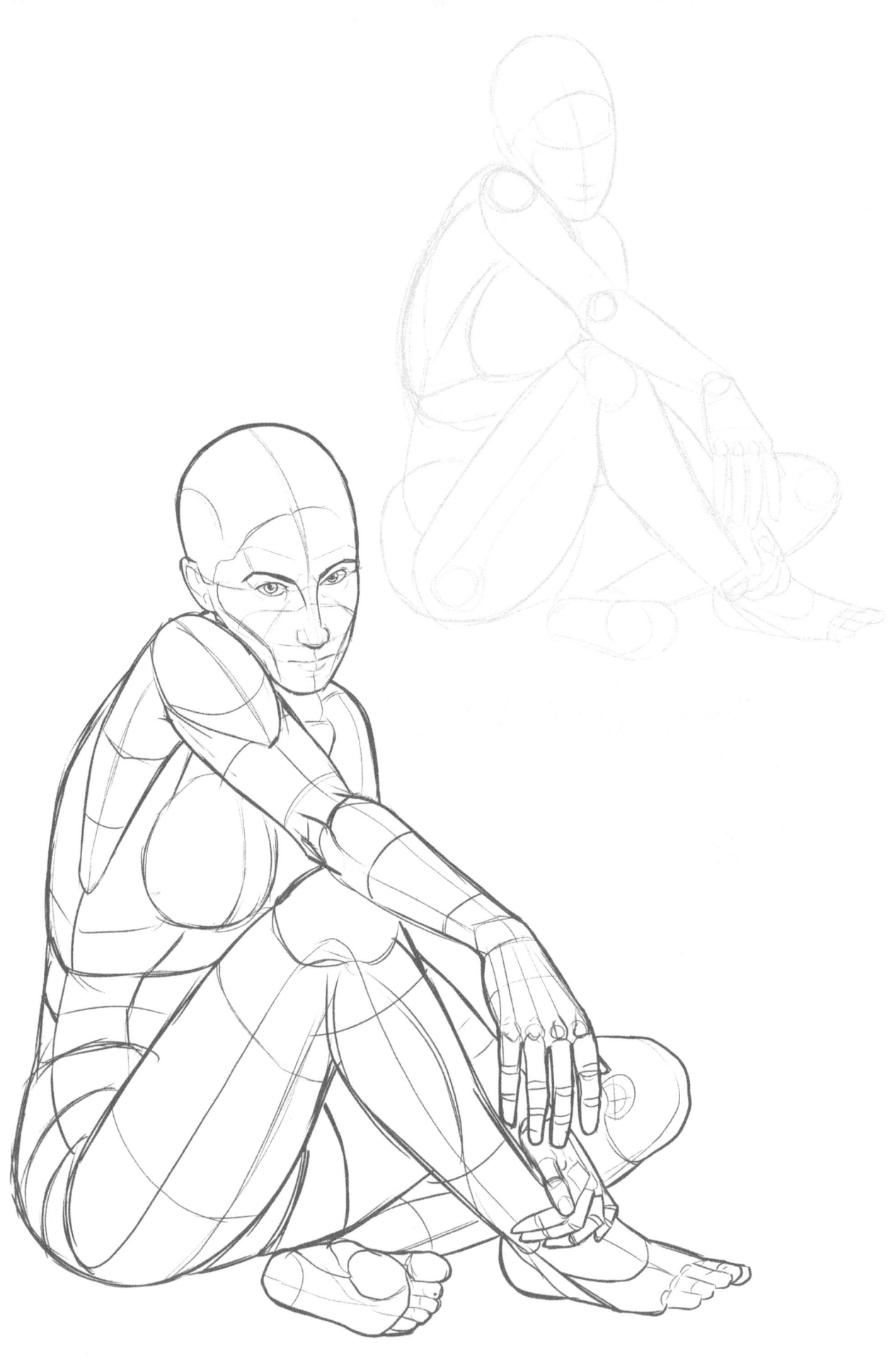

Sitting Poses -Page 68

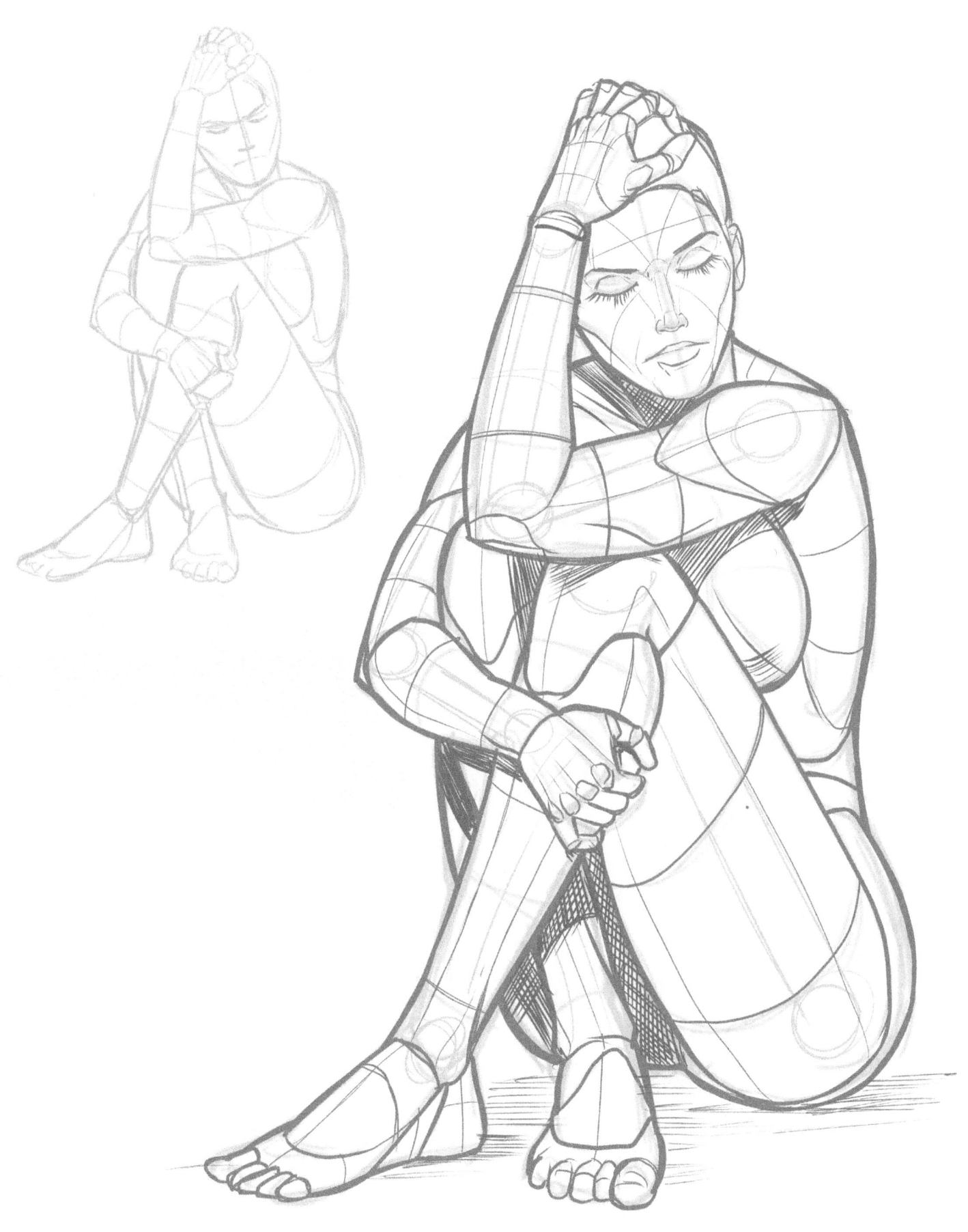

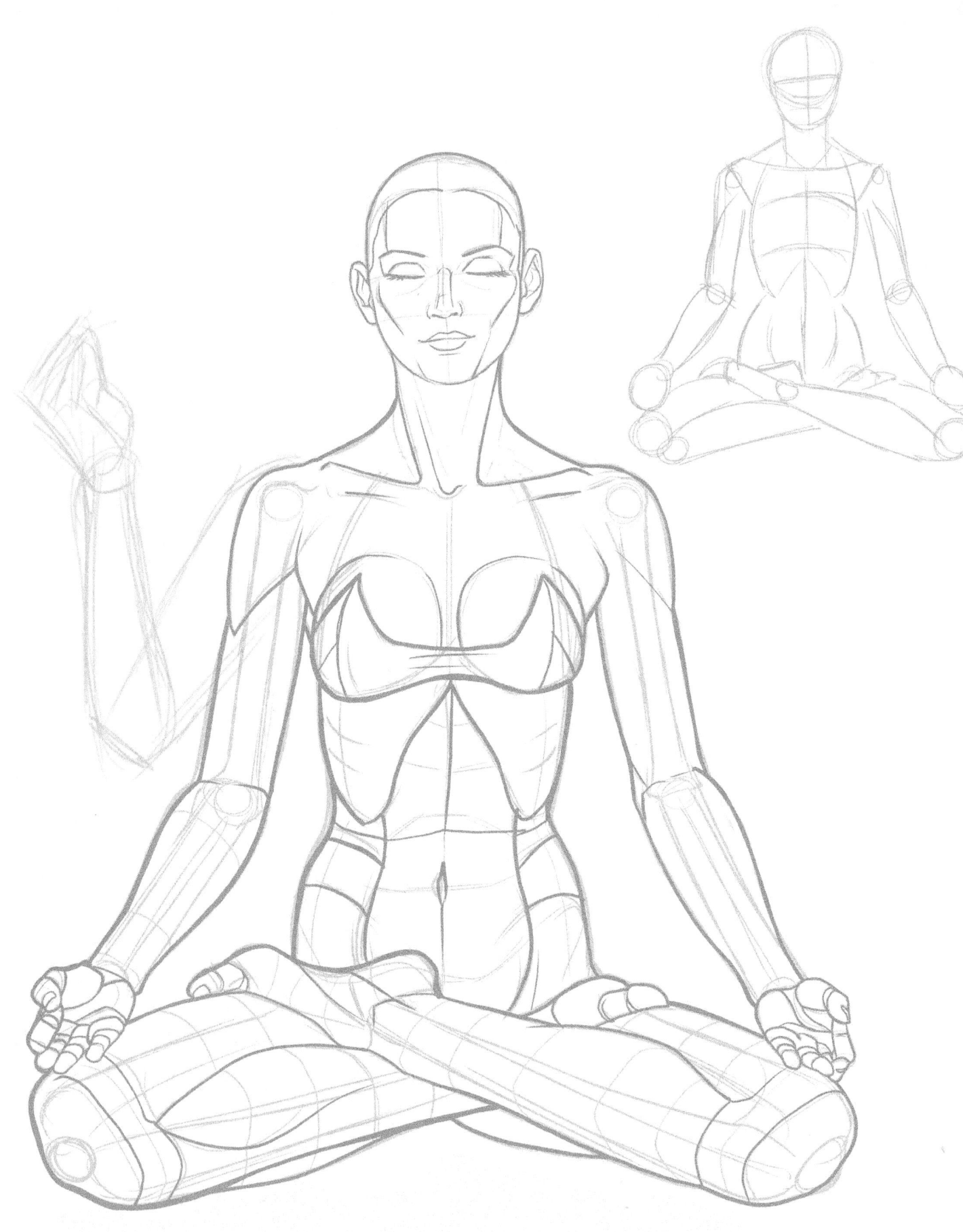

Sitting Poses -Page 70

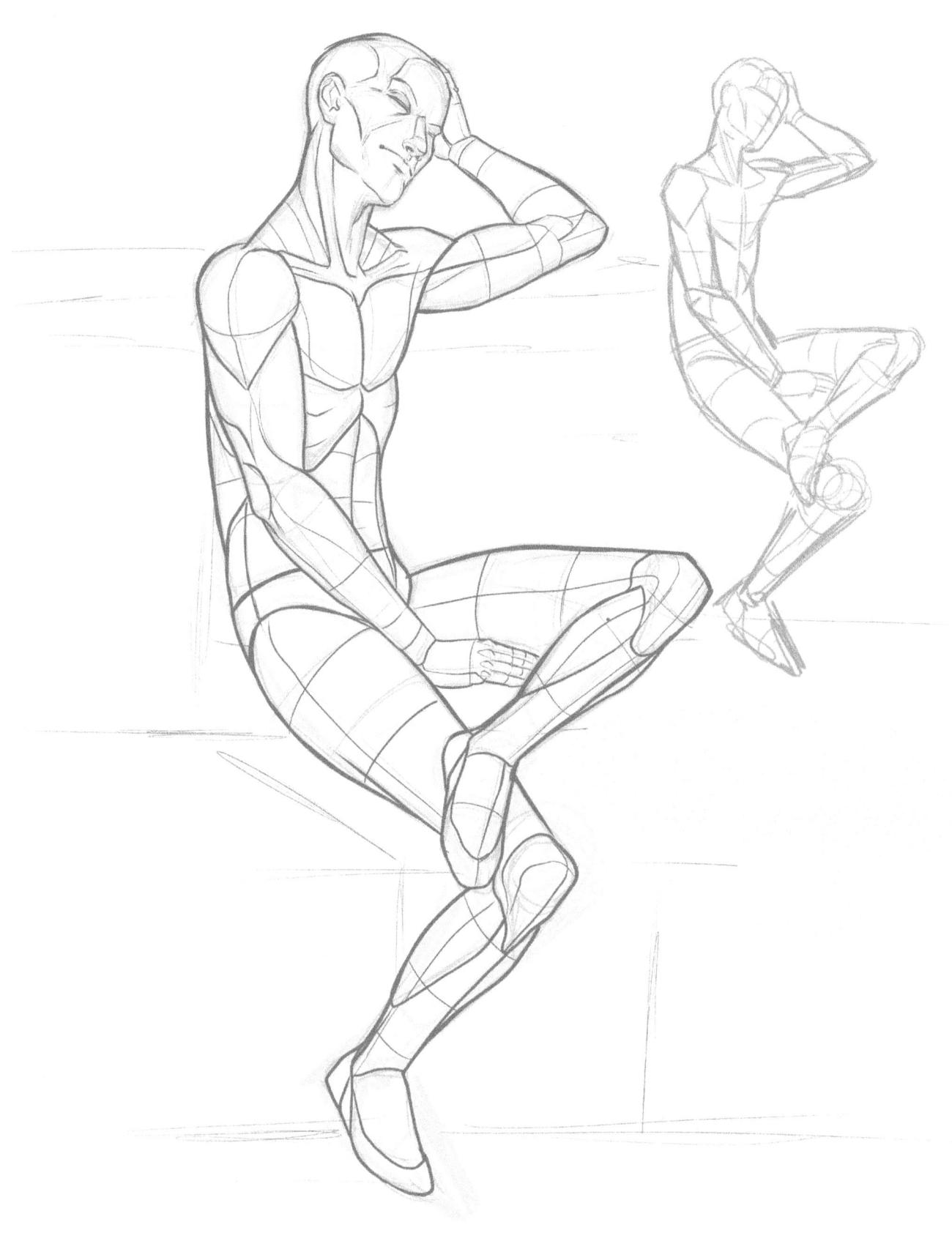

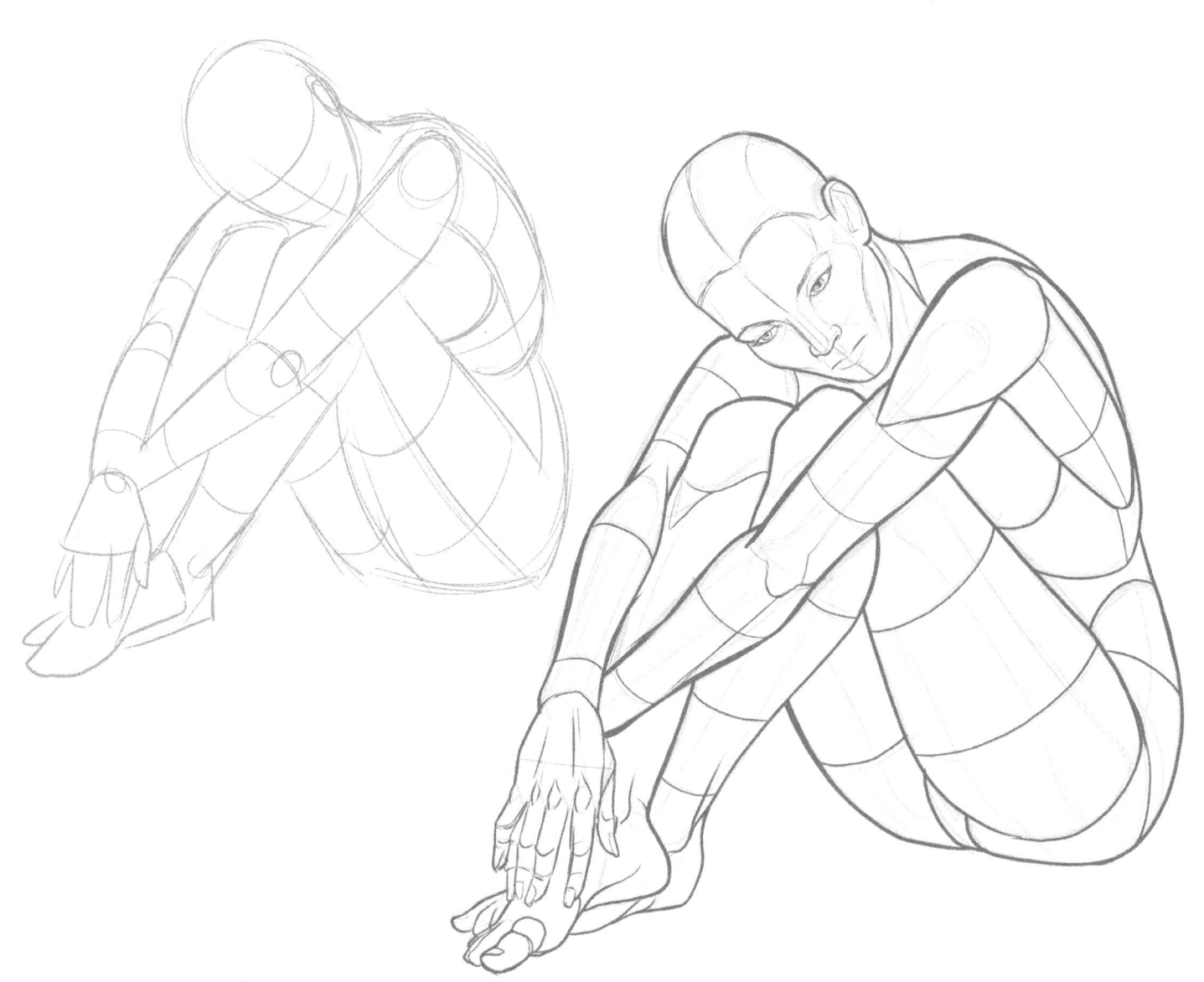

Sitting Poses -Page 72

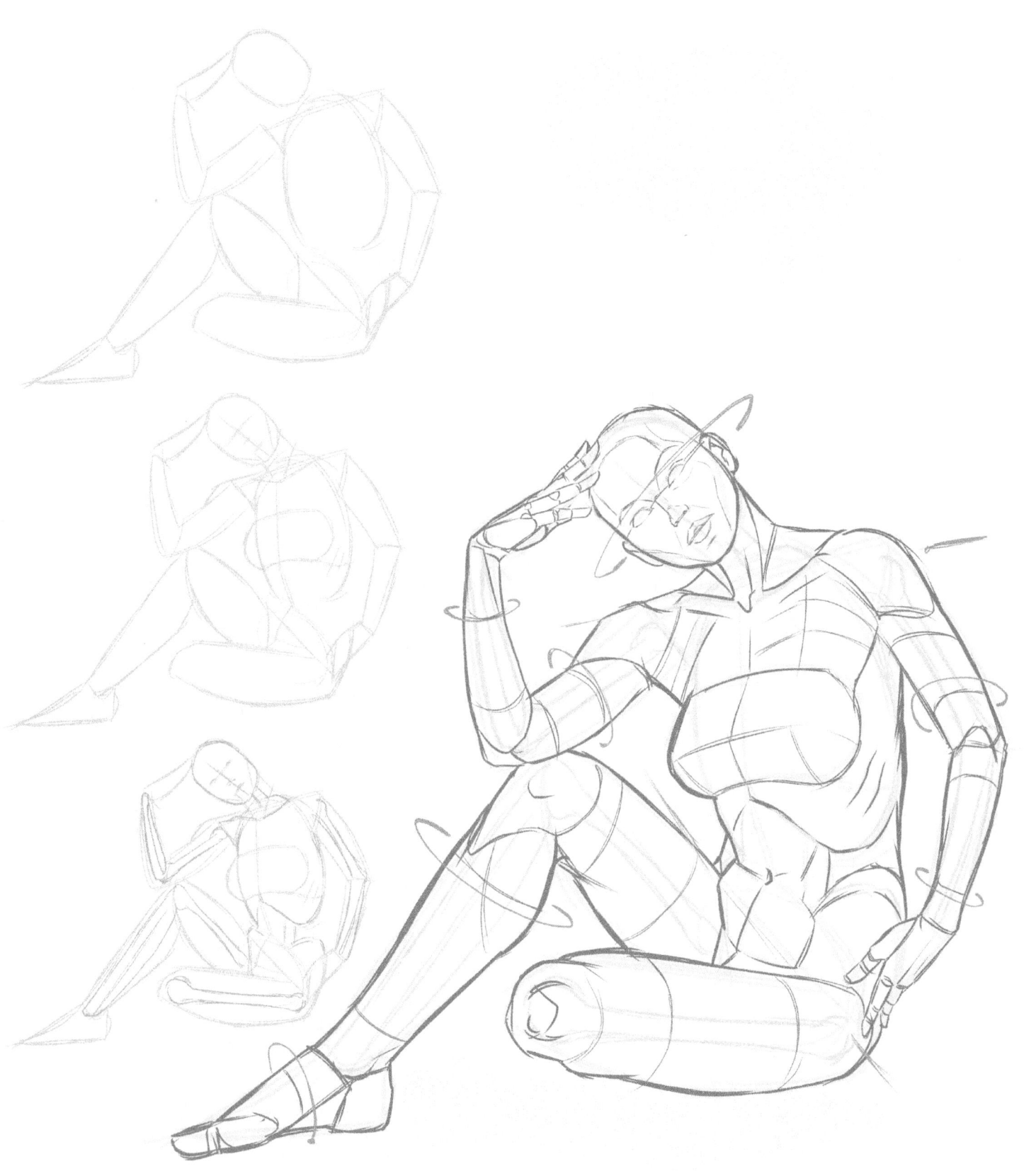

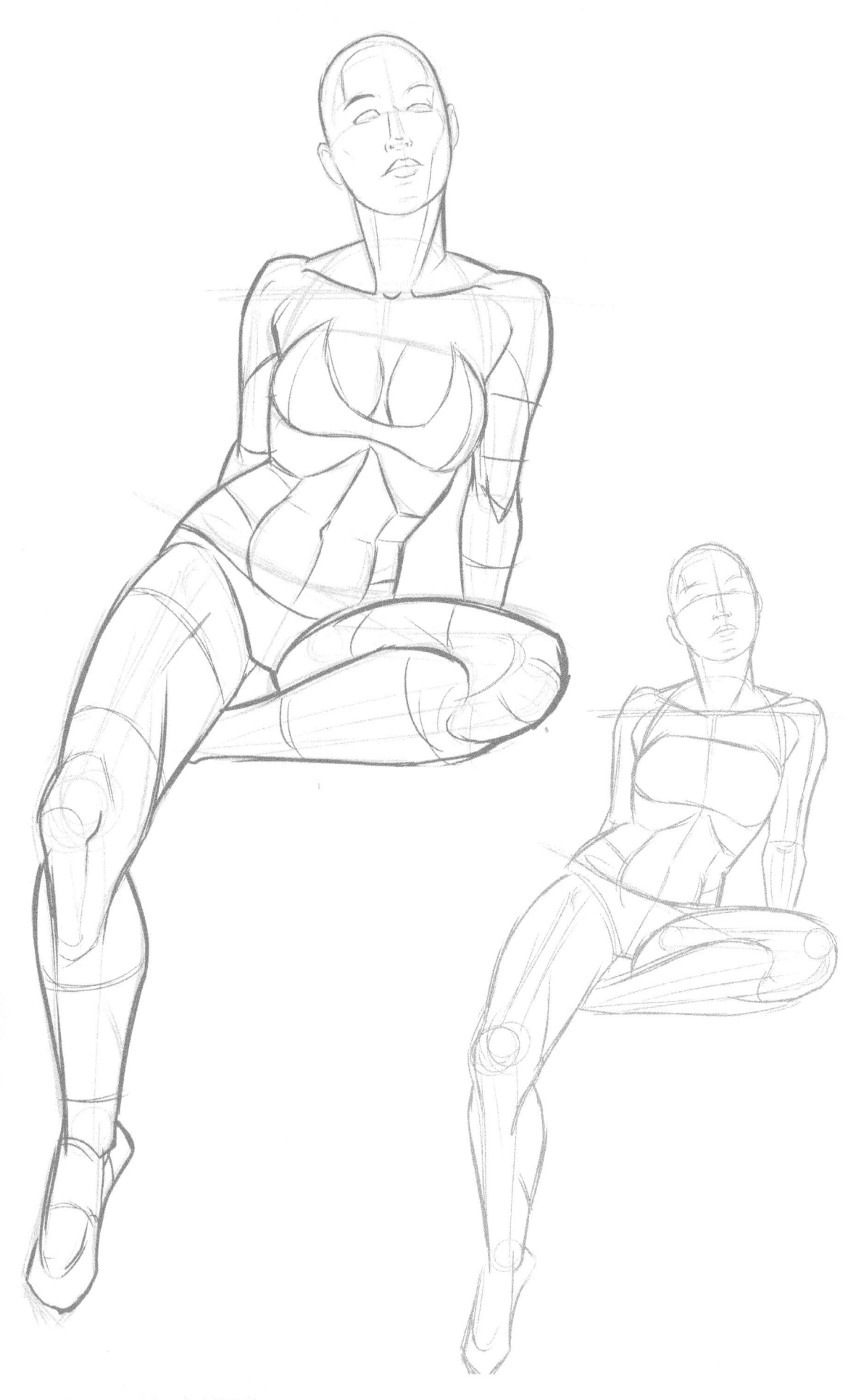

Sitting Poses -Page 74

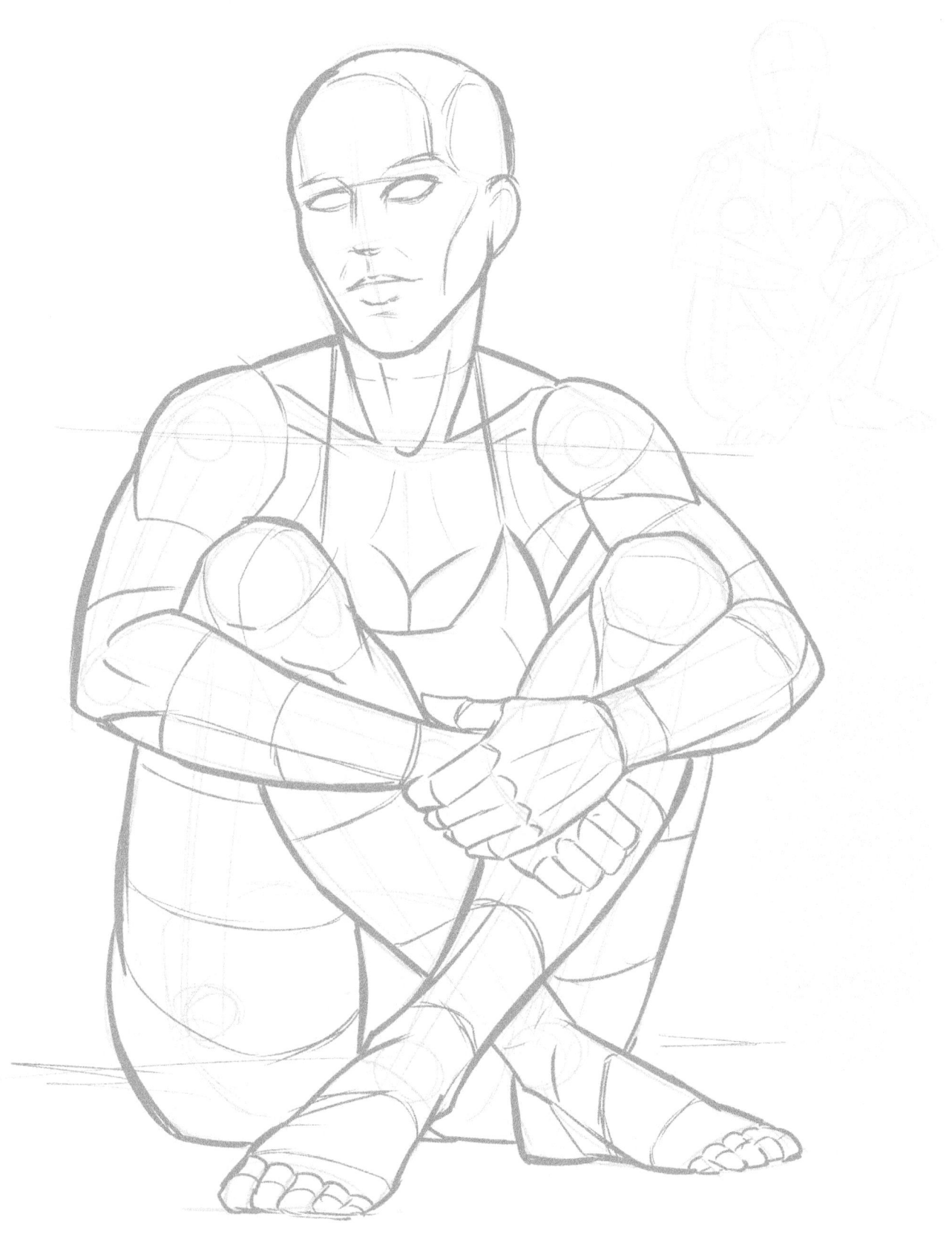

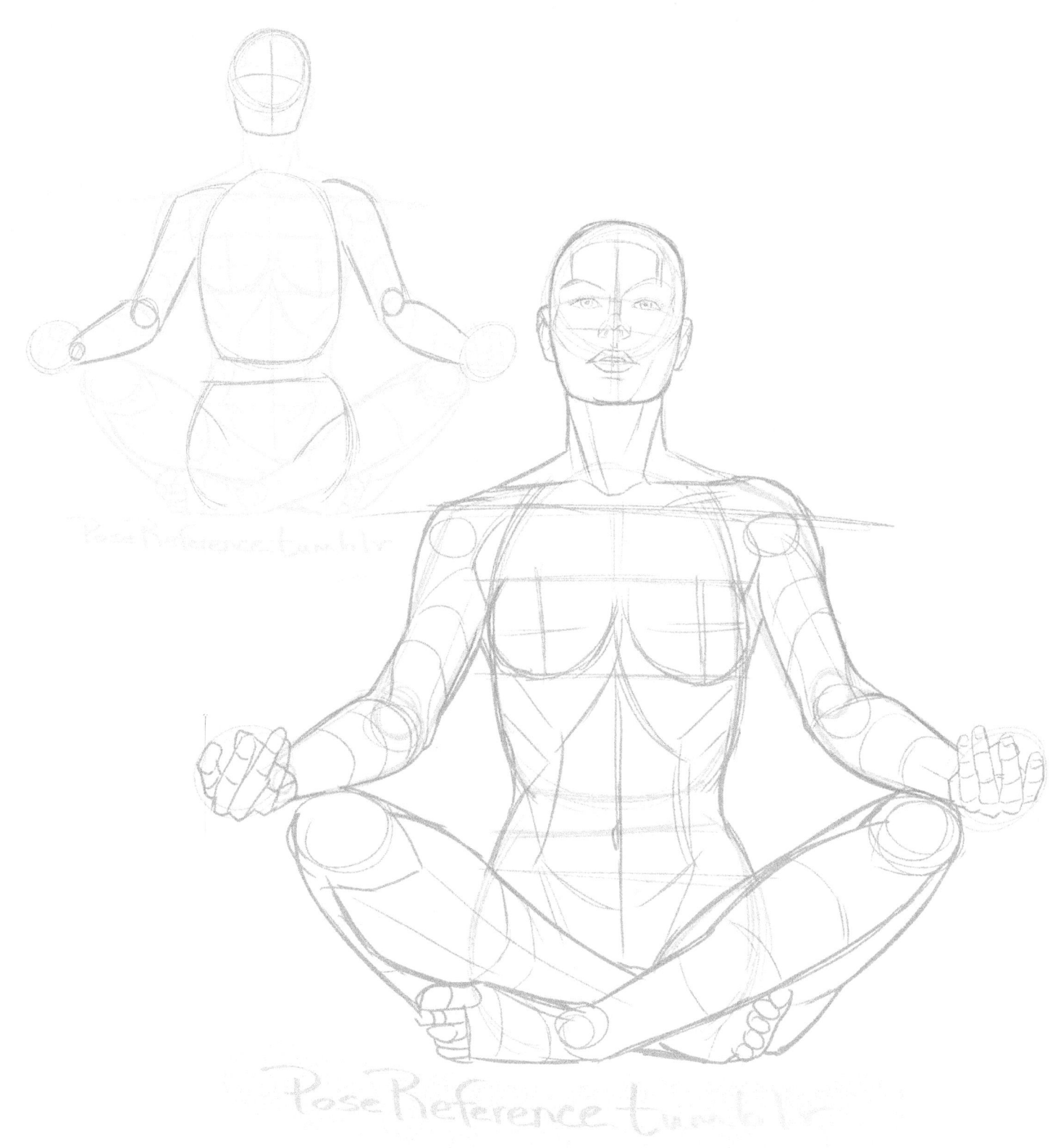

PoseReference tumblr

PoseReference tumblr

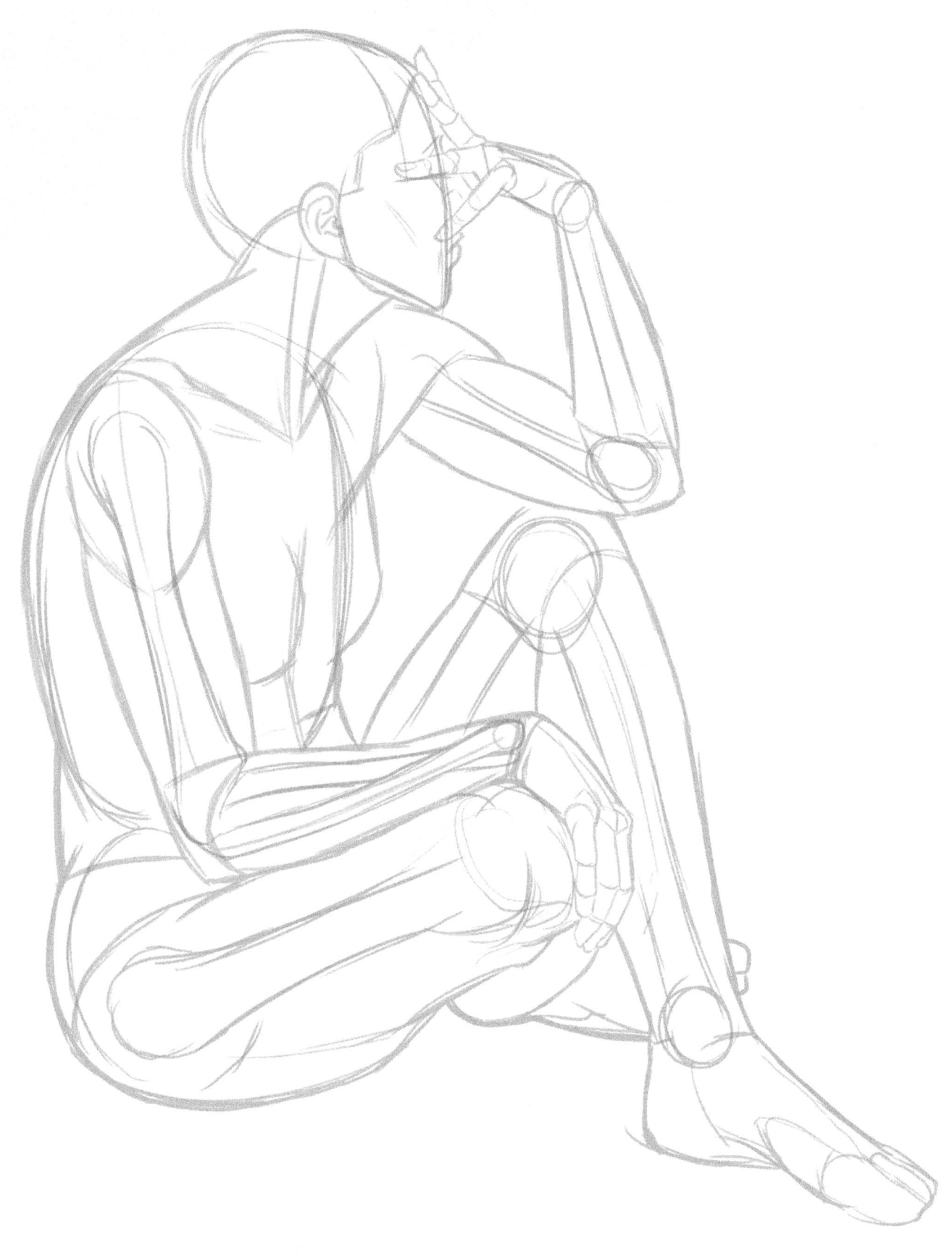

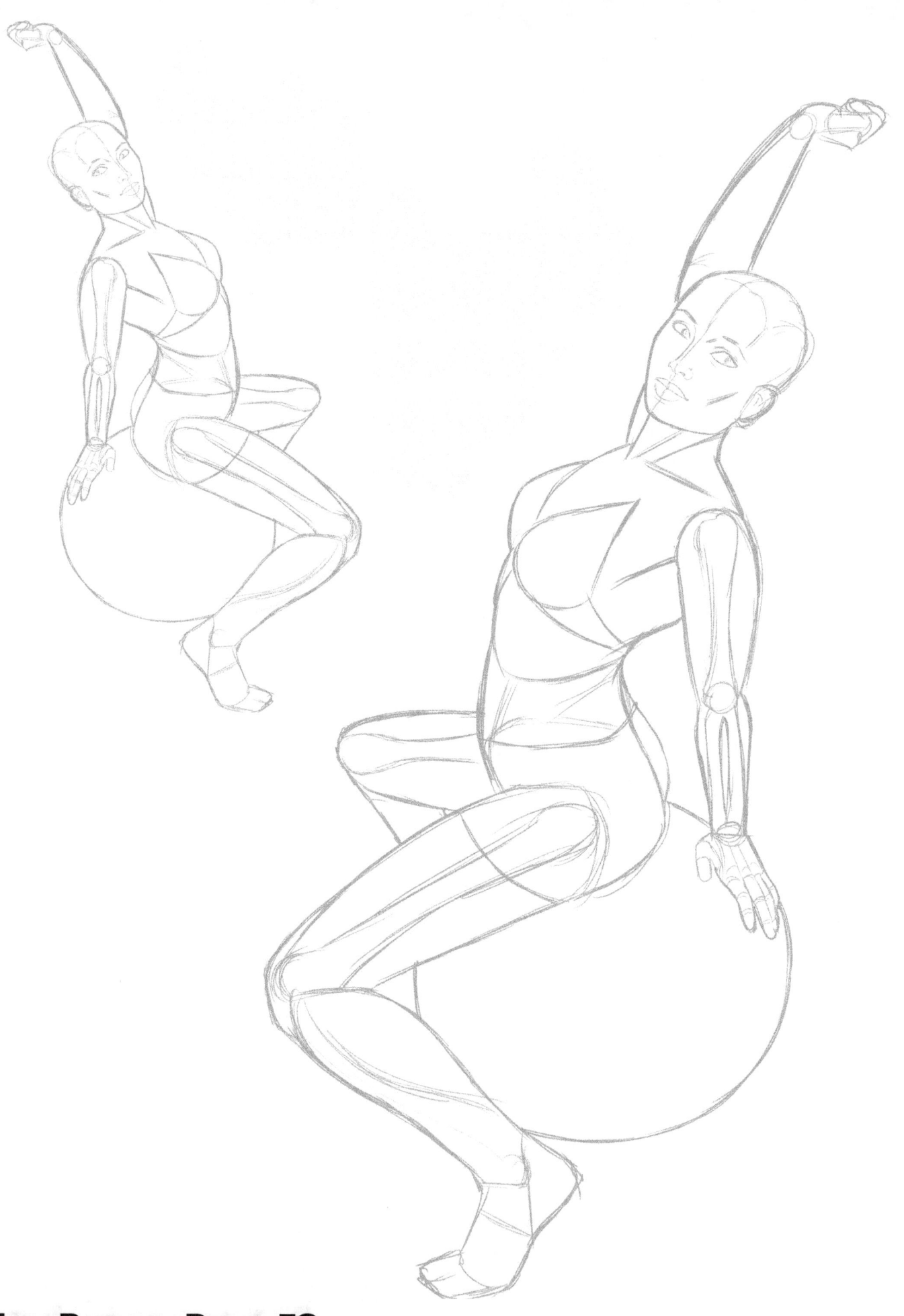

Sitting Poses -Page 78

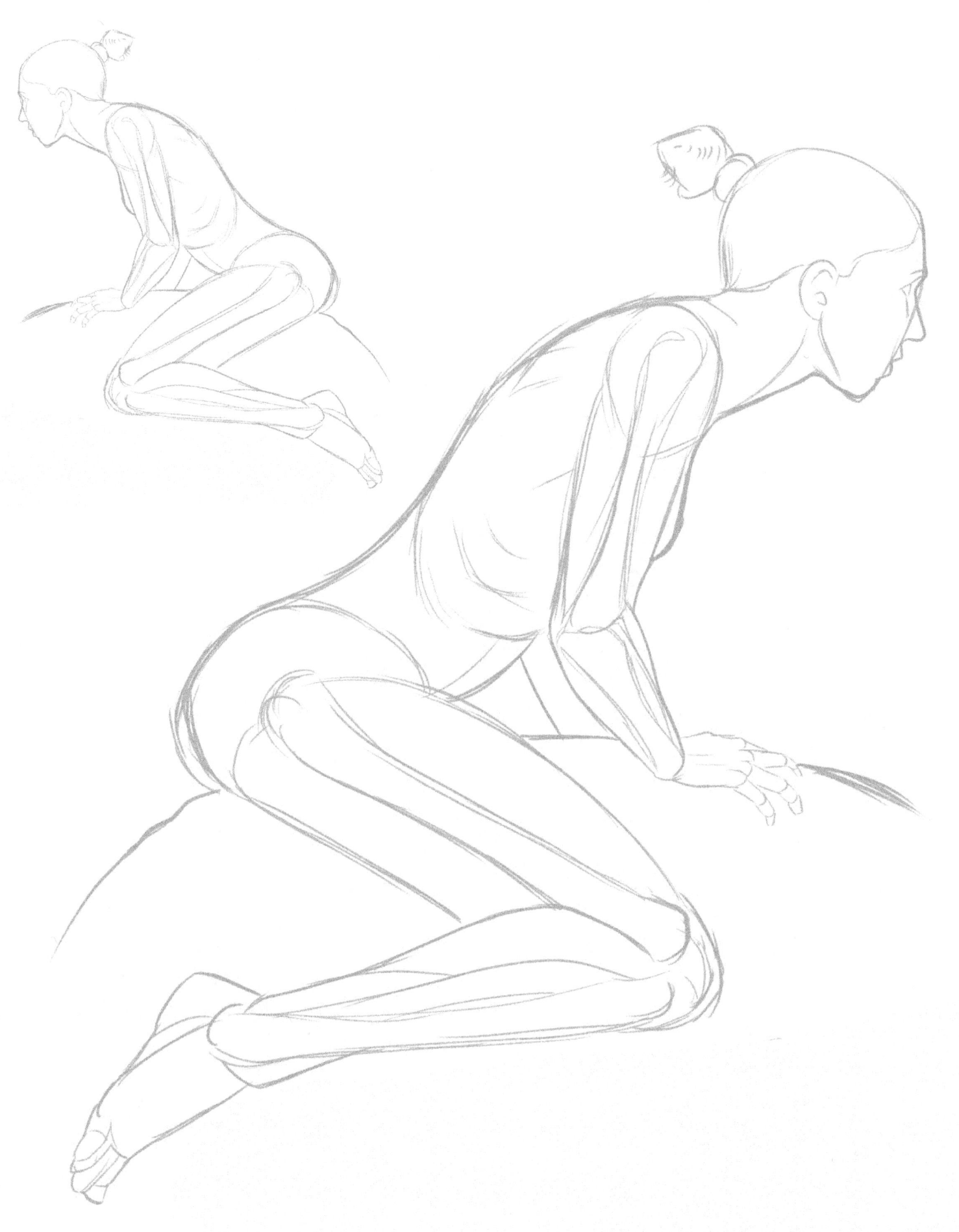

Sitting Poses -Page 79

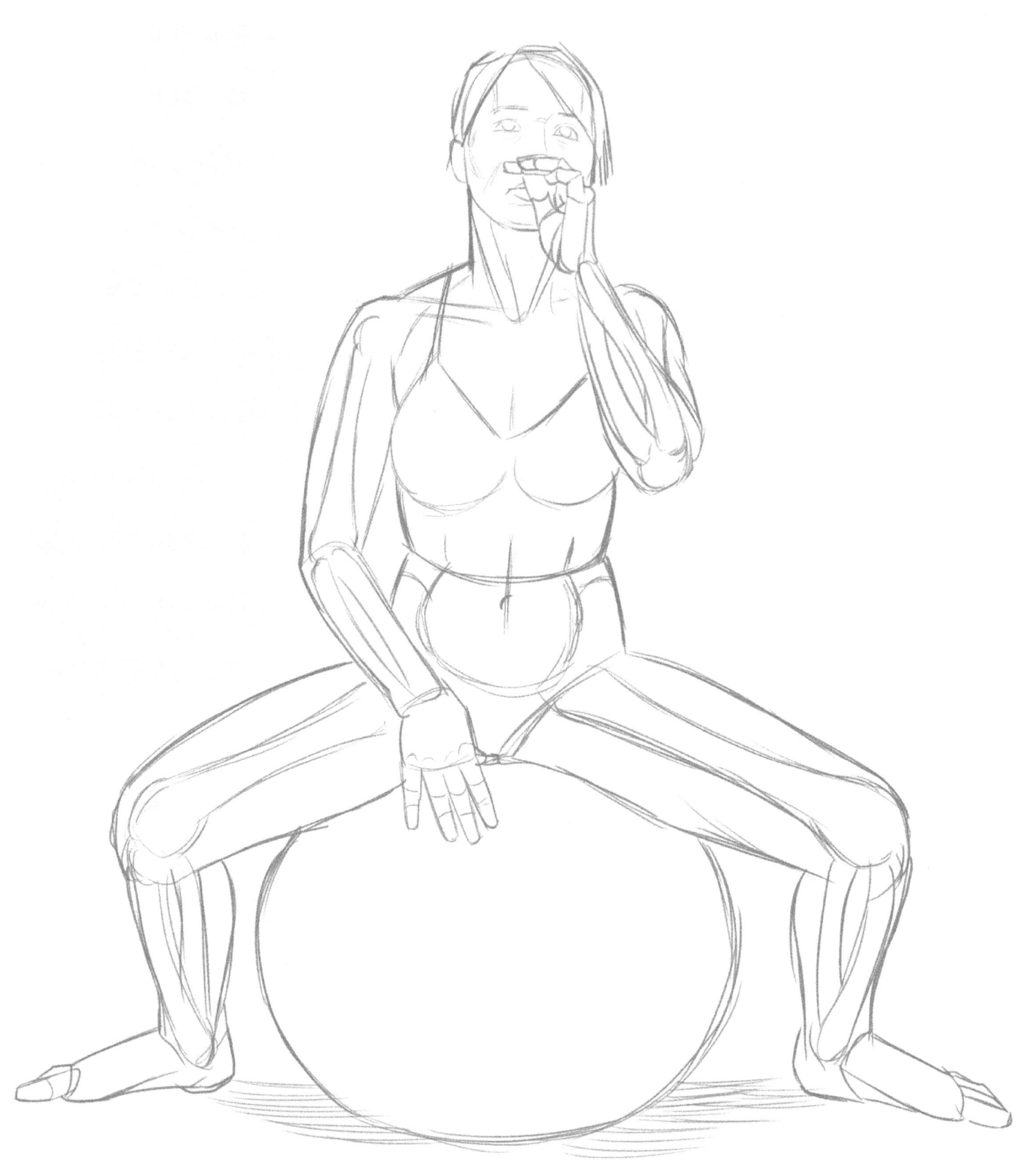

Sitting Poses -Page 80

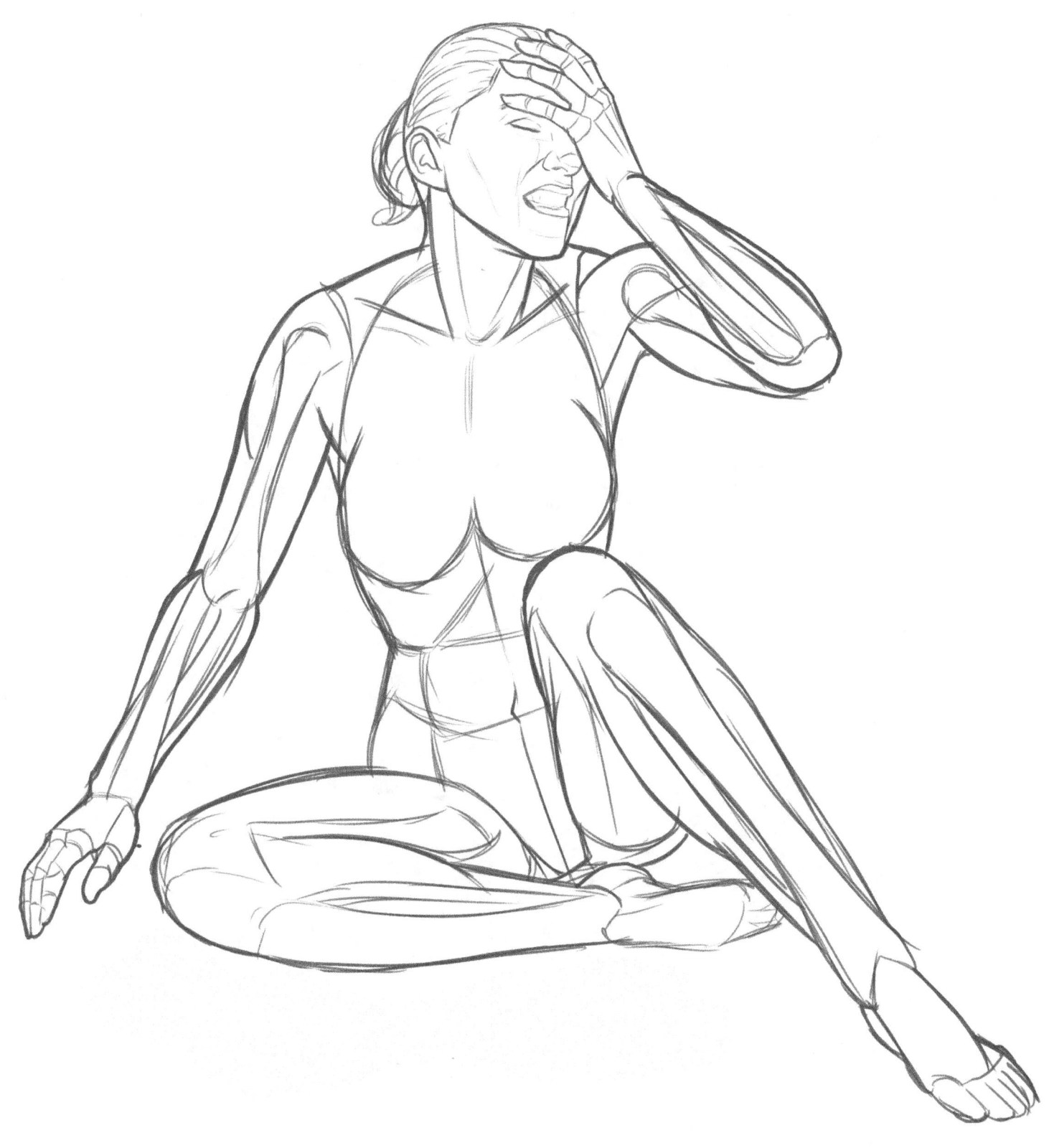

Sitting Poses -Page 81

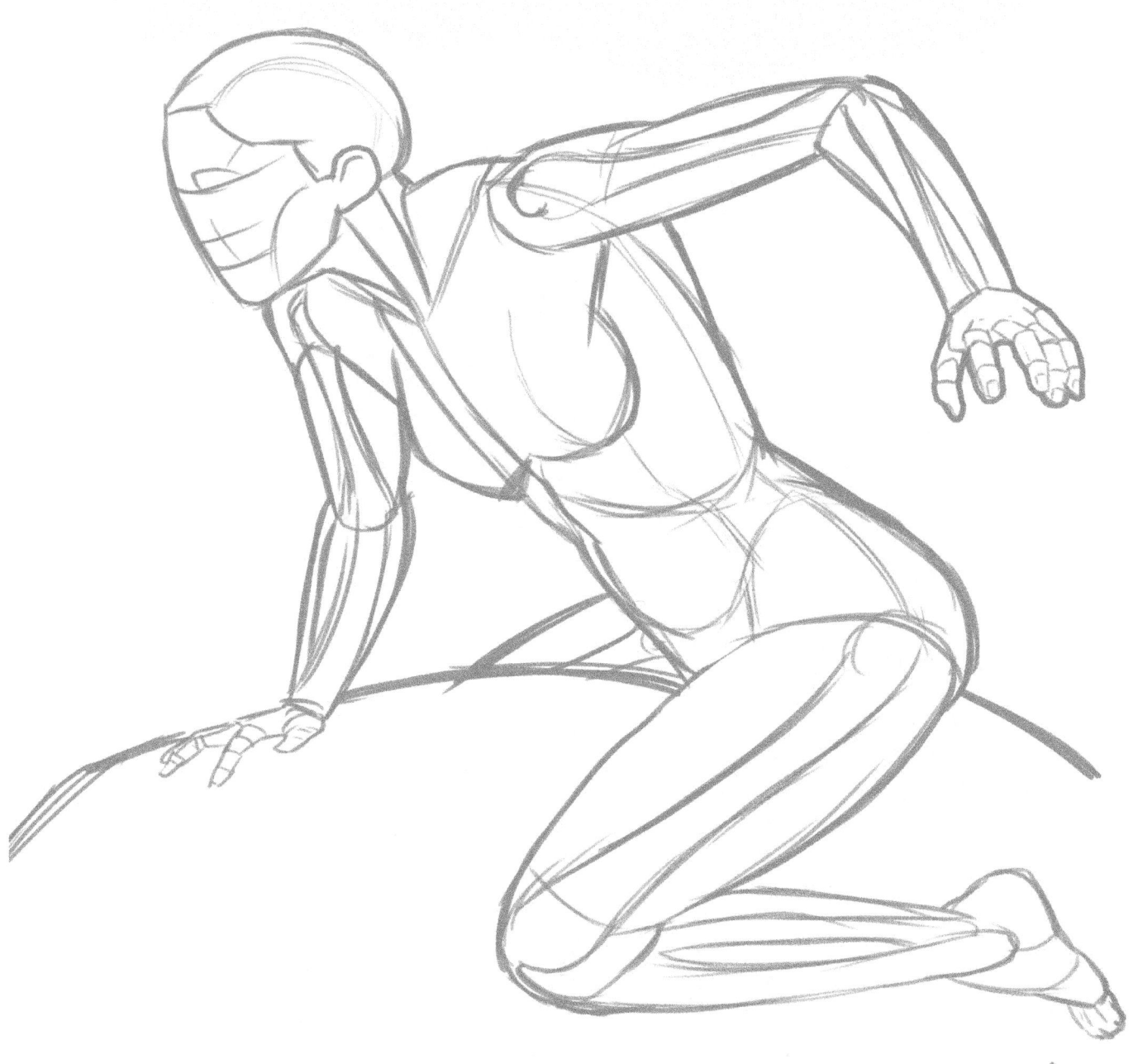

Sitting Poses -Page 82

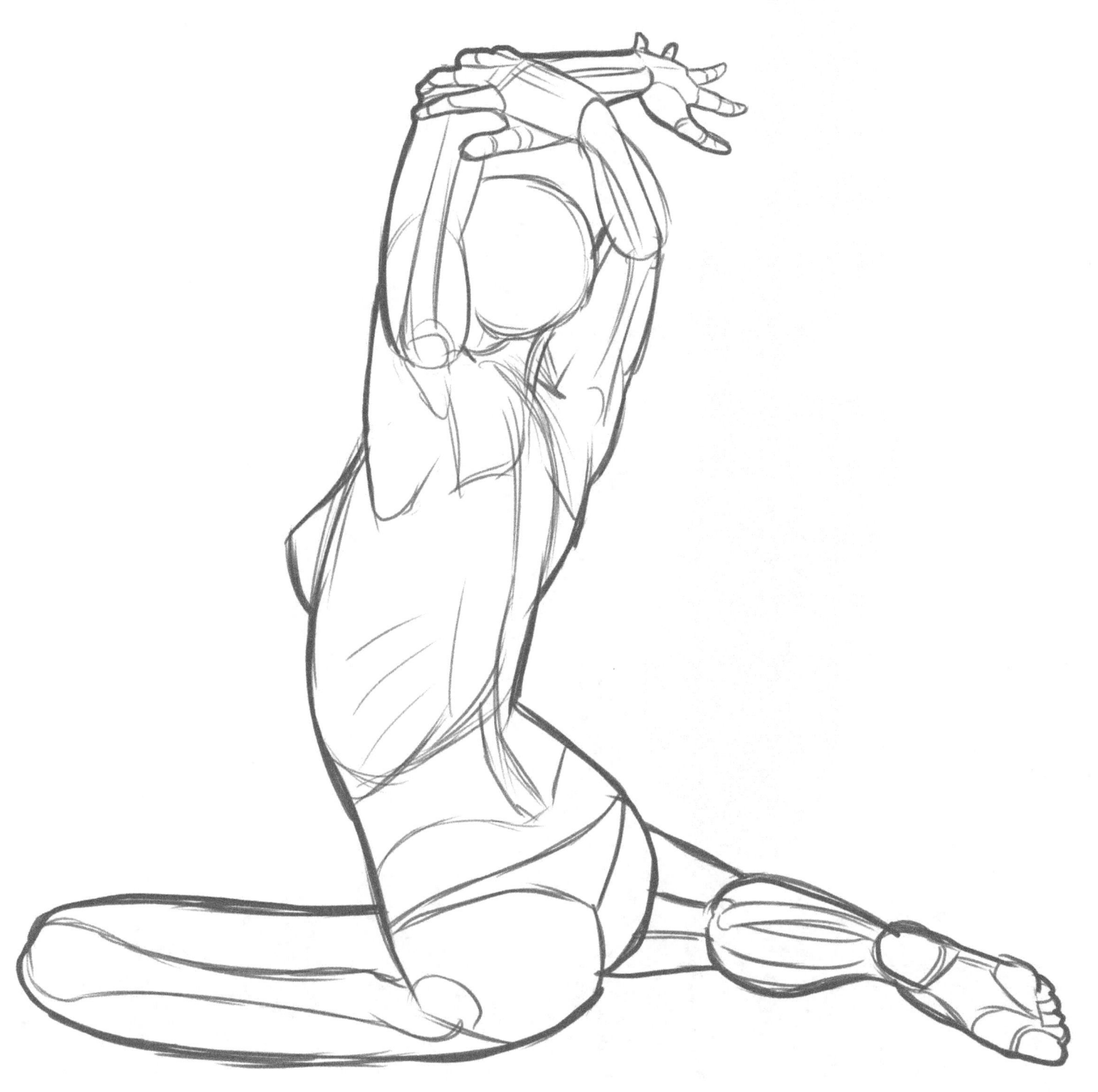

Sitting Poses -Page 83

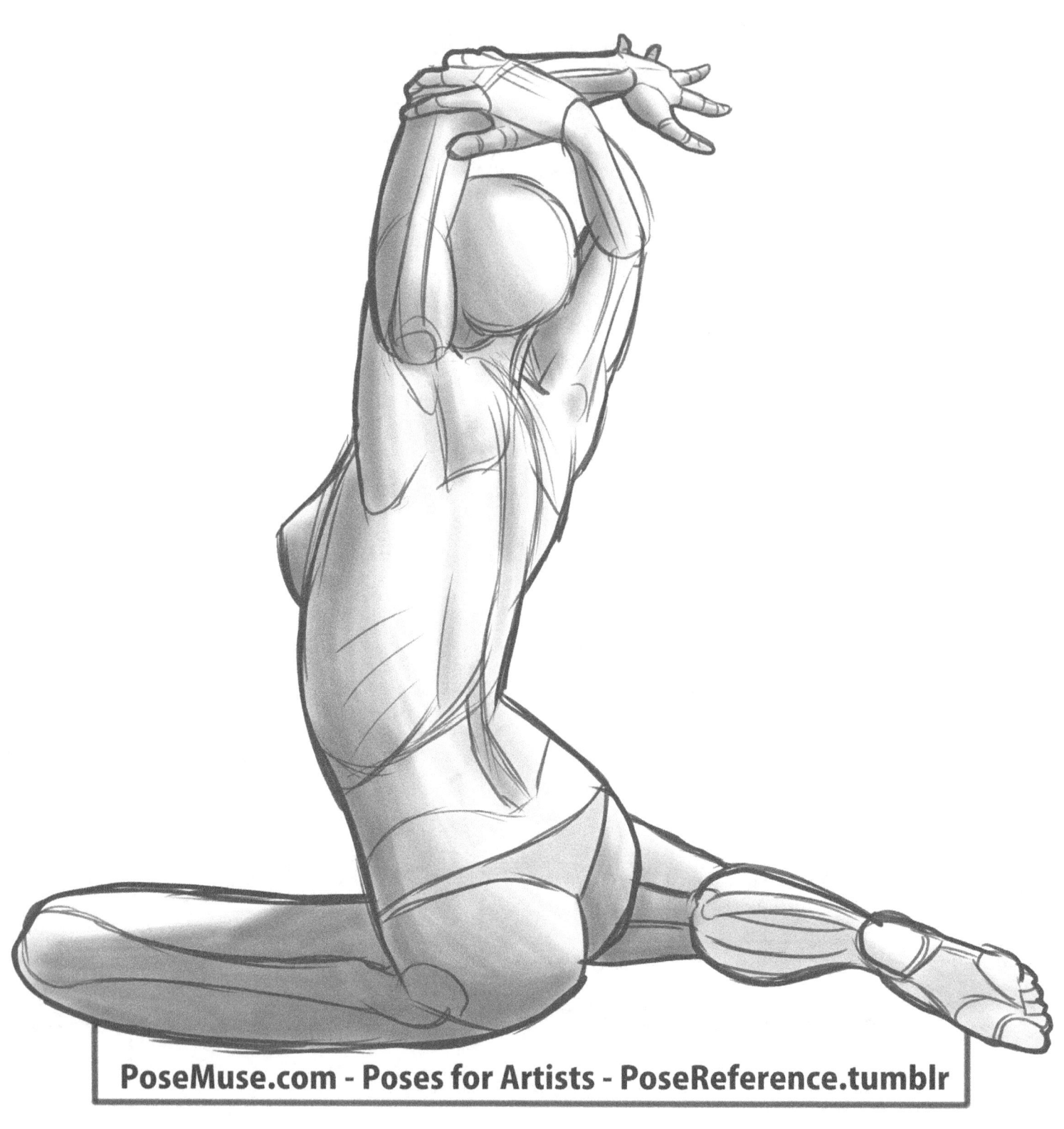

Sitting Poses -Page 84

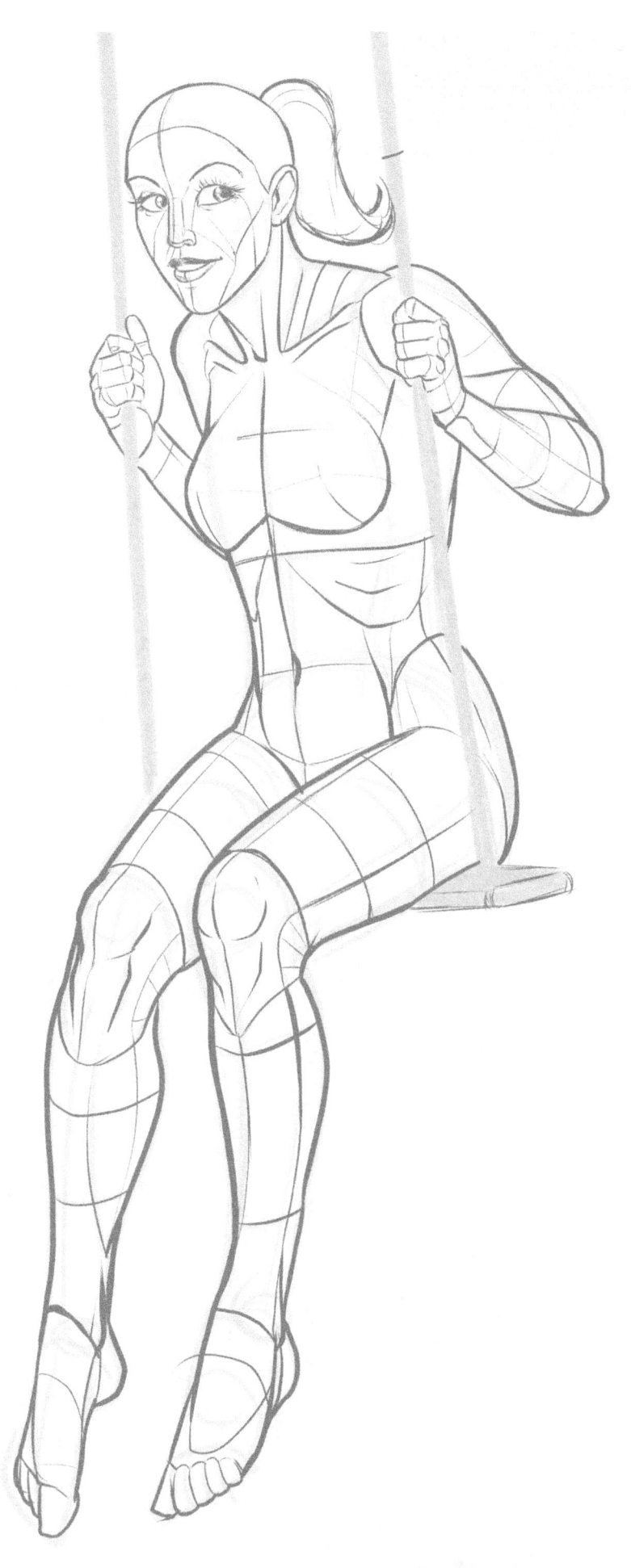

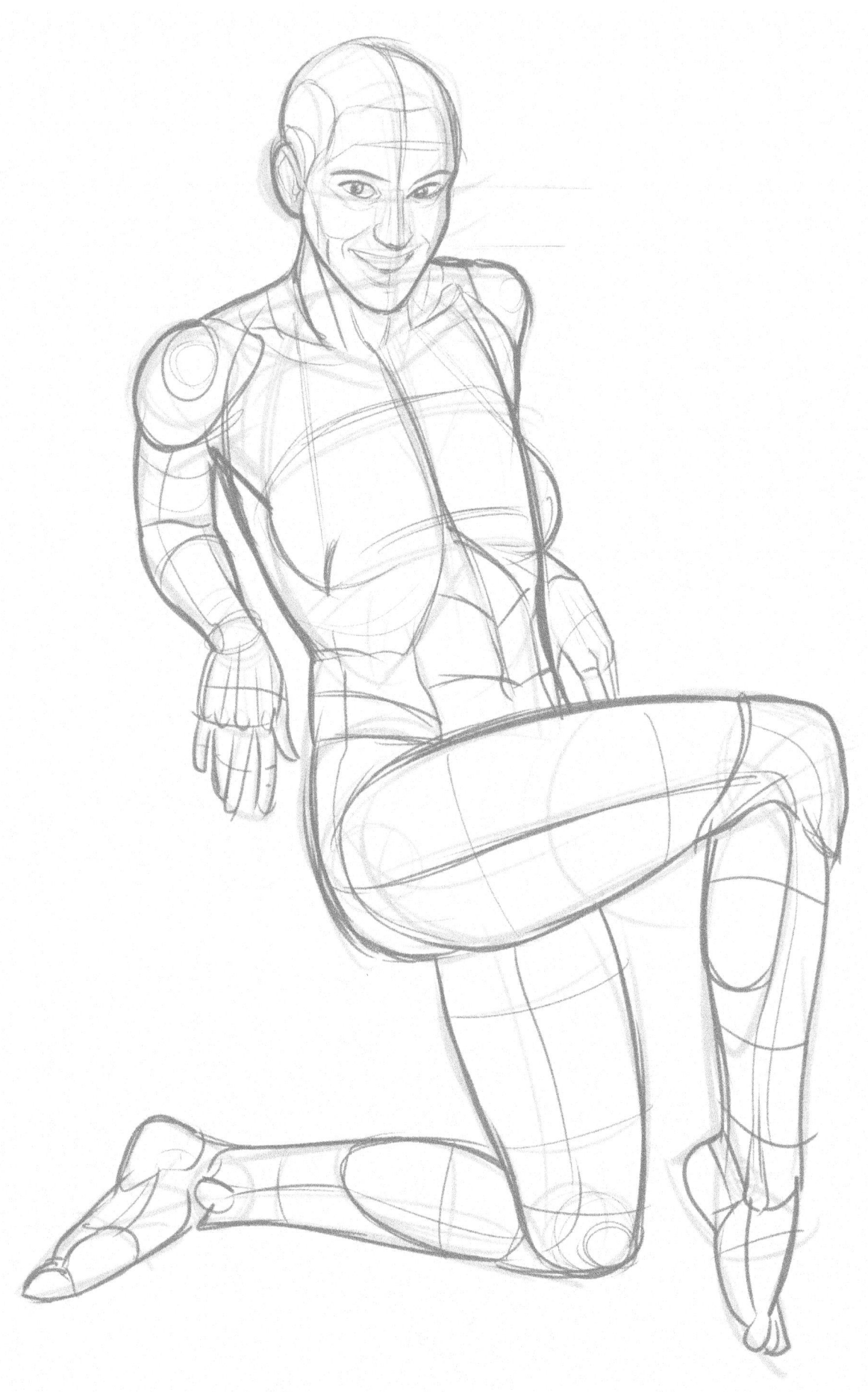

Sitting Poses -Page 86

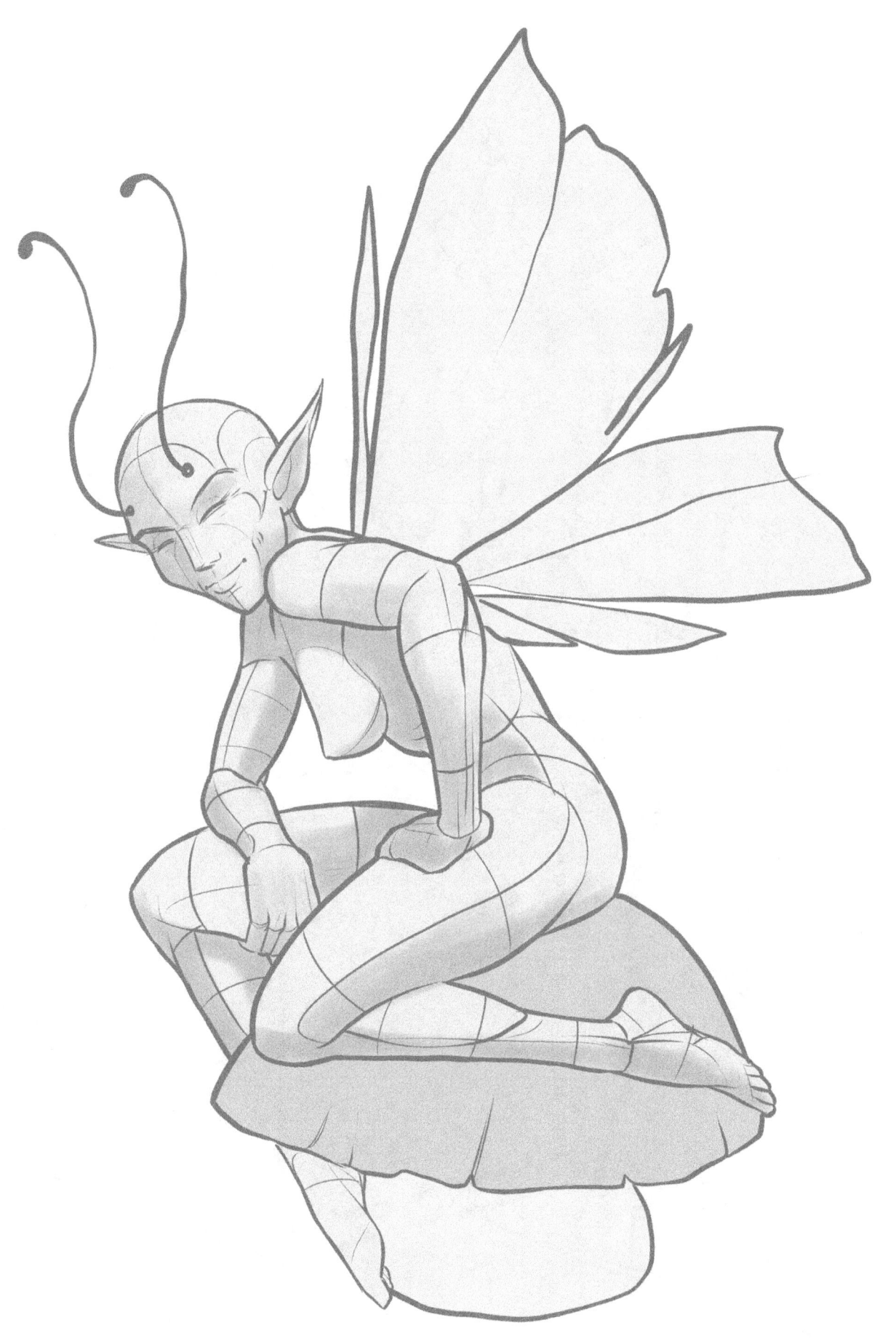

Sitting Poses -Page 87

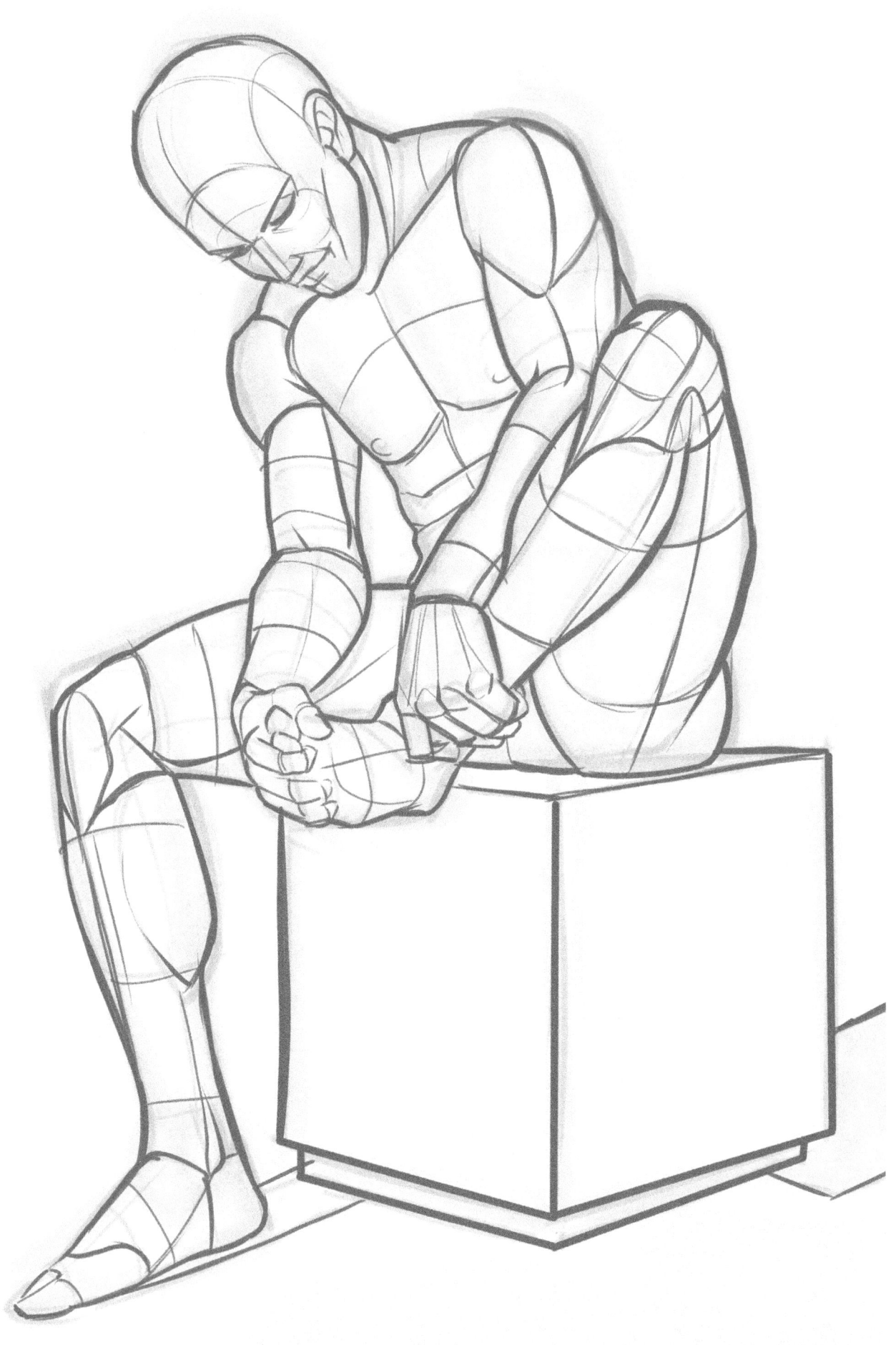

Sitting Poses -Page 88

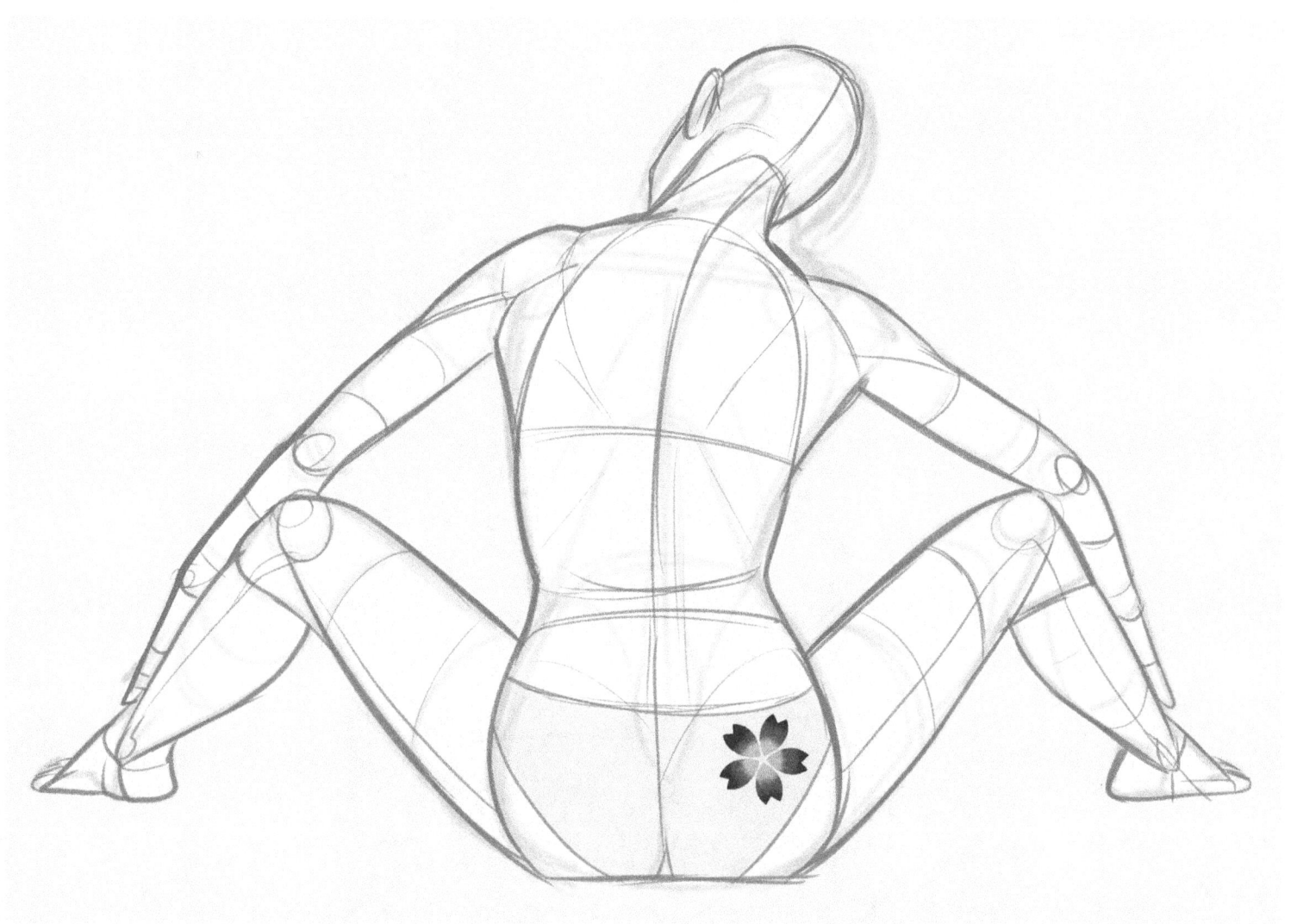

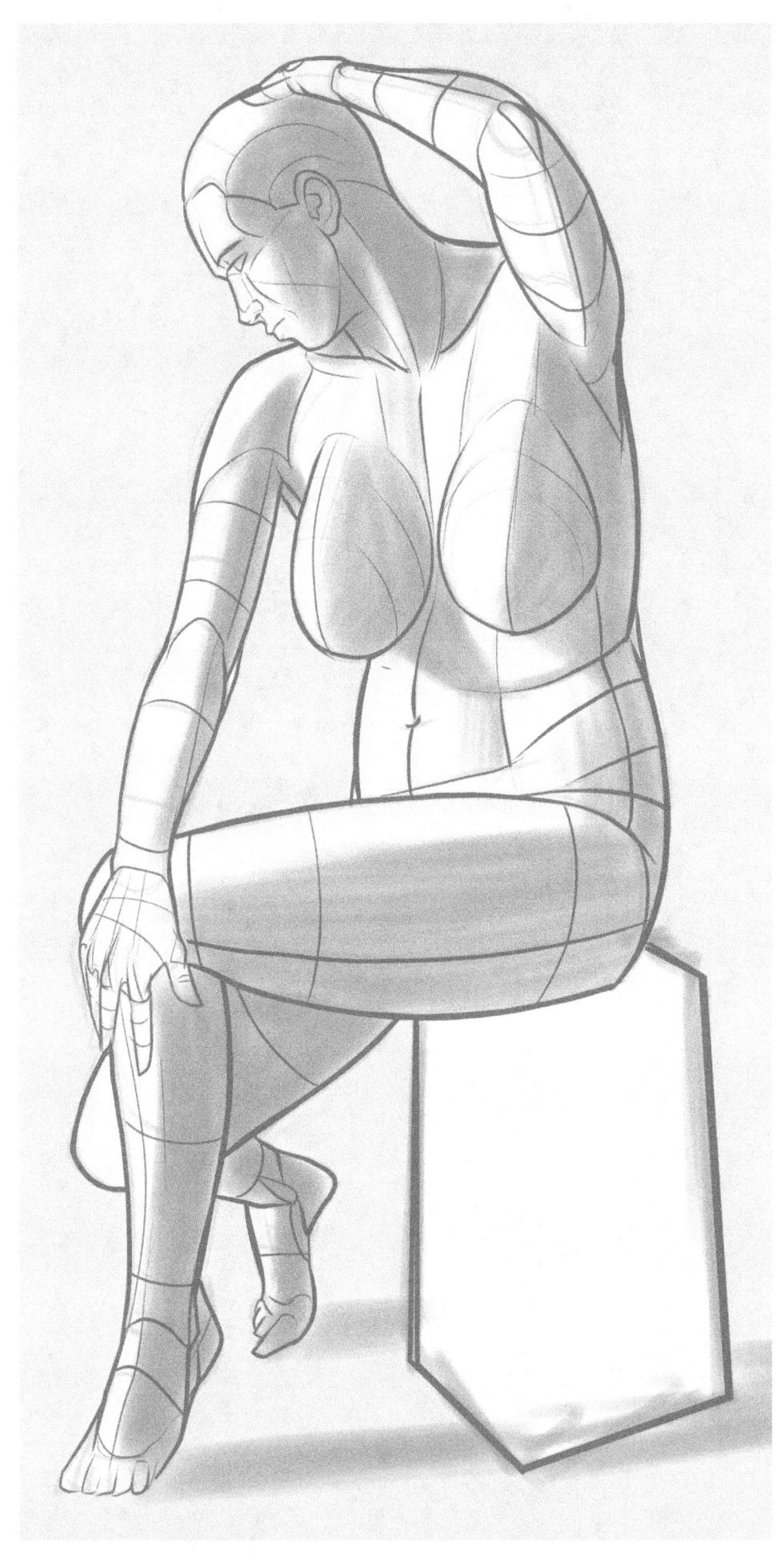

Sitting Poses -Page 90

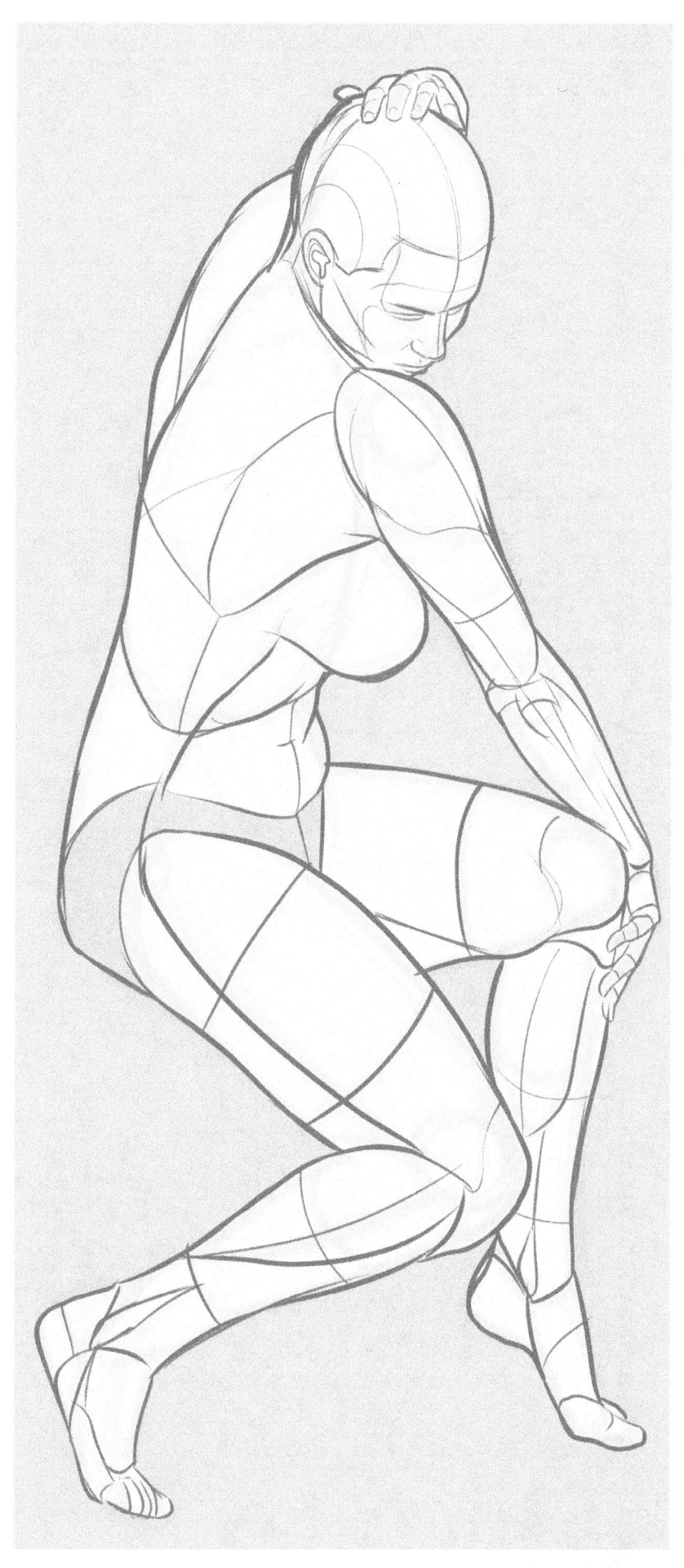

Sitting Poses -Page 91

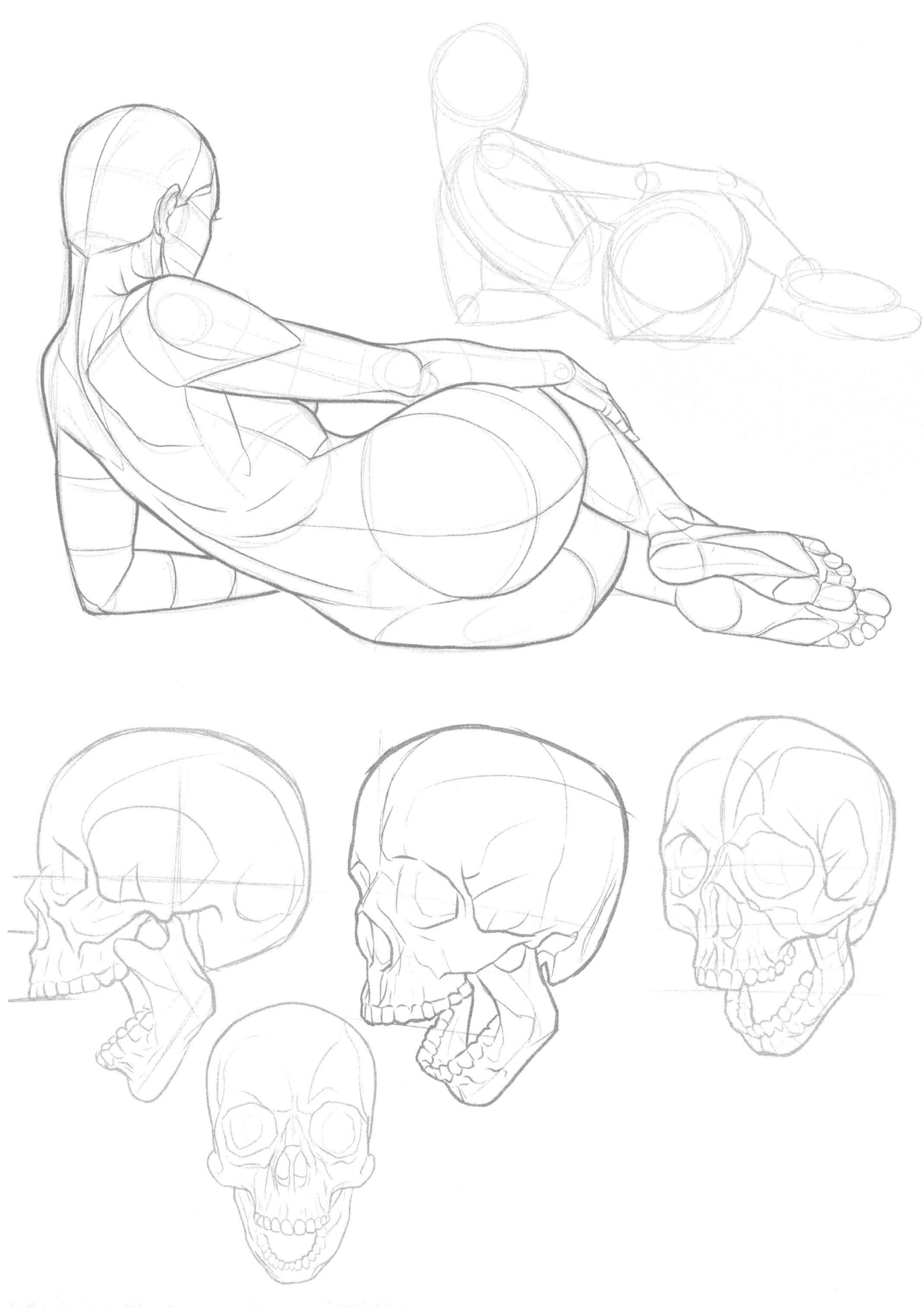

Various Poses -Page 92

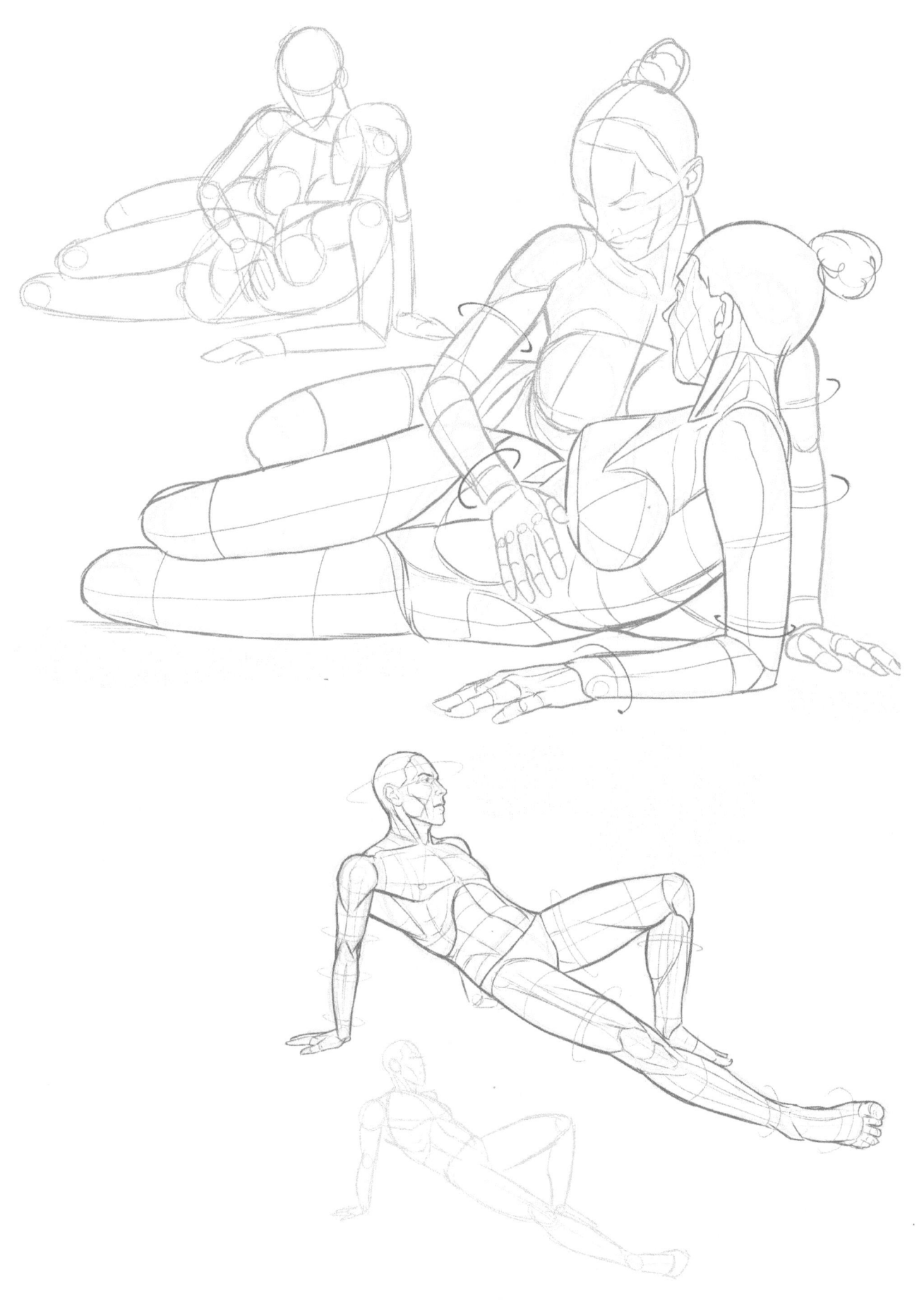

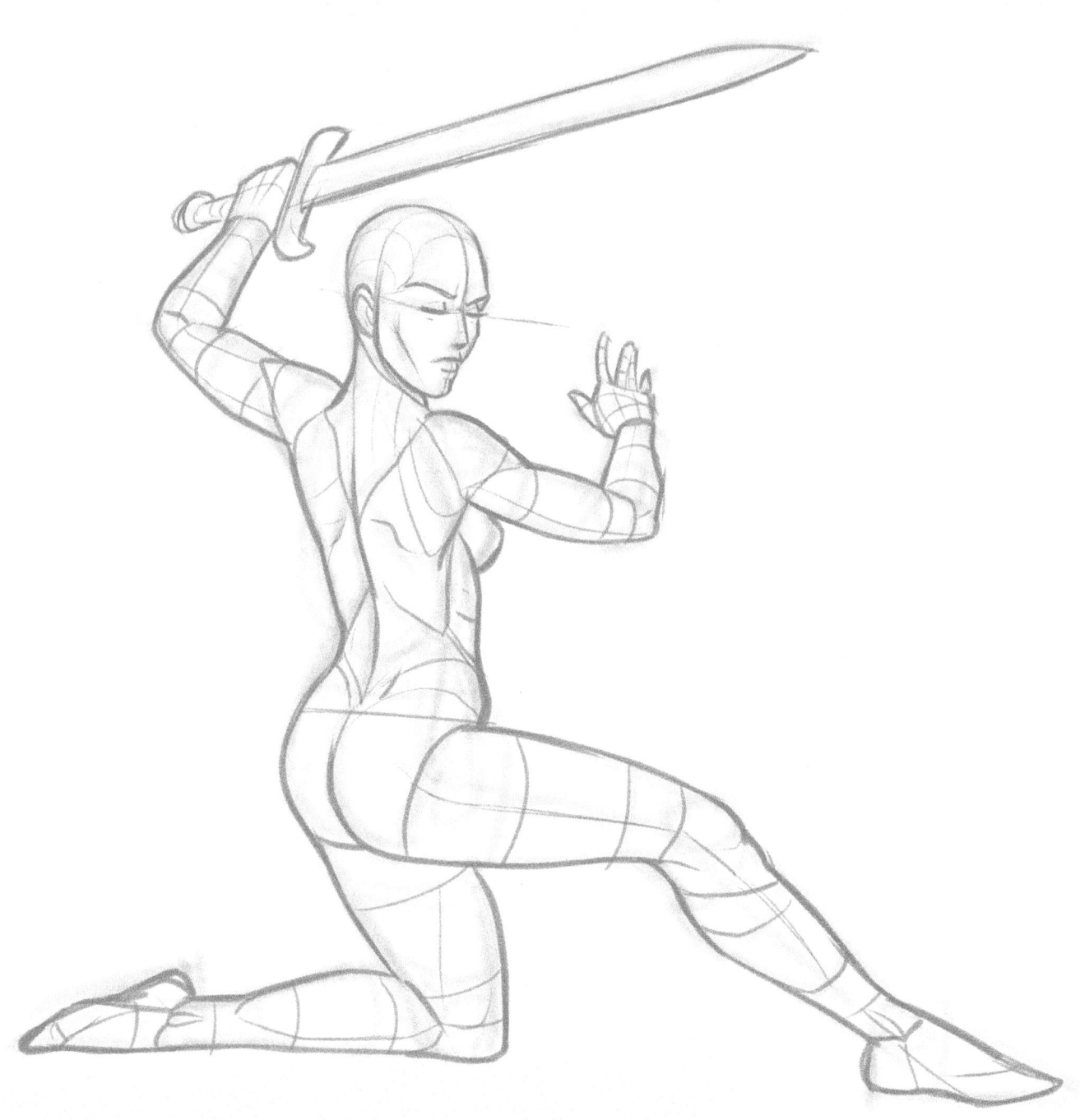

Various Poses -Page 94

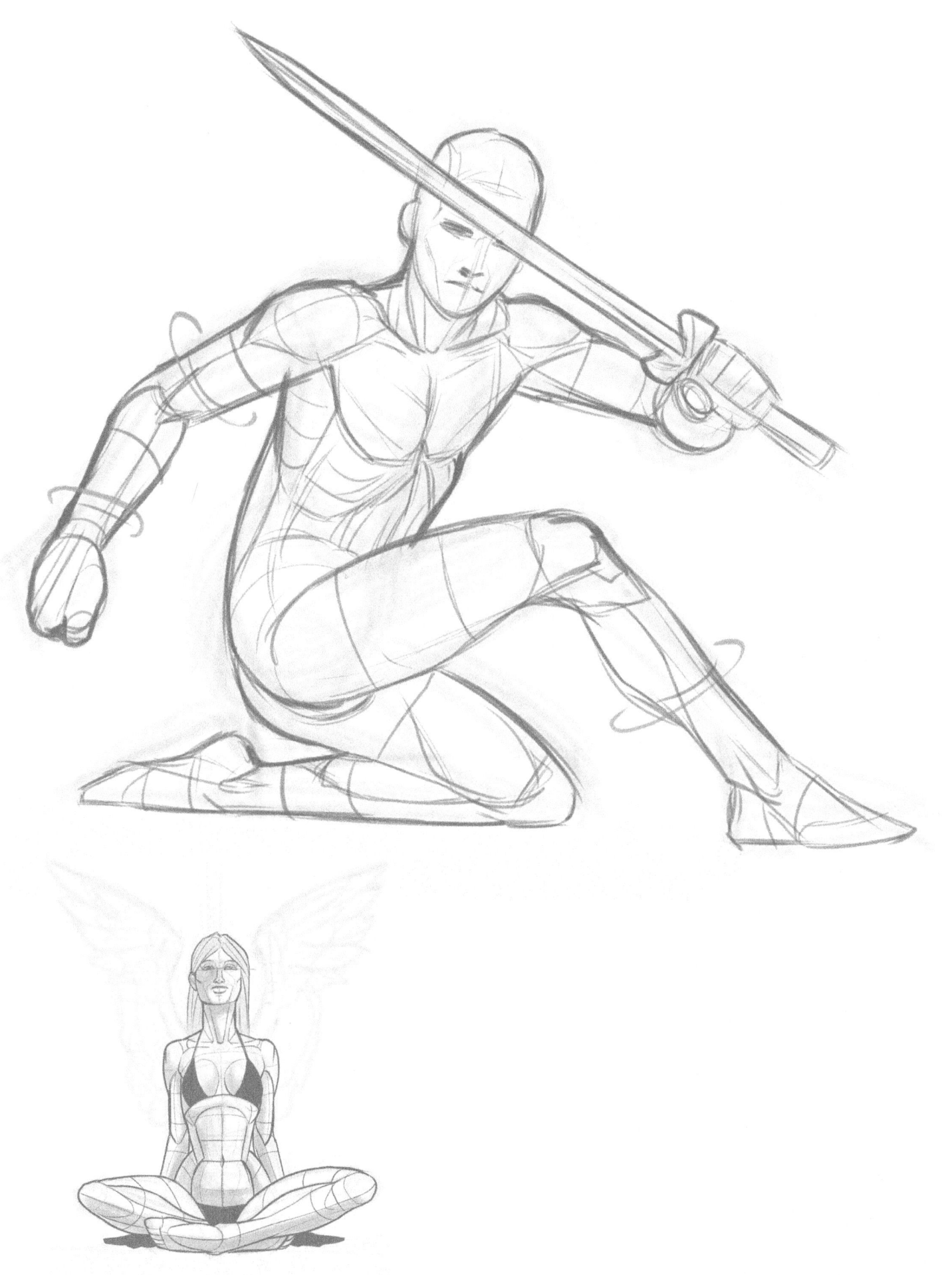

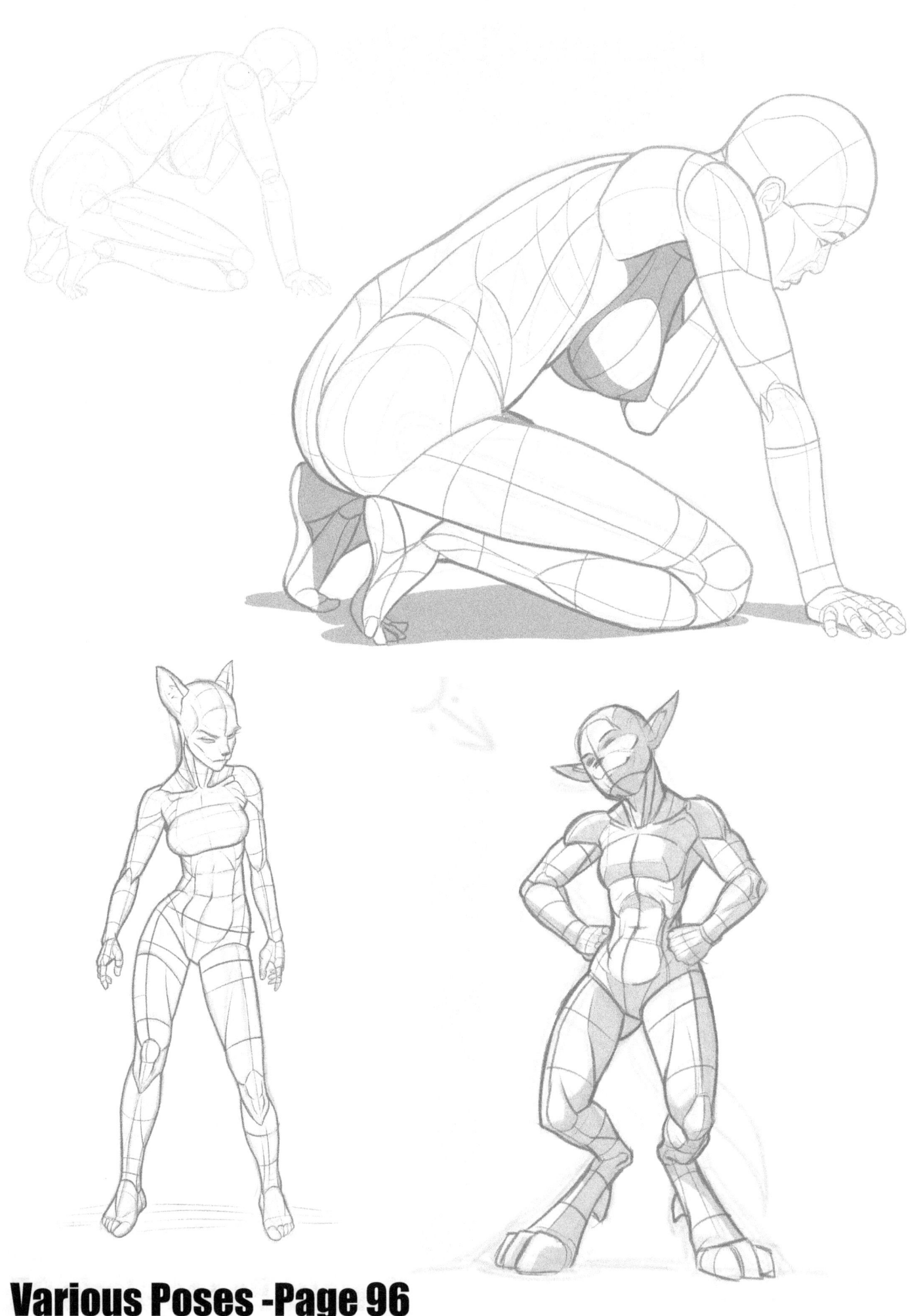

Various Poses -Page 96

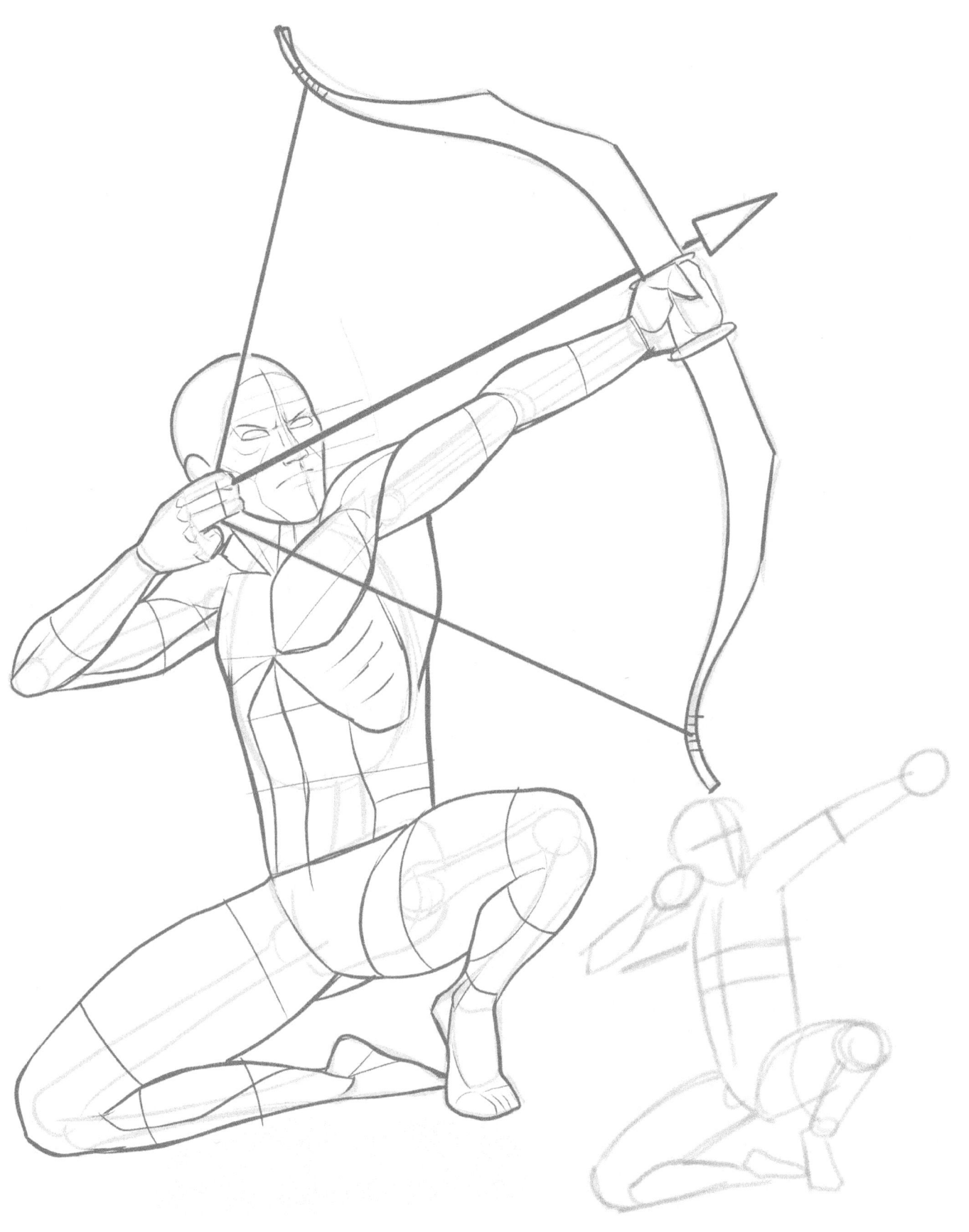

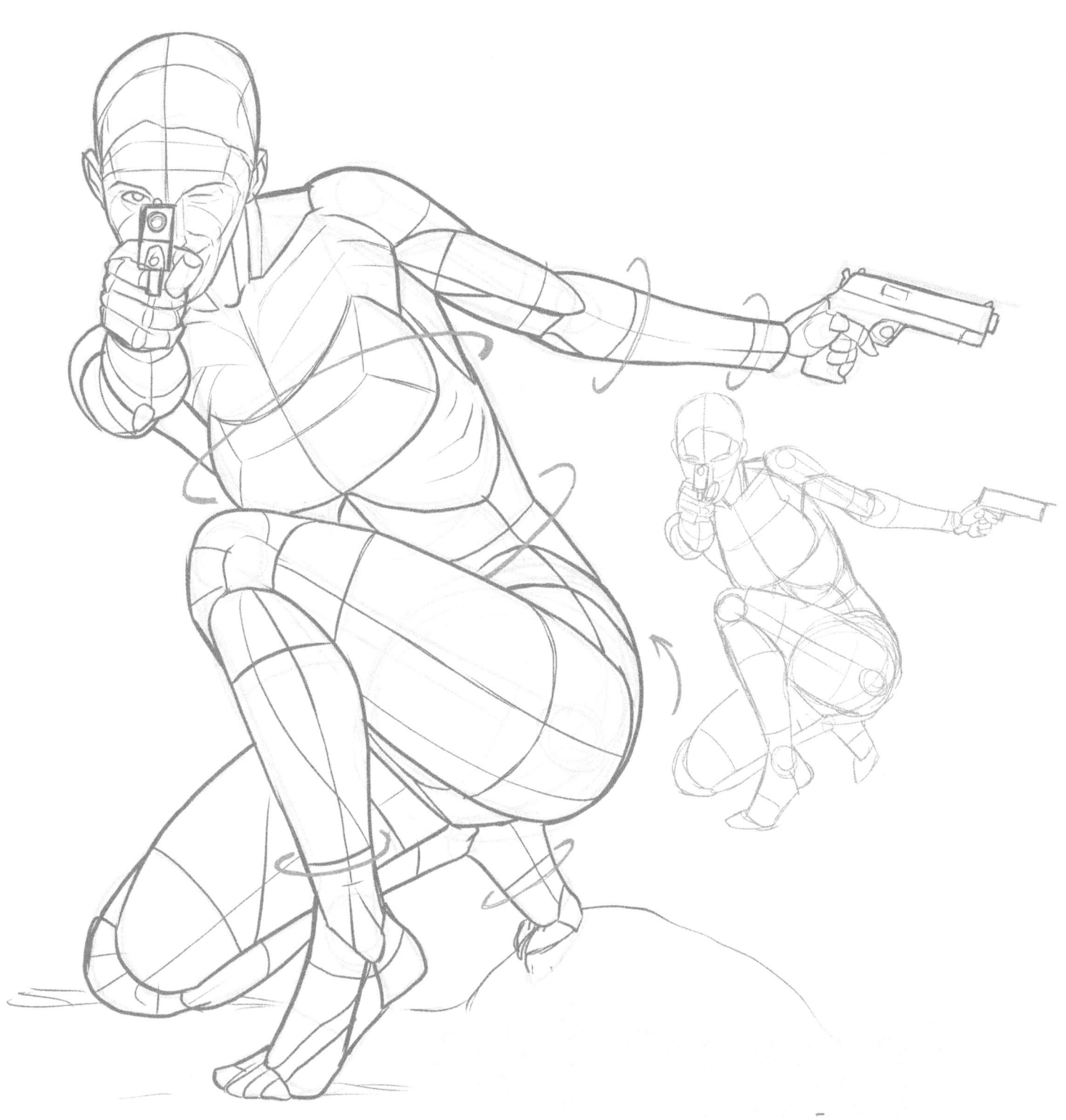

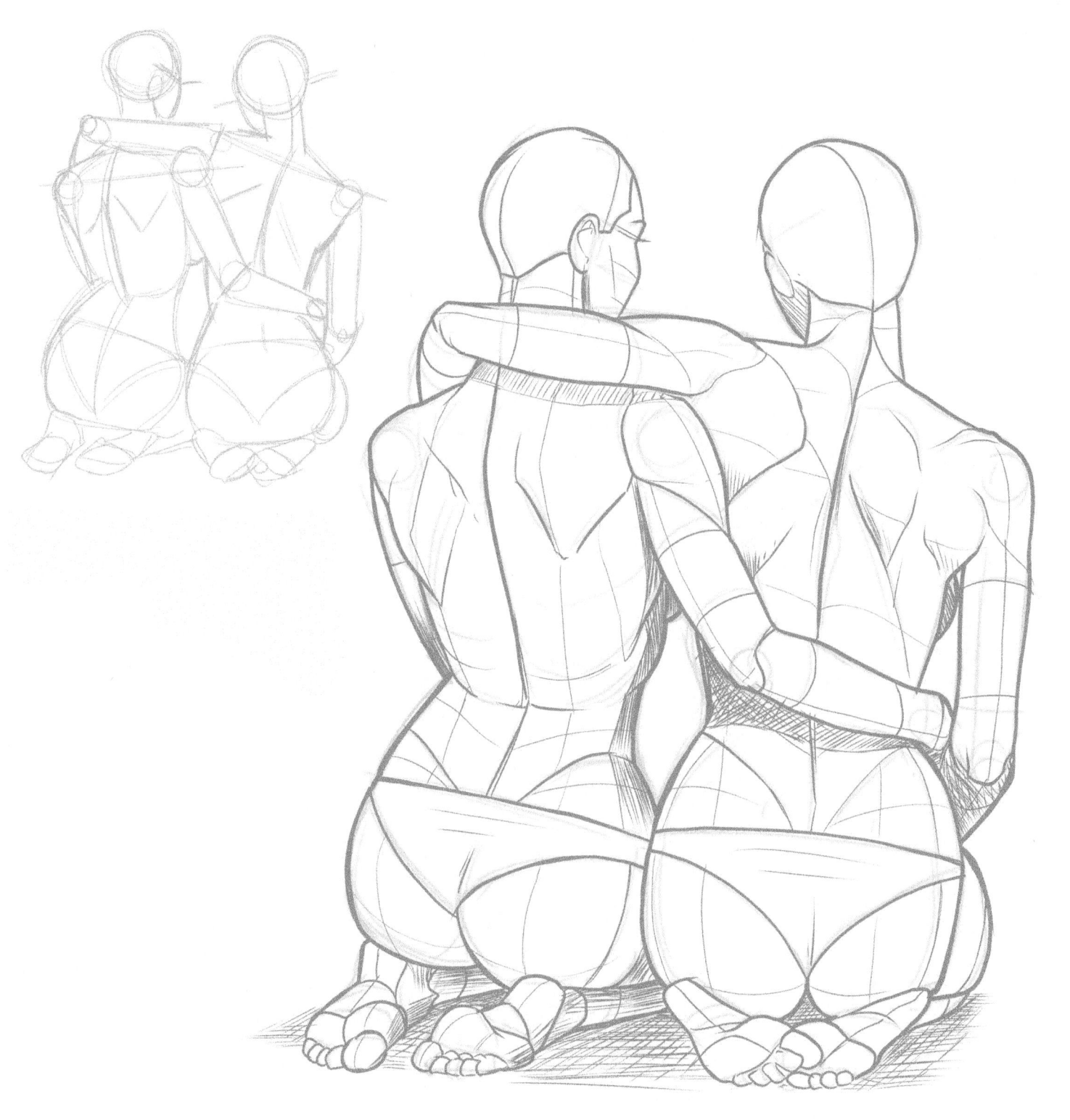

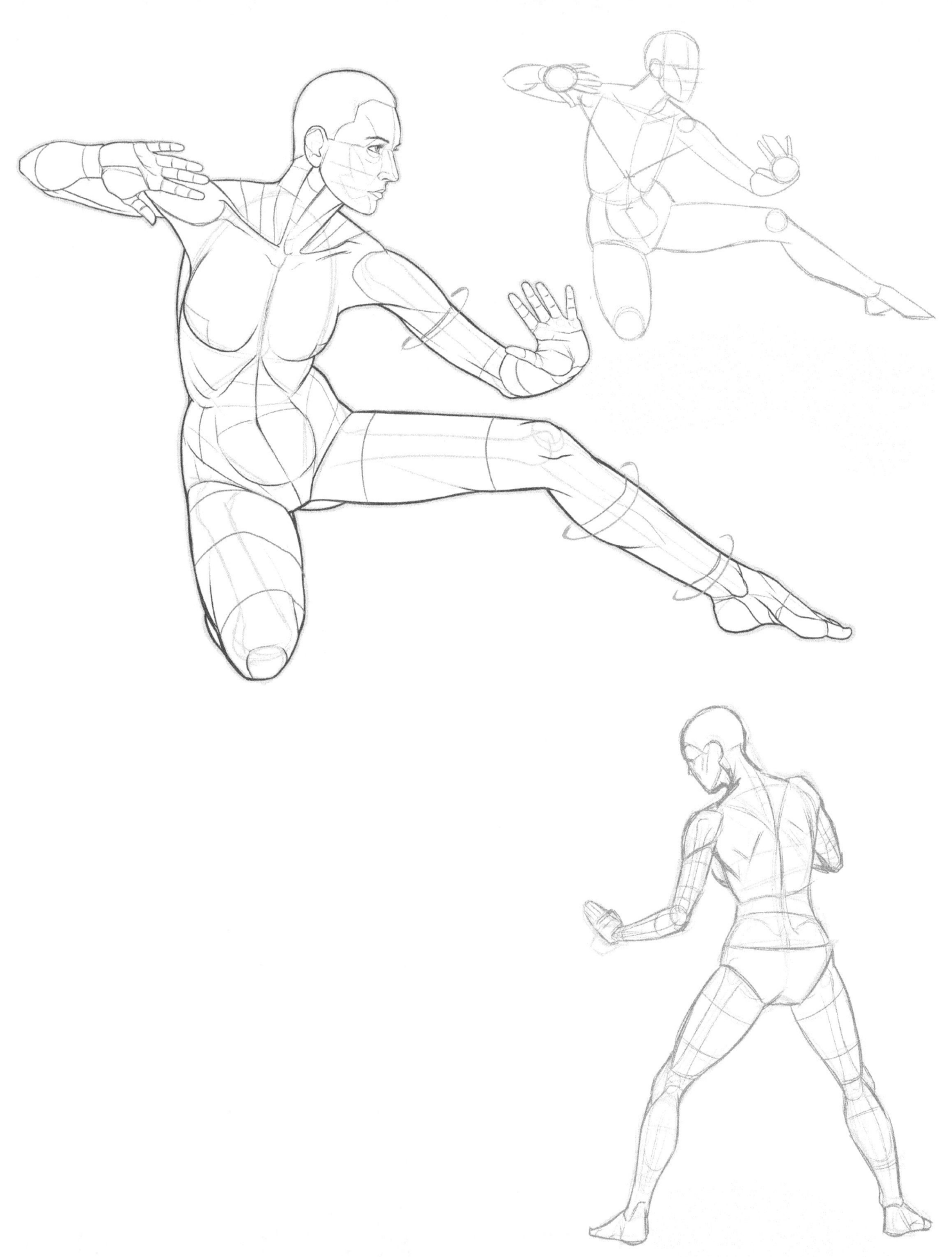

Various Poses -Page 100

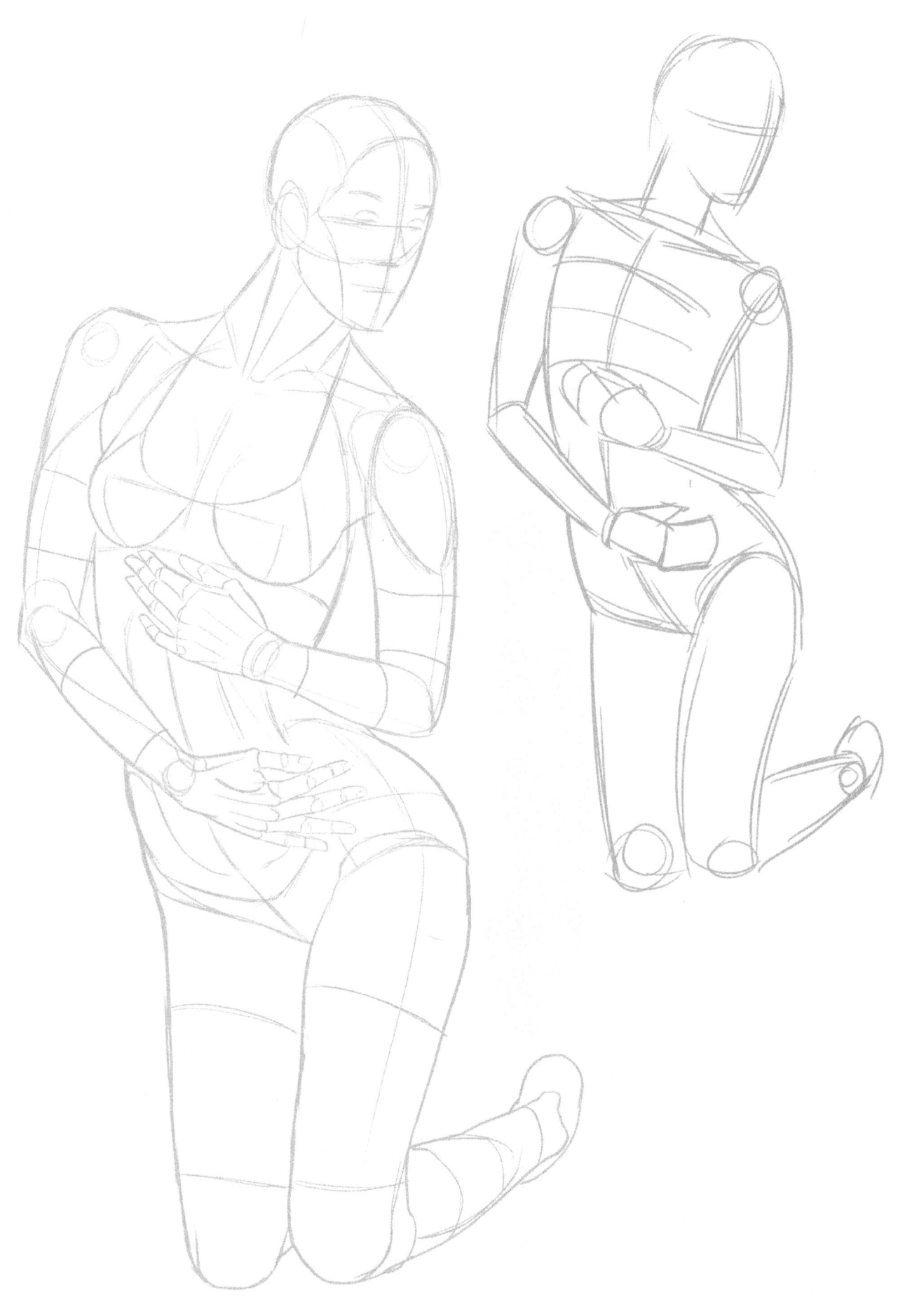

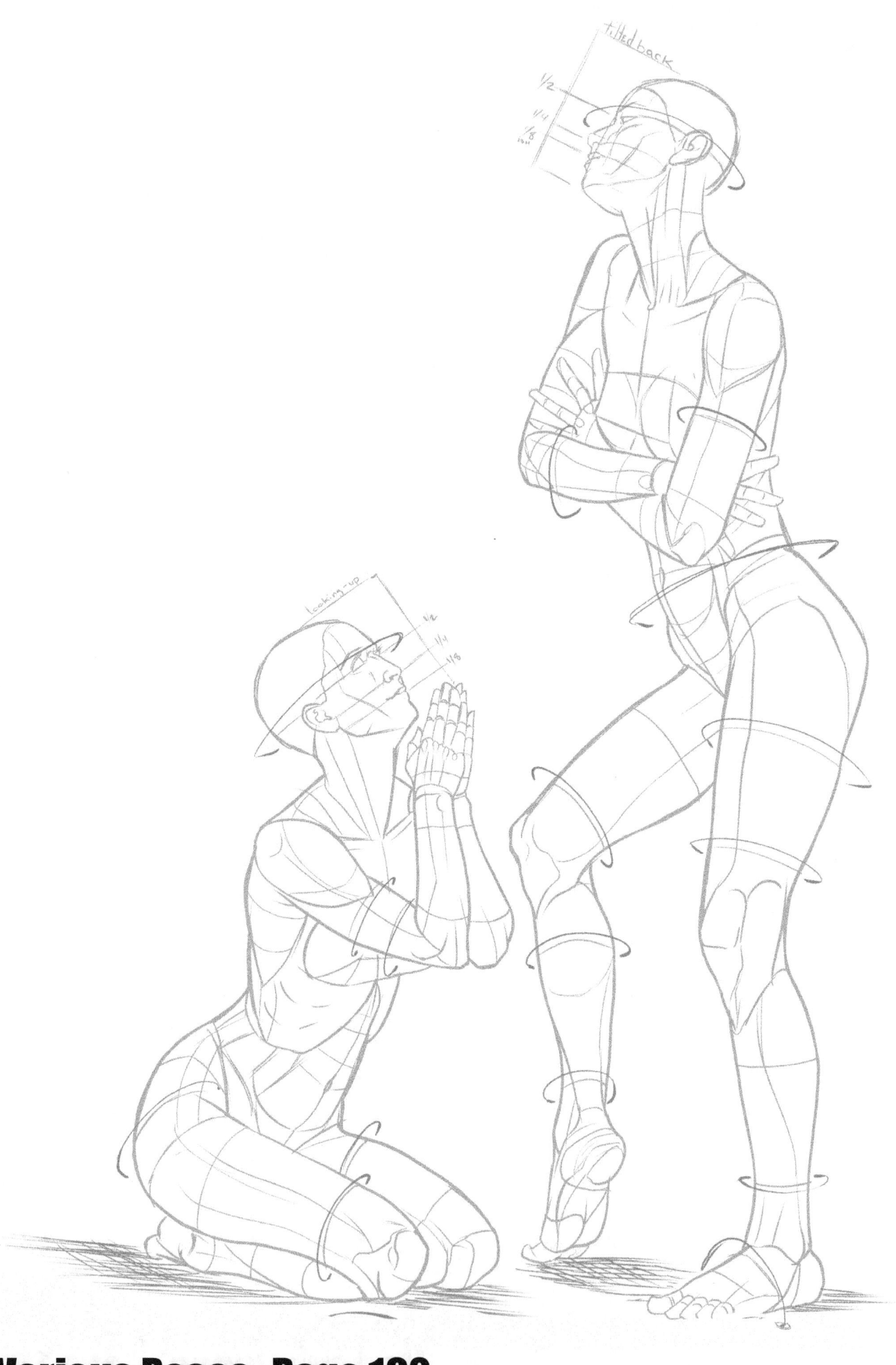

Various Poses -Page 102

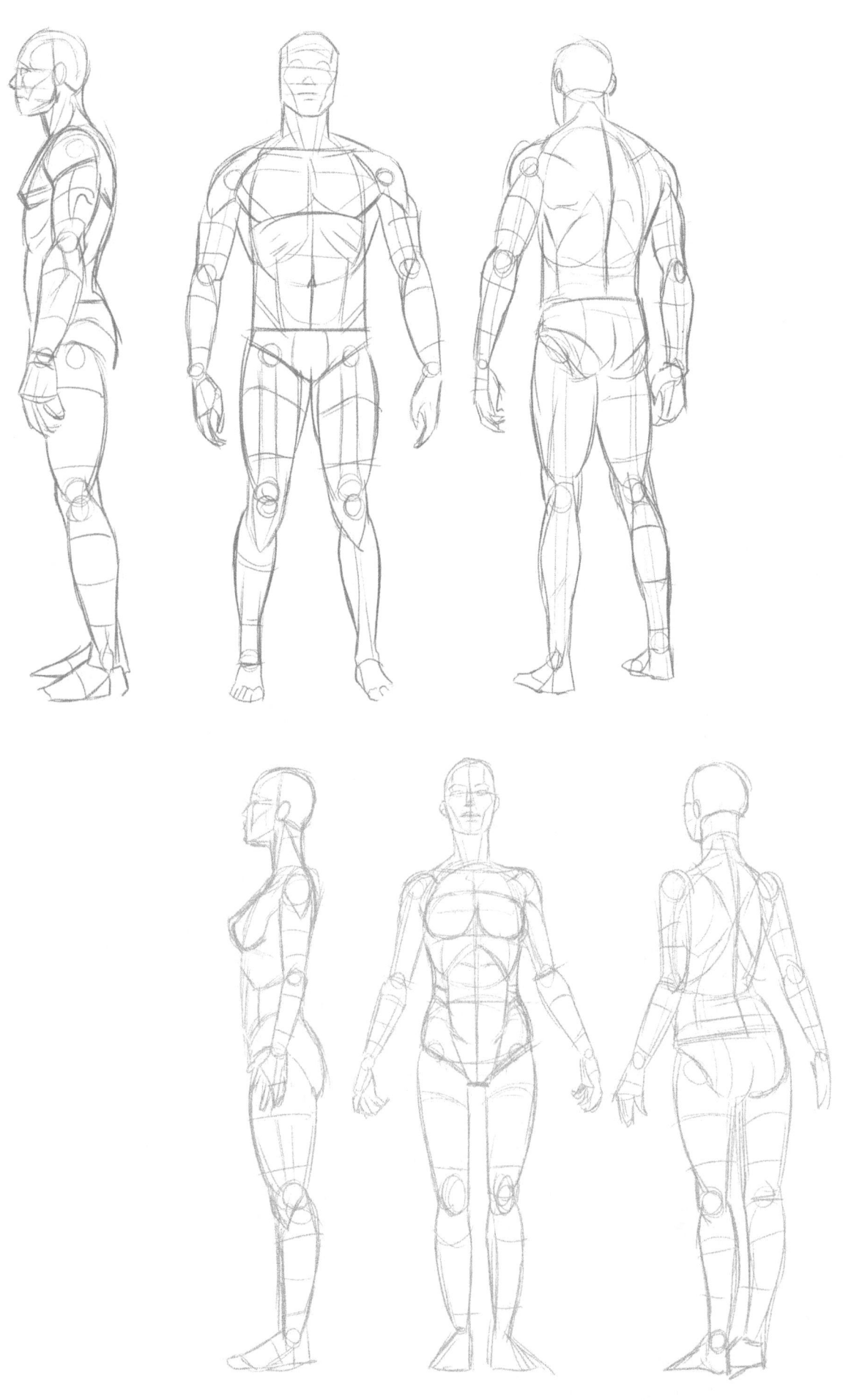

Various Poses - Page 103

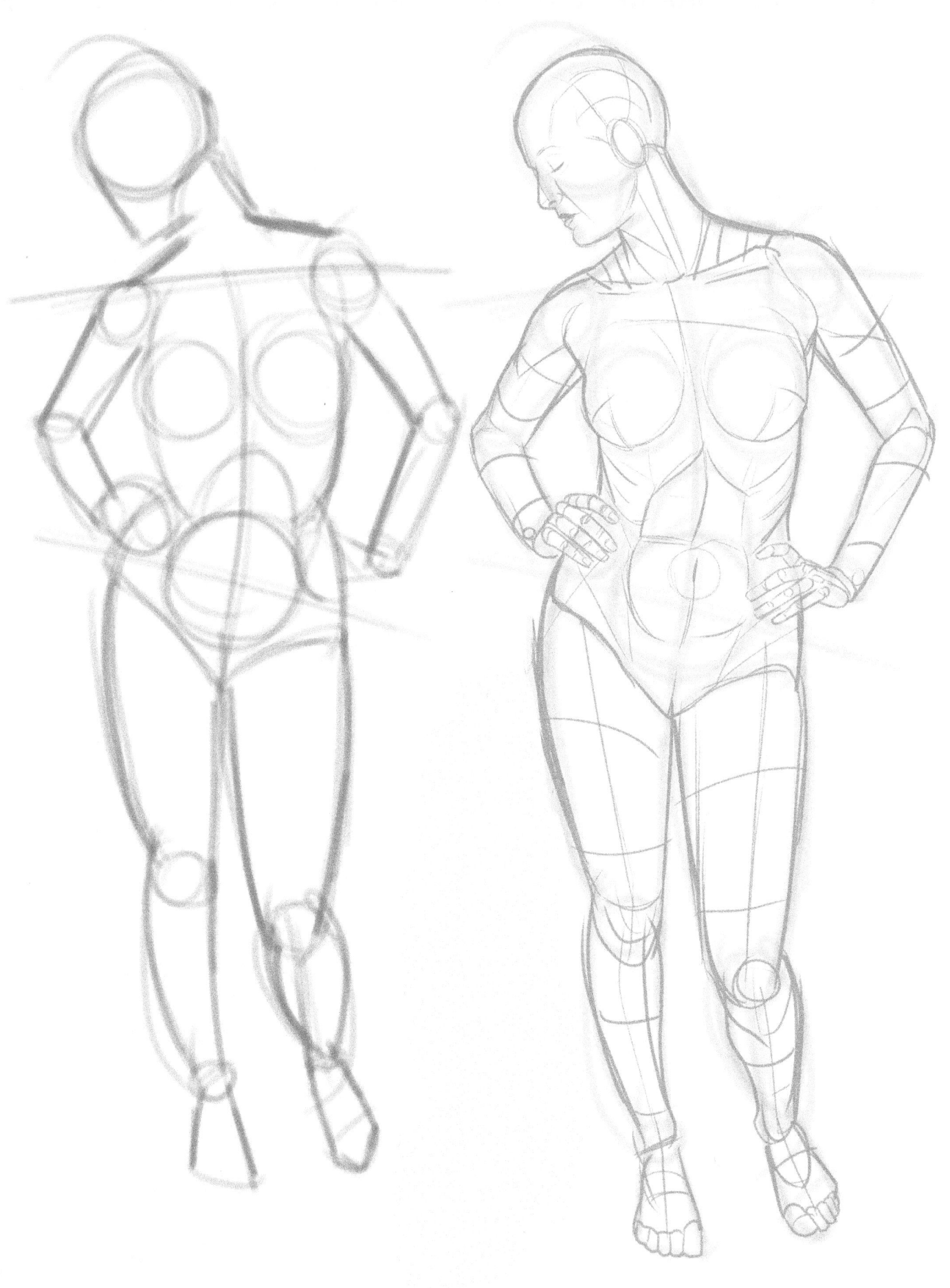

Various Poses -Page 104

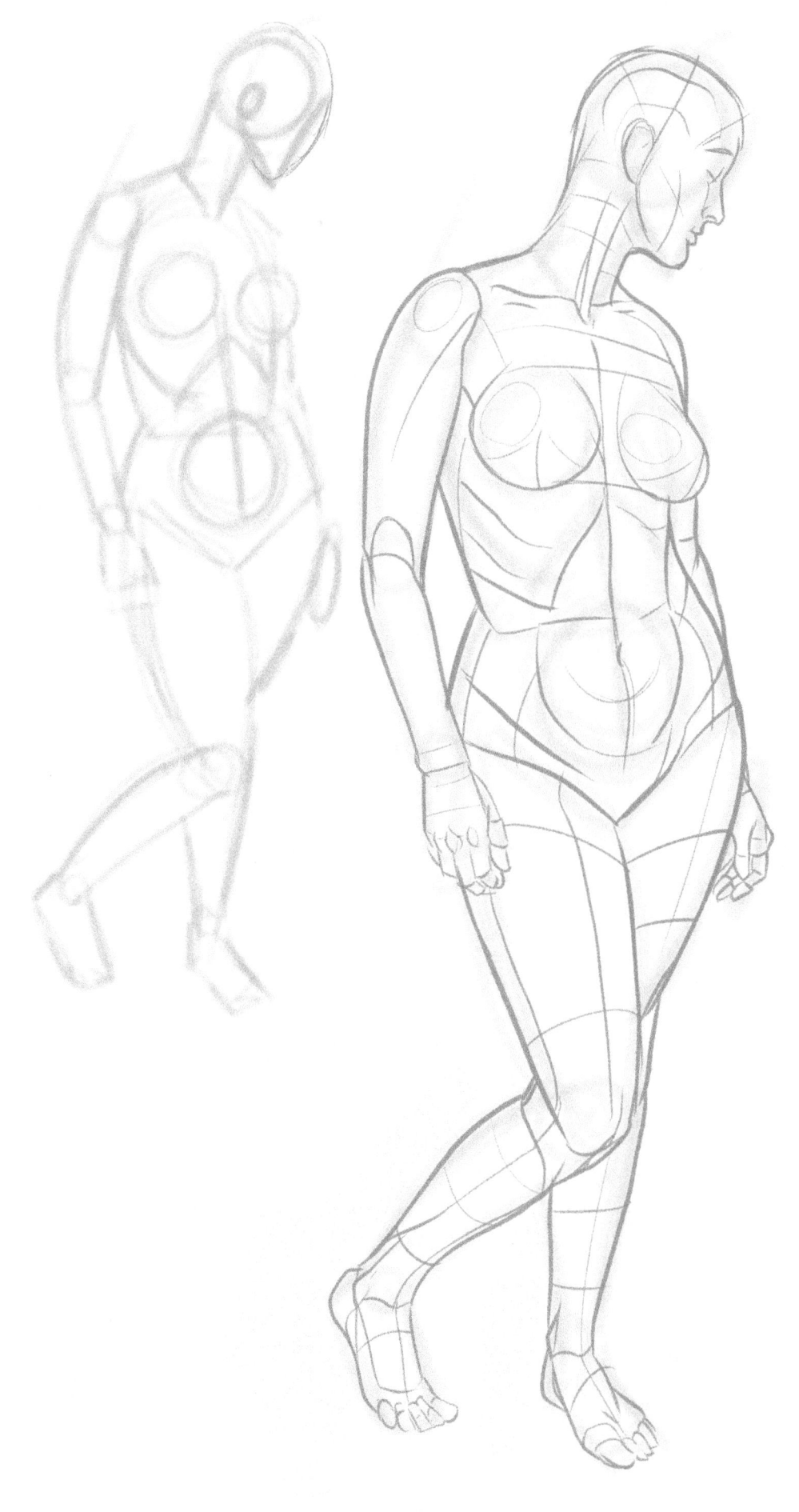

Various Poses -Page 105

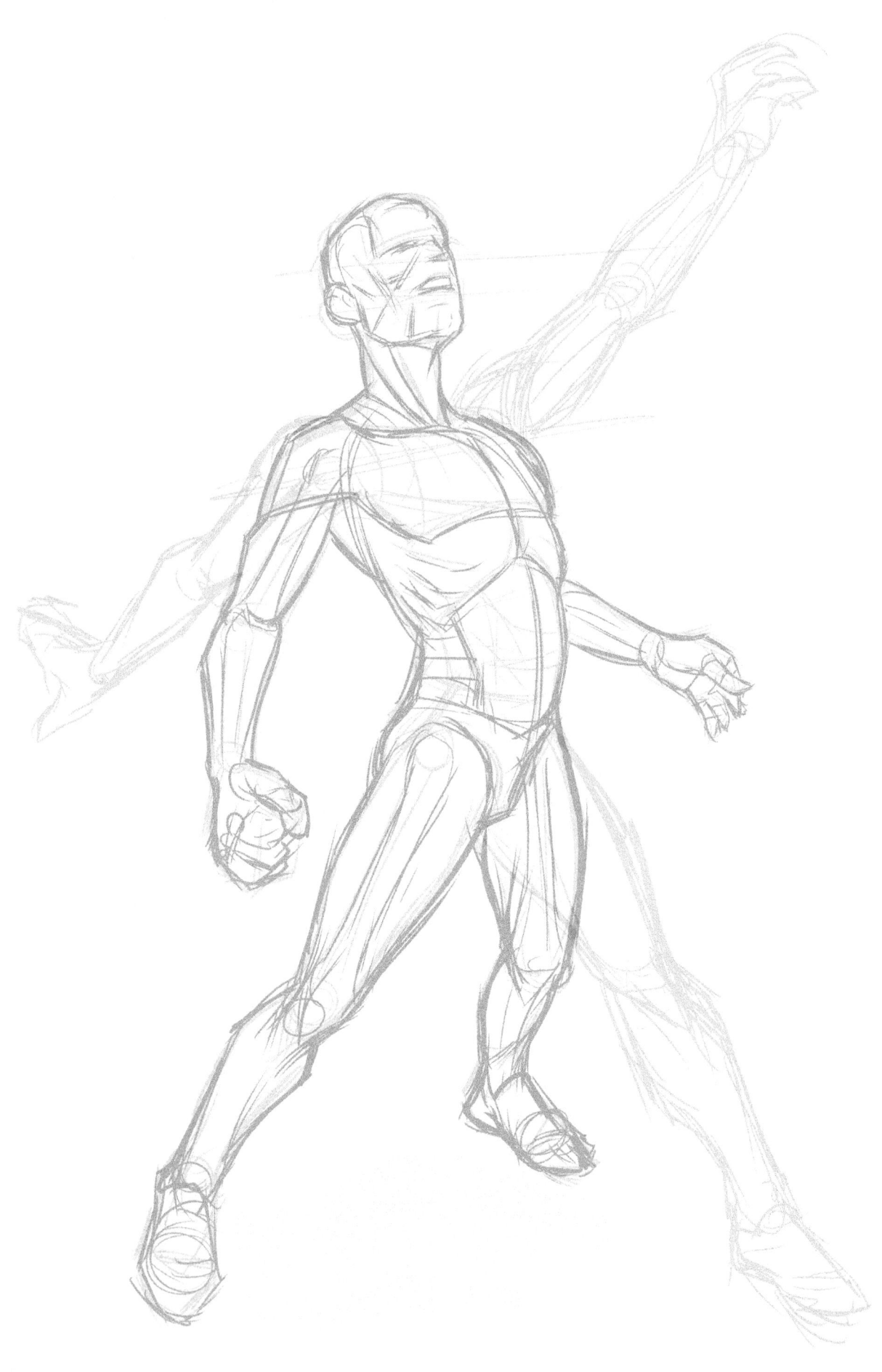

Various Poses -Page 106

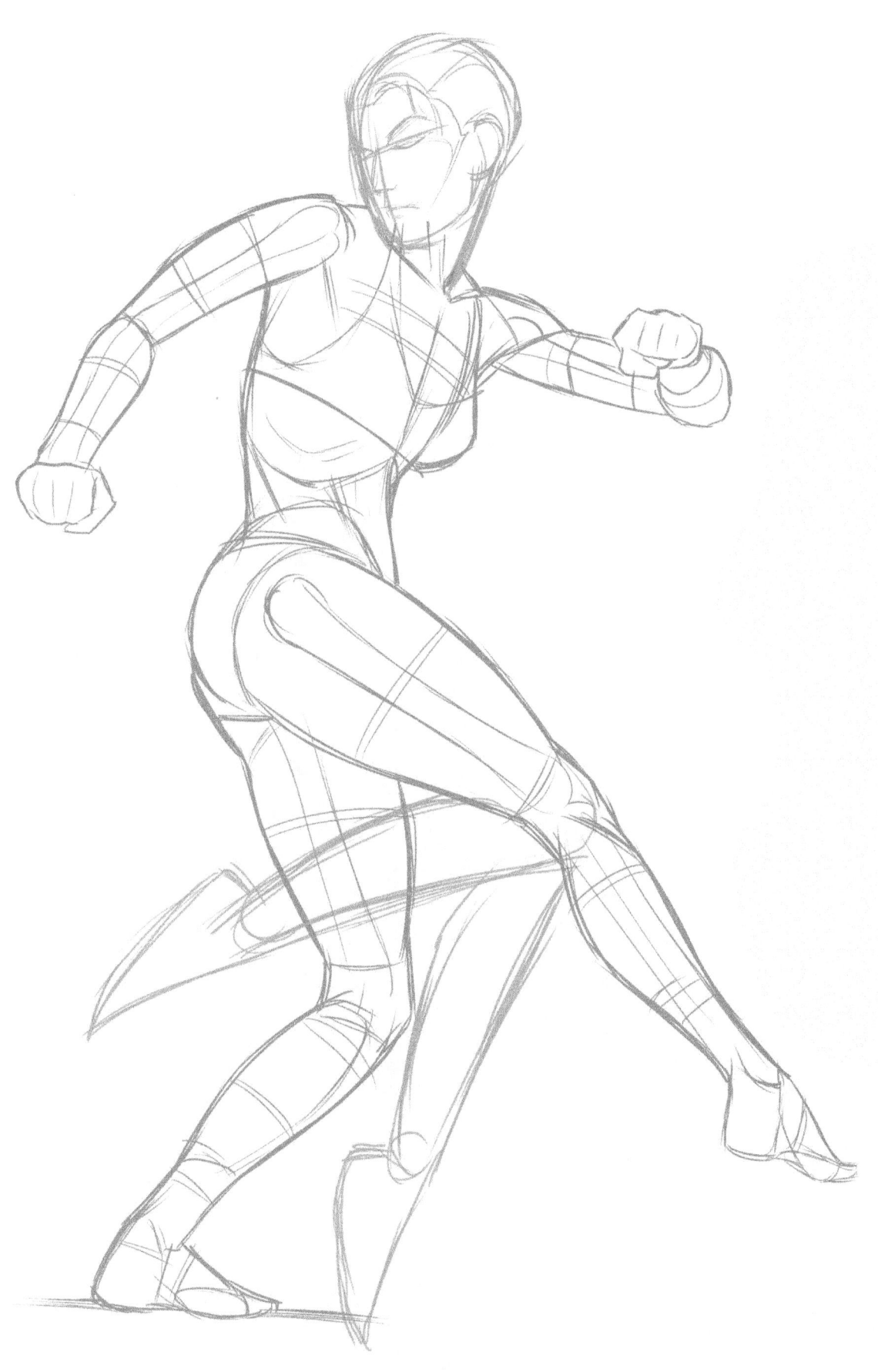

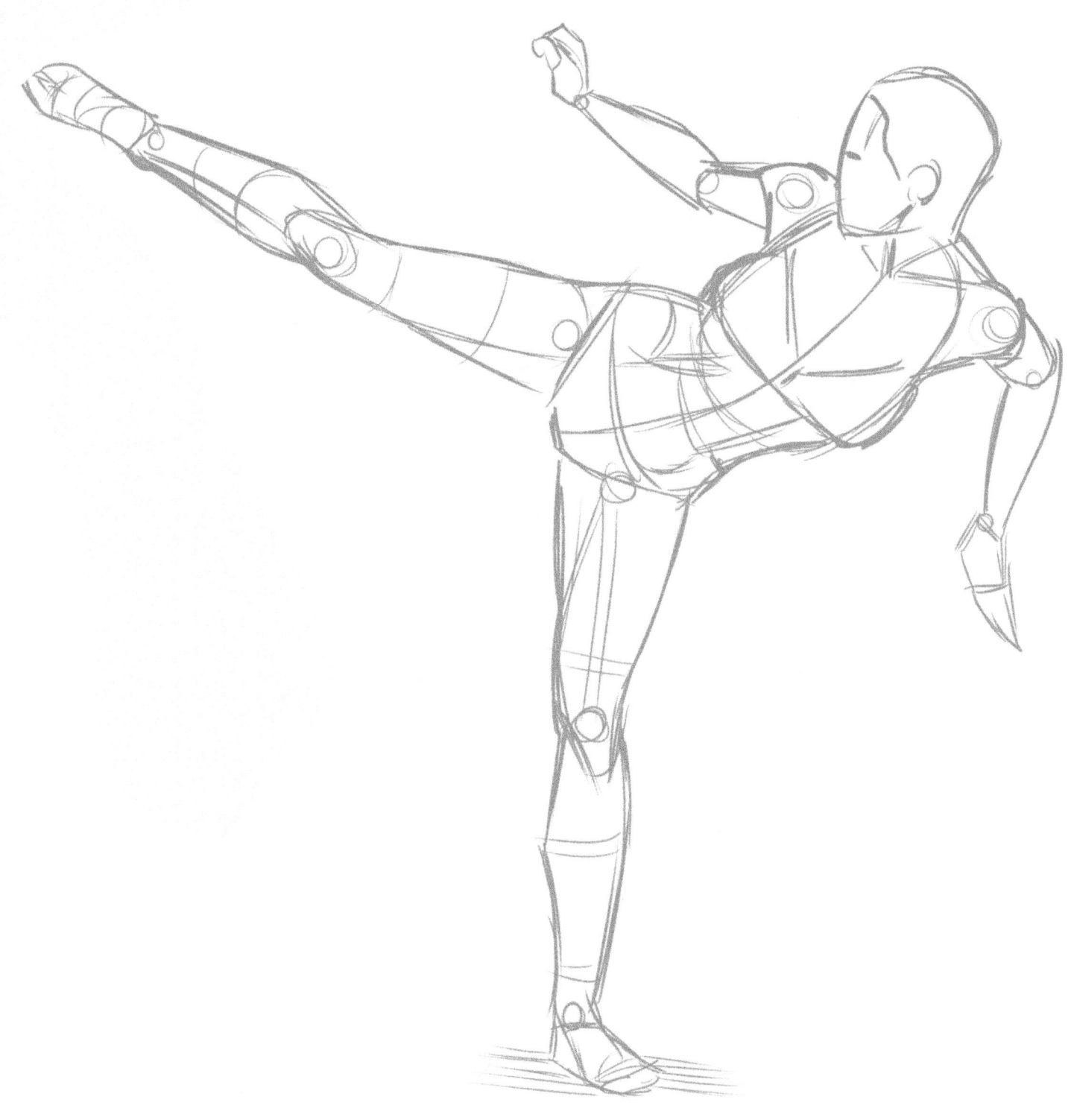

Various Poses -Page 108

Thank You

By purchasing this book, you have become part of a large community of people seeking to be inspired...seeking their "muse".

I am one of those people.

My muse has eluded me my whole life.

Success in art has been hard-won. Like you, my friends love my work, and rarely did the outside world take note.

To learn to draw people I have attended figure drawing classes, purchased books and reference photos, worked unpaid internships, pestered "professionals"...and in the end, it turns-out, I just needed to sit-down and draw.

In January 2015, I started the TUMBLR blog, @PoseReference and posted my goal of 10,000 poses....

...and we "trended".

April...May...June...July...

20,000 followers. Fan-mail. People throwing out questions, like, "Will you draw (insert idea here)?", How do I draw hands?", "When will you publish a book?"

...a book? ...and we come to now.

This is the first "volume" of many.

Watch POSEmuse.com for updates.

Upcoming books:

Poses for Artists Vol. 2: Standing Poses

Poses for Artists Vol. 3: The rest of 2015

Vol. 4: Hands and Couples

Vol. 5: Perspective and Guns

Vol. 6: Furries and Creatures

Vol. 7:???

This ongoing project is completely possible because of the support we get from all of you, so, thanks.

All the best,
Justin Martin
Feb 2016

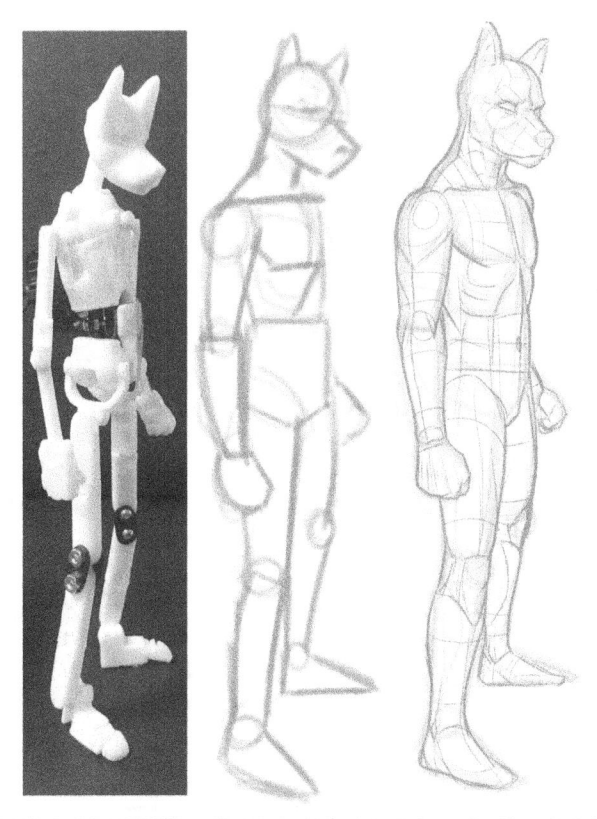

www.ingramcontent.com/pod-product-compliance
Lightning Source LLC
Chambersburg PA
CBHW080706190526
45169CB00006B/2266

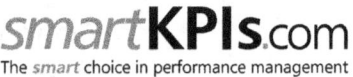

Table of contents

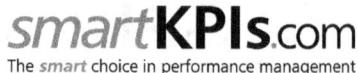

Executive Summary

Key Performance Indicators (KPIs) are today some of the most popular management tools. From the National Museum of Australia, to the First Bank of Nigeria, from the Panama Canal Authority to Rolls Royce, from the Ministry of Education in Brunei Darussalam to the American Medical Association, KPIs are used to understand, learn and improve performance across industries, departments and teams.

In this environment marked by the coming of age of KPIs as management tools, smartKPIs.com represents the go to place for information about the use of KPIs across the world. As a research driven online platform for performance management knowledge integration, the website contains over 20,000 examples of KPIs used at organizational and individual level, pre-populated Strategy Maps, KPI Dashboards and Scorecards, interviews with practitioners, consultants and academics and references 1000 reports illustrating the use of KPIs and organizational objectives in practice. At its core is the largest online database of thoroughly documented KPI examples from 15 business functional areas and 24 industries. The smartKPIs.com research program is supported by a community formed of tens of thousands of members from over 190 countries and territories.

Interest in KPIs and their use across industries is on the rise around the world, driven by both government regulations and by the benefits they bring in terms of accountability, transparency and achievement of results. This trend was reflected in 2011 by the hundreds of thousands of visits to the smartKPIs.com website and the many KPIs visited, bookmarked and rated by members of the smartKPIs.com community.

The Top 10 KPIs of 2011-2012 report is a synthesis of what smartKPIs.com is all about: it brings together an overview of how KPIs are used in practice today, by combining input from the smartKPIs.com community with research and analysis from the editorial team. While centered around the KPIs that in 2011 received the highest number of visits on smartKPIs.com, the report also contains analysis and insight regarding performance management today:

Section 1: "KPIs … Naturally", an article that sets the context through a discussion on what is old and what is new in the use of KPIs
Section 2: Presents the profile of the smartKPIs.com community, illustrating membership by role, country, industry and organization size
Section 3: Outlines the taxonomy of functional areas and industries used for grouping KPIs in smartKPIs.com
Section 4: Introduces a short analysis of each KPI from Top 10 most viewed KPIs in 2011 on smartKPIs.com
Section 5: Lists the names of the Top 10 KPI examples in 2011 on smartKPIs.com
Section 6: Contains the detailed description of each KPI listed in the report, as documented in smartKPIs Premium (the premium content section of smartKPIs.com)

In 2011, the list of the most viewed KPIs in smartKPIs.com was dominated by KPIs specific to functional areas (7 out of 10), which was expected considering their pervasiveness across industries:

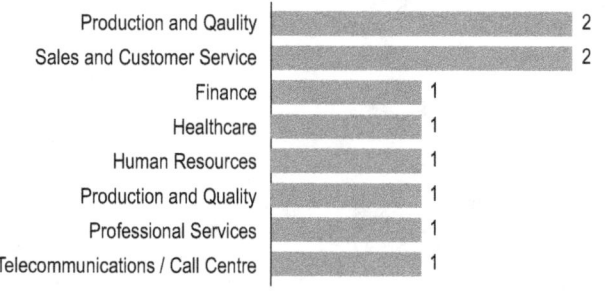

Top 3 KPIs

% Hospital bed occupancy rate

% Call setup success rate (CSSR)

Realization rate

The other 3 KPIs completing the top 10 came from 3 different industries: Healthcare, Telecommunications and Professional Services.

By discussing the use of KPIs today, presenting the best practice in documenting them and listing the most popular KPIs in 2011, this report can be a useful resource in promoting the adoption of KPIs or refreshing the existing performance measurement and management practice in any organization. Both the free and premium content available on smartKPIs.com can be useful guides on this journey.

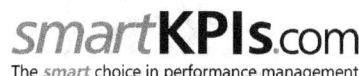
About Key Performance Indicators (KPIs)

In many domains of human activity, the use of tools is essential for the achievement of results. Measurement and evaluation make no exception, being equipped with both conceptual and physical tools. Of the first category, at the core of any performance measurement and management system are the measures, metrics, indicators or KPIs used.

Both academic and practitioner literature uses interchangeably these terms, oftentimes even within the same organization.

At smartKPIs.com, we have adopted the following definitions for these terms:

Measure - A number or a quantity that records a directly observable value. All measures are composed of a number and a unit of measure. The number provides magnitude (how much) for the measure, while the unit gives number a meaning (what). Examples of unit measures are: dollars, hours, meters, inches, etc.

Indicator - Indicators are defined in many ways, but the common meaning for all of them is that they refer to specific information. Thus, the Organisation for Economic Co-operation and Development (OECD) defines an indicator as *"a qualitative or quantitative factor or variable that provides a simple and reliable means to measure achievement, to reflect changes connected to an intervention, or to help assess the performance of a development actor"*.[1]

Metric, Performance Measure or Performance Indicator - A generic term encompassing the quantitative basis by which objectives are established and performance is assessed. It helps quantify the achievement of a result, the quantifiable component of an organization's performance. In the context of measuring and managing performance these terms are use interchangeably.

Key Performance Indicator (KPI) - A selected indicator considered key for monitoring the performance of a strategic objective, outcome, or key result area important to the success of an activity and growth of the organization overall. KPIs make objectives quantifiable, providing visibility into the performance of individuals, teams, departments and organizations and enabling decision makers to take action in achieving the desired outcomes. Typically, KPIs are monitored and communicated through dashboards, scorecards and other forms of performance reports.

While on paper the terms listed above can be differentiated, in practice, the difference between them is blurred and, at some extent, irrelevant. As long as their purpose and use is clear and understood by members of the organization, whether they are called performance measures or KPIs is a matter of preference.

At smartKPIs.com, we assess each example entered in the online database and label it as measure, performance indicator or KPI. It is an empirical and subjective approach to catalogue each entry based on relevance. Ultimately, all entries in the online database are considered KPI examples. In addition, to single out the entries that stand out in terms of relevance, we introduced a new label:

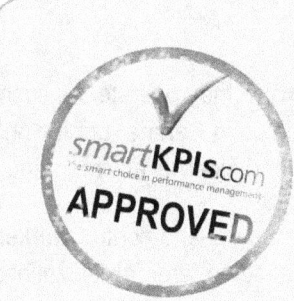

smartKPI - A Key Performance Indicator example available on smartKPIs.com, that is recommended as being the most relevant and truly "Key" for organizational performance. They are selected by the editorial team of the website based on criteria such as:

- Listing in academic and practitioner publications that analyse their usefulness;

- Frequency of use by Functional Area / Industry;

- Fulfillment of the criteria of how good KPIs should be defined and used.

---

1. Organisation for Economic Co-operation and Development, 2002, Glossary of Key Terms in Evaluation and Results Based Management, OECD Publications, Paris, France

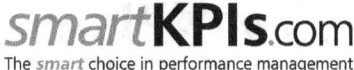
KPIs ... Naturally

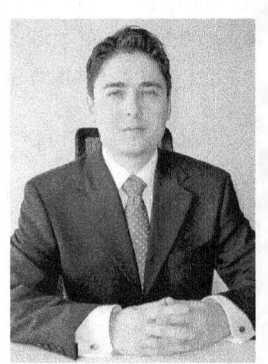

Measurement as a human activity is not new. It emerged in early history as means for discovery and sense making. Archaeologists consider the first measurement tool used in human history to be the Lebombo bone, a baboon fibula containing 29 cut notches. Dated 35,000 BC, this tally stick was discovered in the Lebombo mountains in Swaziland.

Evaluation, as a form of measurement was used as early as the 3rd century AD, when emperors of the Wei Dynasty rated the performance of the official family members. The biased nature of individual performance evaluation was noticed by Chinese philosopher Sin Yu, who reportedly criticized a rater employed by the Wei Dynasty with the following words: "The Imperial Rater of Nine Grade seldom rates men according to their merits, but always according to his likes and dislikes".

A major milestone in making the connection between measuring as a human activity and performance was in 1494, when Luca Pacioli published in Venice *'Summa de arithmetica, geometrica, proportioni et proportionalita'* (*'Everything on arithmetic, geometry, proportions and proportionality'*). It detailed a practice the Venetian sailors had in place to evaluate the performance of their sailing expeditions, which became the basis of the double-entry accounting system.

In time, the subjective nature of individual performance evaluations and the dominance of financial indicators for evaluating enterprise performance became stepstones for performance management in human activities.

The industrial revolution added to this combination the *"organization as a machine"* metaphor that played a major role in driving improvements in efficiencies and effectiveness. The result was an organizational performance management model based on mechanistic, command-and-control thinking, driven by subjective individual performance assessments and financial indicators and crowned by pay-for-performance arrangements.

Did it work? To a certain extent, yes. Many organisations flourished and matured based on this model.

Does it have flaws? Many. And while historical circumstances attenuated them in time, today's environment amplifies and exposes them at an accelerated rate.

Is there a better way? Yes, but it is not simple. It requires a change at multiple levels, from the underlying philosophy of performance, to mentalities and processes. This is not easy.

Over time, the use of Key Performance Indicators (KPIs) became synonym to performance measurement and management. KPIs are the link between the old and the new in performance management. Their use, however, is much richer and rewarding in an environment based on organic performance architecture principles:

Organizations are echo-systems in their own right. They vary in terms of maturity and the environment in which they operate. As such, their use of performance management systems should reflect their own "personality". You can try to build an igloo in Sahara, but it won't be sustainable. The performance architecture of each organisation needs to be unique and to reflect its internal and external environment.

Systems thinking provides a much richer context for understanding and improving performance. Command-and-control worked in time for the army, for increasing productivity of unskilled workers during the industrial revolution and for managing large organizations (such as the public service). Today, knowledge workers form the majority of the workforce in developed economies, operate in a much more interconnected environment and have to make decisions at an accelerated pace. Understanding the systems in which we operate, analysing flow and learning based on data become ever more important today and complement the traditional simplistic managerial approach of executing orders from above.

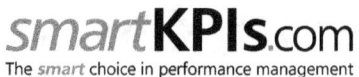
KPIs should be used primarily for learning. The role of KPIs should be the one of providing the required information to assist in navigating towards the desired results. The same principle is used by ants, who leave pheromone trails to assist each other in navigating towards the food source. Similarly, the nerve impulses travel through the different points of the nervous system, transmitting information. KPIs results should travel through the organisation, facilitating communication, providing a base for analysis / synthesis and ultimately decision making across all levels of the organisation.

Data accuracy in human administration is an elusive desideratum. Neils Bohr once said: *"Accuracy and clarity of statement are mutually exclusive"*. Accuracy is a challenge in exact sciences and even more in human administration. Striving to obtain any KPI data is a challenge in itself for many organisations and data accuracy is an even bigger ask. The use of KPIs should acknowledge this aspect and be oriented towards making the most out of existent data, oftentimes by using variance intervals. This approach is used by the human body. If the temperature drops under a safe limit, we shiver. If the temperature increases, we sweat. Both are performance improvement initiatives of the body, aimed to regulate its temperature back to safe limits. The KPI here is the temperature. While it is not a constant, its trend is good when within certain safe limits.

The use of KPIs for rewards and punishment should be limited and driven by self-assessment. Purposeful oriented behaviour is a characteristic of living organisms. For humans and many other species, this behaviour is amplified by rewards and punishment. Along with this amplification, risks are amplified, too. Gaming of results, lack of cooperation, decreased morale and work accidents are some of the undesired consequences. On the other hand, the majority of nerve impulses in the human body transmit general information. Only in particular situations pleasure or pain signals. Similarly, the use of KPIs for rewards and punishment should be the exception to the rule, rather than the norm.

Embedding KPIs in organisations through visualization and communication of KPIs results is the key to maximising their value added. Variations in the KPIs used by the human body are felt by our senses as their impact is sensory rich. Similarly, KPIs used in an organizational context should be embedded in everyday use and be a part of the working experience. The most important aspect of communicating KPI results is their visual representation. This is key, both in terms of optimising the layout of the data representation and the presence of visual displays in the working environment. The range of media is diverse today: posters, whiteboards, banners, LED and LCD monitors should be combined to bring results to life across the organization. KPI results should not be restricted to paper reports and computer screens anymore.

New philosophy of performance, driven by self-assessment and purposeful achievement as a mean to happiness. While happiness means many things to many, a common expression of this feeling is the result of the purposeful achievement of a desiderate. Achieving something we want, while shared with others, is about us and reverberates strongly in our inner self. Transposing this powerful catalyst of performance in both our personal and organizational life is facilitated by a new paradigm: Happiness is driven by achievement. Achievement is an expression of performance. If we want to be in control of our happiness, we should be in control of our performance.

Self-assessment of performance results is not easy. However, if more emphasis is placed on building this capability in each employee, organisations can benefit by creating a rewarding environment conducive to happiness. In this environment, managers can focus on understanding and improving the working system, while employees can focus on self-assessment of the results' achievement, learning and communicating. Purposeful achievement of results in a well-structured working system would bring both individuals and organisation much closer to happiness and fulfillment compared to the payment of bonuses in the current command-and-control driven dominant paradigm.

KPIs are here to stay. The question we have to answer is how do we want to use them: mechanistically or naturally?

Aurel Brudan,
Performance Architect
smartKPIs.com

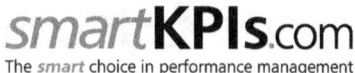
smartKPIs.com Community Profile

Since its launch in 2009, smartKPIs.com established itself as the favourite destination of professionals from around the world interested in high quality documented examples of performance measures. With hundreds of thousands of page views and tens of thousands of visitors from over 190 countries each month, www.smartKPIs.com is one of the most used performance management resources on the Internet.

What sets the smartKPIs.com community apart is the profile of its members.

smartKPIs.com is a truly global community, with relatively uniformly spread representation in terms of membership around the world. While the highest number of members comes from English speaking countries, no single country dominates in terms of representation. The same applies in terms of the size of the organizations to which smartKPIs.com members belong. While membership is the highest among companies with 11 to 500 employees, both small and large organizations in terms of headcount are well represented.

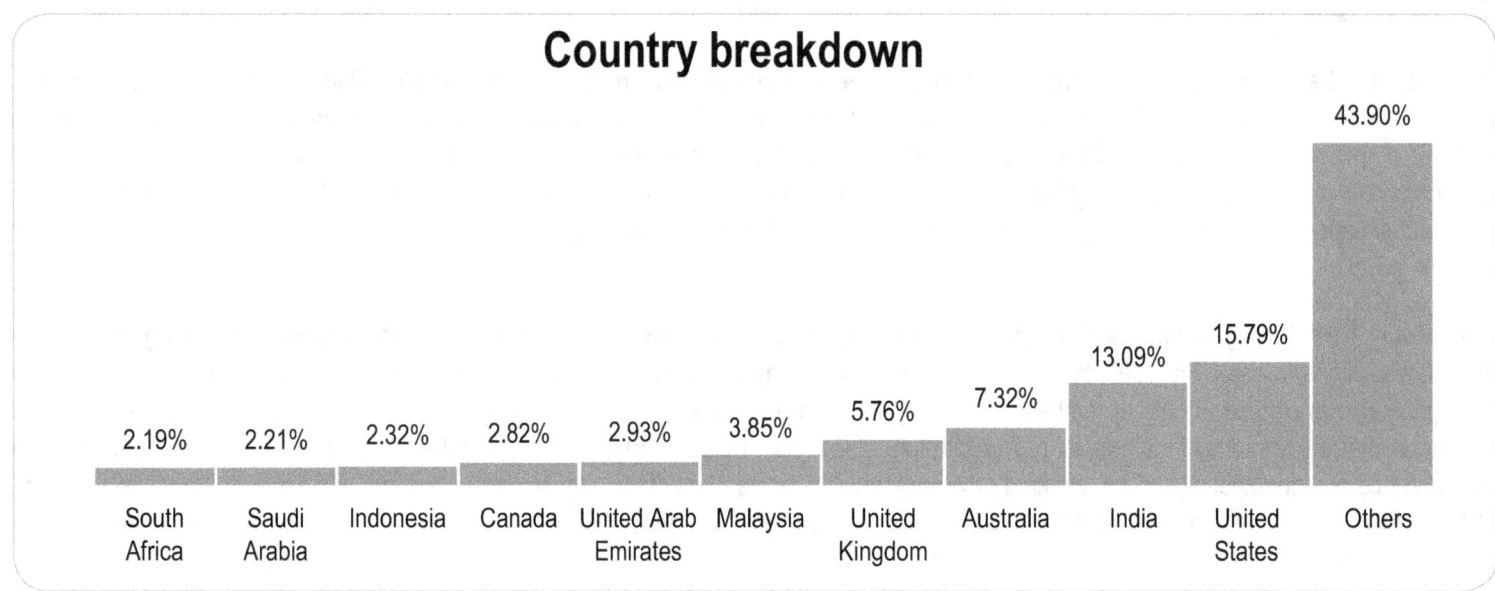

Country breakdown

South Africa	Saudi Arabia	Indonesia	Canada	United Arab Emirates	Malaysia	United Kingdom	Australia	India	United States	Others
2.19%	2.21%	2.32%	2.82%	2.93%	3.85%	5.76%	7.32%	13.09%	15.79%	43.90%

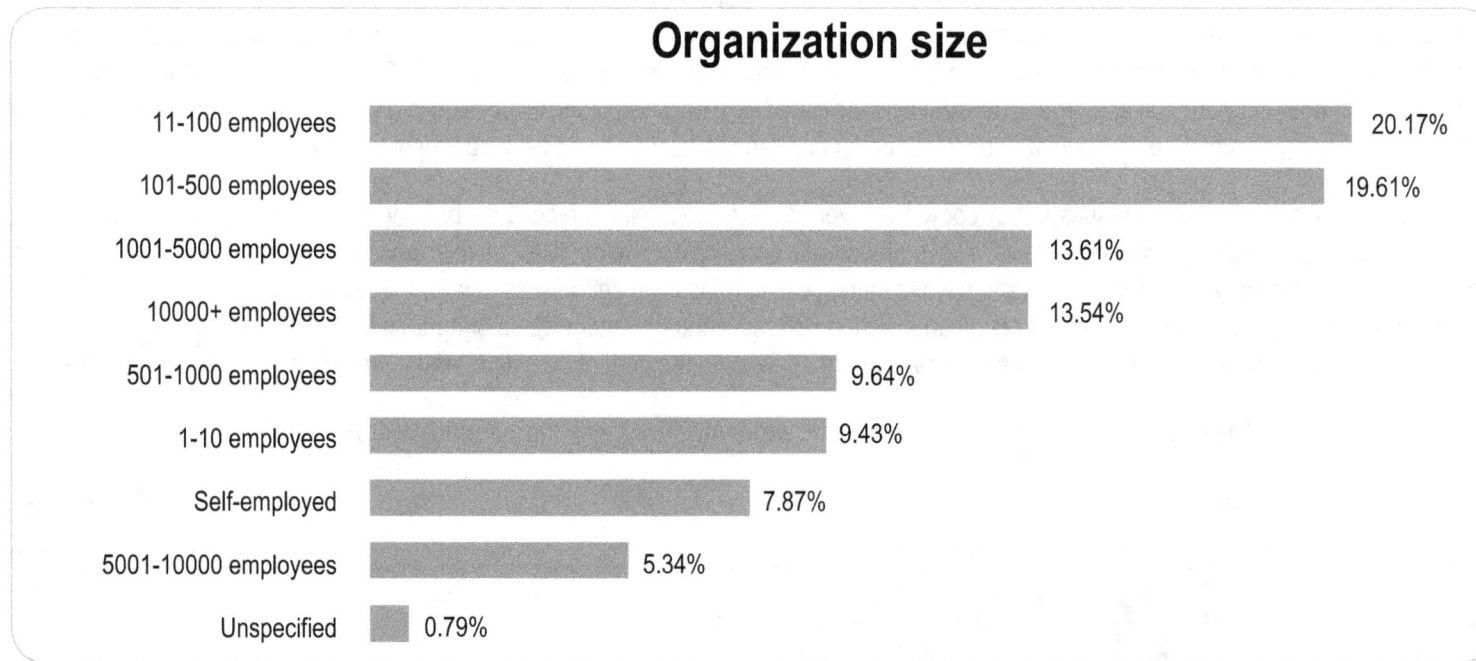

Organization size

11-100 employees	20.17%
101-500 employees	19.61%
1001-5000 employees	13.61%
10000+ employees	13.54%
501-1000 employees	9.64%
1-10 employees	9.43%
Self-employed	7.87%
5001-10000 employees	5.34%
Unspecified	0.79%

Top 10 KPIs of 2011-2012

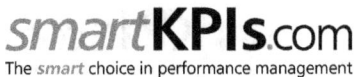

Industry affiliation

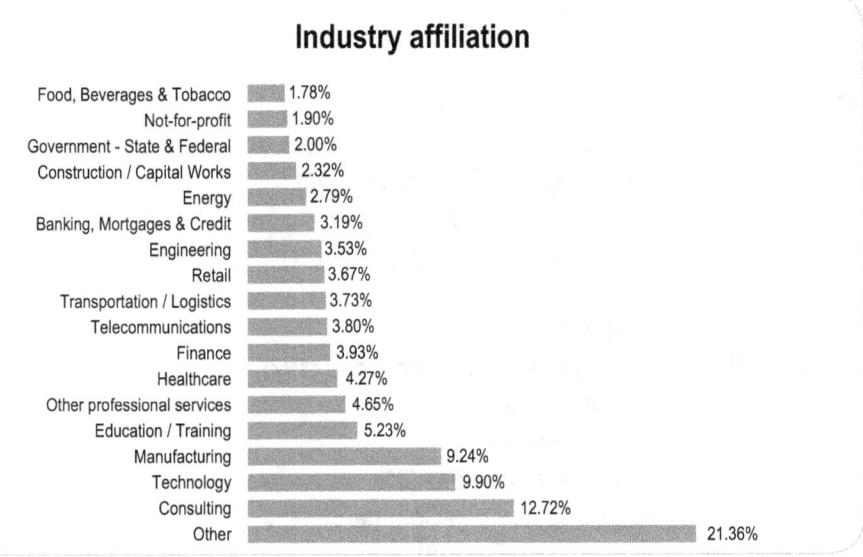

Food, Beverages & Tobacco	1.78%
Not-for-profit	1.90%
Government - State & Federal	2.00%
Construction / Capital Works	2.32%
Energy	2.79%
Banking, Mortgages & Credit	3.19%
Engineering	3.53%
Retail	3.67%
Transportation / Logistics	3.73%
Telecommunications	3.80%
Finance	3.93%
Healthcare	4.27%
Other professional services	4.65%
Education / Training	5.23%
Manufacturing	9.24%
Technology	9.90%
Consulting	12.72%
Other	21.36%

In terms of industry affiliation, the majority of smartKPIs.com community members operate in the consulting industry. The ICT, manufacturing and education / training sectors follow in this hierarchy, which also reflects wide interest from both the public and not-for-profit sectors.

Job title

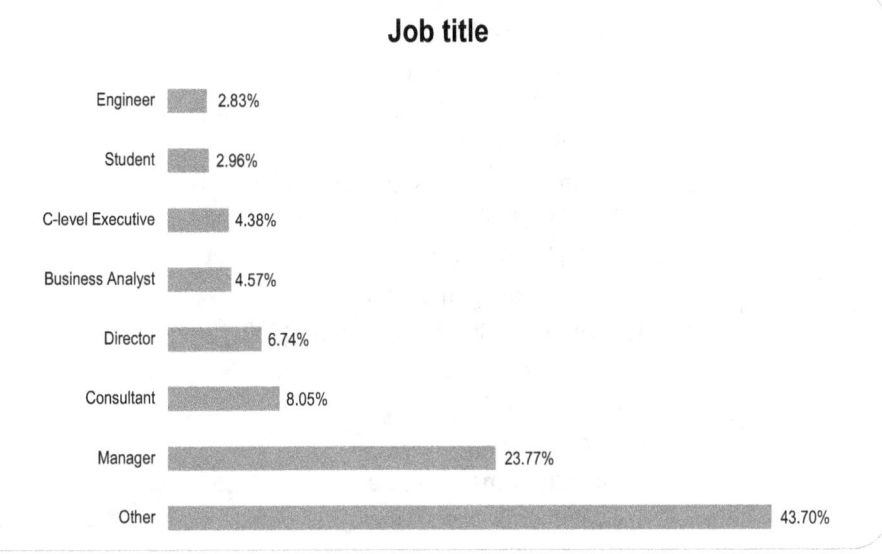

Engineer	2.83%
Student	2.96%
C-level Executive	4.38%
Business Analyst	4.57%
Director	6.74%
Consultant	8.05%
Manager	23.77%
Other	43.70%

The membership of smartKPIs.com community is dominated by managers and consultants, which reflect a high level of professional expertise. The breakdown of managerial positions by function reflects a higher than the average representation from HR, Project and IT managers.

Managerial role

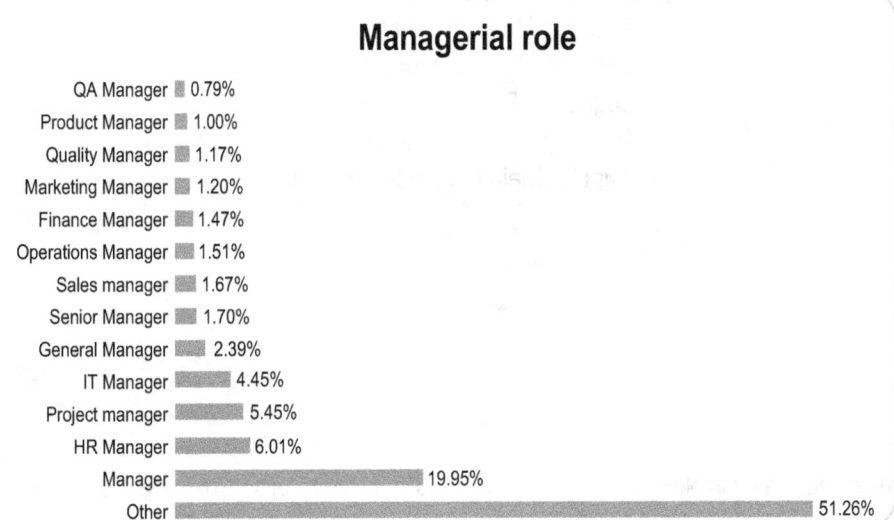

QA Manager	0.79%
Product Manager	1.00%
Quality Manager	1.17%
Marketing Manager	1.20%
Finance Manager	1.47%
Operations Manager	1.51%
Sales manager	1.67%
Senior Manager	1.70%
General Manager	2.39%
IT Manager	4.45%
Project manager	5.45%
HR Manager	6.01%
Manager	19.95%
Other	51.26%

Overall, the profile of the smartKPIs.com community paints the picture of a global, diverse and highly qualified membership base. Tapping into the collective intelligence of this community by analyzing visit trends is a reflection of both trends in performance management at international level across industries / functional areas and of the relevance of the smartKPIs.com content.

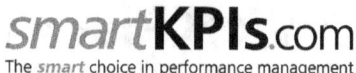

2011-2012 smartKPIs.com Functional Areas Taxonomy

15 Functional Areas with 60 Sub-categories

Accounting (269)
- Accounting Systems (35)
- Cash Management (25)
- Control (12)
- Cost Analysis (44)
- Planning and Reporting (65)
- Transactions / Accounts Payable / Accounts Receivable (88)

Corporate Services (134)
- Administration / Office Support (24)
- Corporate Travel (27)
- Facilities / Property Management (75)
- Legal Services (8)

CSR / Sustainability / Environmental Care (225)
- Corporate Social Responsibility (54)
- Environmental Care (171)

Finance (219)
- Asset / Portfolio management (49)
- Financial stability (42)
- Forecasts & Valuation (56)
- Liquidity (19)
- Profitability (53)

Governance, Compliance and Risk (146)
- Compliance and Audit Management (52)
- Governance (40)
- Risk Management (54)

Human Resources (476)
- Compensation and Benefits (52)
- Efficiency and Effectiveness (48)
- Recruitment (71)
- Retention (29)
- Service Delivery (31)
- Talent Development (109)
- Workforce (48)
- Working Environment (88)

Information Technology (609)
- Application Development (81)
- Data Center (36)
- Enterprise Architecture (46)
- IT - General (47)
- IT - Security (118)
- Network Management (59)

- Service Management (222)

Knowledge and Innovation (198)
- Innovation (45)
- Knowledge Management (71)
- R & D (82)

Management (53)

Marketing & Communications (192)
- Advertising (34)
- Marketing (127)
- Public Relations (31)

Online Presence - eCommerce (203)
- eCommerce (48)
- Email Marketing (25)
- Online Advertising (34)
- Online Publishing - Weblogs (18)
- Search Engine Optimisation (SEO) (15)
- Web Analytics (63)

Portfolio and Project Management (116)
- Benefits Realisation Management (6)
- Portfolio Management (54)
- Project Management (56)

Production & Quality Management (200)
- Maintenance (34)
- Production (97)
- Quality Management (69)

Sales and Customer Service (314)
- Customer Service (138)
- Sales (176)

Supply Chain, Procurement, Distribution (420)
- Contract Management (50)
- Inventory Management (85)
- Logistics / Distribution (138)
- Procurement / Purchasing (86)
- Supply Chain Management (61)

* The figures in the brackets represent the number of documented KPI examples available on www.smartKPIs.com as of 11 November 2012. For up to date statistics follow the hyperlinks.

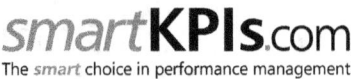
2011-2012 smartKPIs.com Industries Taxonomy

24 Industries with 89 Sub-categories

Agriculture (297)
- Crops (118)
- Forestry and Logging (32)
- Livestock, Hunting and Fishing (148)

Arts and Culture (410)
- Event Production and Promotion (5)
- Libraries and Archives (354)
- Museums (51)

Construction & Capital Works (76)
- Civil Engineering (27)
- Construction of Buildings (69)

Education & Training (703)
- Academic Education (250)
- Colleges and Universities (145)
- Primary and Secondary Schools / K-12 (250)
- Training and Other Education (43)

Financial Institutions (495)
- Banking and Credit (146)
- Insurance (75)
- Investments (62)
- Mortgages (155)
- Pension Funds (65)

Government - Local (814)
- Budget and Finance (38)
- Community - Quality of Life (34)
- Culture, Recreation and Entertainment (40)
- Economic & Business Affairs (92)
- Environment (112)
- General Local Administration (60)
- Public Safety (123)
- Public Services (174)
- Social Services (143)
- Sports (1)

Government - State / Federal (824)
- Agriculture, Fisheries and Forestry (49)
- Education (107)
- Employment and Workplace Relations (92)
- Finance / Treasury (25)
- Foreign Affairs and Trade (9)

- General State Administration (84)
- Healthcare (117)
- Human / Social Services (32)
- Law and Justice (111)
- Military, Security and Defense (21)
- Resources and Energy (50)
- Tourism (76)
- Transportation and Infrastructure (54)

Healthcare (1445)
- Emergency Response / Ambulance Services (36)
- Healthcare Support Services (29)
- Hospitals (1075)
- Medical Laboratory (18)
- Medical Practice (291)
- Preventive Healthcare (32)
- Veterinary Medicine (7)

Hospitality & Tourism (315)
- Food and Beverage Service (163)
- Hotel / Accommodation (137)
- Tour Operator (23)
- Travel Agency (24)

Infrastructure Operations (707)
- Airports (345)
- Ports (283)
- Railways (26)
- Roads (68)

Manufacturing (97)

Media (146)
- Broadcasting (TV and Radio) (60)
- Film and Music (45)
- Social Media (42)

Non-profit / Non-governmental (513)

Postal and Courier Services (295)

Professional Services (388)
- Accounting Services (32)
- Business Consulting (81)
- Engineering (42)
- Legal Practice (273)
- Recruitment / Employment Activities (51)

Publishing (47)

Real Estate / Property (181)

- Property Management (83)
- Real Estate Development (67)
- Real Estate Transactions (34)

Resources (442)
- Coal and Minerals Mining (327)
- Oil and Gas (62)
- Sustainability / Green Energy (56)

Retail (151)

Sport Management (131)
- Coaching / Training (14)
- Sport Club Management (61)
- Sport Event Organisation (41)

Sports (146)
- American Football (10)
- Badminton (10)
- Baseball (28)
- Basketball (18)
- Cricket (10)
- Football / Soccer (27)
- Rugby (10)
- Tennis (34)

Telecommunications / Call Center (123)
- Call Center (81)
- Telecommunications (43)

Transportation (1509)
- Airlines (487)
- Land Transport (Road & Rail) (469)
- Local Public Transport (367)
- Marine Transport / Shipping (235)

Utilities (560)
- Electricity (114)
- Natural Gas (331)
- Water and Sewage (141)

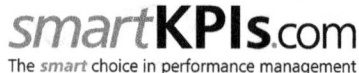
KPI Documentation Form Template as Used by smartKPIs.com

Organizational capability or department that fulfils a specific business function.

Sub-grouping of the functional area or industry.

Aggregate of organizations operating in a particular field, often named after its principal product or service.

Functional Areas	Sub-categories	Industries
N/A	Hospitals	Healthcare
KPI record	**Indicator type**	**Unit type**
sK41	smartKPI	%

Key Performance Indicator (KPI) example unique identification number assigned automatically when entered in the database.

Classification of performance indicators based on their relevance and level of analysis.

Type of measurement unit to reflect results (number, percentage, monetary value).

Name of the indicator, a brief representation of its role.

Succinct description of the indicator, clarifying in business terms its name.

Other versions of the indicator name, as used in practice.

Name

% Hospital bed occupancy rate

Definition and variations

Definition
Measures the percentage of beds in the hospital that are occupied by patients, from overall number of hospital beds.

Variations
% Bed occupancy rate - long-term patients
% Bed occupancy rate - short-term patients

Related KPIs
Hospital bed capacity
$ Hospital operating profit per bed
# Hospital admission rate per 10,000 inhabitants

Tags
hospital, occupancy

List of other related indicators in the database, either upstream (influenced by this indicator), or downstream (with influence on this indicator).

Keywords relevant to the indicator, useful for navigating by thematic clusters of similar examples.

Names of the measures used in calculating the indicator (if applicable).

Calculation

Subordinate measures used for calculation
A = # Hospital inpatient beds occupied
B = # Hospital inpatient beds

Calculation formula	Formula type	Trend is good when
(A/B)*100	Rate	Increasing

Expresses the indicator as a formula linking the subordinate measures (if applicable).

Type of calculation formula, based on the combination of subordinate measures (rate, ratio, index, composition).

Direction in which the results of the indicator need to move for a positive result.

Explanation of the reason or business justification for using the indicator.

Classification of performance indicators based on what dimension of an activity or result they are measuring.

Strength of the indicator based on the stage of evaluation: input, process, output or outcome.

Focus

Purpose
To indicate the hospital's efficiency regarding bed management and its spare capacity.

BSC perspective	Measurement focus	Impact stage
Customer	Volume	Process
Indicator focus	**Measurment type**	**Level**
Leading	Quantitative	Strategic

Standard Balanced Scorecard perspective where the indicator fits best.

Type of indicator based on the emphasis of past activity or future performance.

Measurement approach for the KPI (Quantitative or qualitative).

Organizational level at which the indicator is measured (strategic or operational).

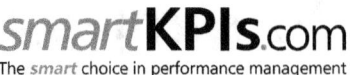

Period for which the results of the indicator have been measured.

Frequency of data gathering and reporting for the indicator.

Subjective evaluation of the integrity characteristics of the data being reported.

Data profile

Data capture period
Spot

Standard reporting frequency
Daily

Data integrity
High

Automation fit
Recommended

Limitations
Accurate reporting for this KPI requires real-time registration of inpatients, so that no lag exists between the actual hospitalization (and the occupancy of the bed) and registering it in the bed management system.

Suitability for automated data gathering by importing data in the centralized reporting tool.

Other limitations (data or reporting system related) to be considered during the use of the indicator.

Subjective evaluation of the suitability for benchmarking based on indicator reporting standardization in the industry.

Additional information related to the target setting for this indicator.

Thresholds outlining the limits for positive and negative results, as well as the tolerance interval.

Targets

Benchmarking fit
Suitable

Notes
Given the universality of the measure, it suits benchmarking very well. High levels of bed occupancy reflect the ability of a hospital to provide safe patient care and indicate an efficient use of a hospital's capacity.

Threshold exemple
Red: <70%

Yellow: 70-90%

Green: >90%

Analysis and resources

Overall notes
Bed occupancy rate is used to assess the demands for hospital beds and hence to gauge an appropriate balance between demand for health care and number of beds available. Managing the bed occupancy rate can be a difficult task due to the demand that cannot be controlled by postponing (like in the case of a guest house, for example).

Additional resources
http://news.bbc.co.uk/2/hi/health/5370336.stm

References

1. Adeyi, O. , Smith,O., Robles, S. & World Bank (2007), "Public policy and the challenge of chronic noncommunicable diseases", available at: http://siteresources.worldbank.org/INTPH/Resources/PublicPolicyandNCDsWorldBank2007FullReport.pdf
2. Health Policy Research Associates & Institute for Health Policy (2007), "Performance Reviews of Provincial and Line Ministry Healthcare Services", available at: http://203.94.76.60/AHF/pdf/CD03/Assesment_Overall_Perfor_bw_Districts02_35-54.pdf
3. Republic of the Philippines, Department of Health (2004),
OTHER HEALTH FACILITIES STATISTICAL REPORT, available at: www.doh.gov.ph/bhfs/images/issuances/psychiatric/statisticalreport.pdf

General remarks about the use of the indicator.

Other recommended online and offline resources for understanding and using the indicator.

List of resources reviewed as part of the documentation process.

Average rating of the indicator by smartKPIs.com community members.

Total number of pageviews for the indicator.

Date stamp of when the indicator page was last updated.

Statistics & bookmarking

Rating
★☆☆☆☆ (1/5)

Views
1780

Last updated
03 February 2011

Add rating
☆☆☆☆☆

Share

Save

Rating button.

Share button, for social media communication.

Option to save the indicator in a preferred list available online at smartKPIs.com.

smartKPIs Community

Other popular KPI examples
• # Average length of stay in ER
• % Emergency Department visits resulting in hospital admissions
• % Employee turnover

Comments

Other indicators saved in the preferred list along with the current example by smartKPIs.com community members.

Option to comment, provide feedback and engage with other members of the smartKPIs.com community on topics relating the documentation and use of the indicator.

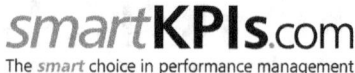
Top 10 KPIs of 2011-2012 Countdown Analysis

10 % Production schedule attainment

Monitoring production schedule attainment can help decision makers in organizations in a variety of ways. As companies increasingly focus on continuous improvement, this KPI helps them assess effectiveness in achieving desired production volumes, while also providing a feedback loop into their planning processes.

9 % Cannibalization rate of new product offering

Marketers and retailers are especially interested in this KPI as it helps them get a better understanding of the customer traffic in stores that sell a certain brand or product, which can further impact decisions regarding product portfolios and distribution channels, key elements of the marketing mix.

8 # Units per man-hour

One of the most common KPIs used to measure productivity levels in most of the industries. Especially in the construction and manufacturing industries, it represents one of the two basic reporting methods used along with the volume of units produced. As productivity is at the core of traditional performance measurement, this KPI is bound to remain one of the most popular KPIs used in operations management.

7 # Inventory to sales ratio (ISR)

Keeping the right balance between the inventory value and volume of sales is one of the major challenges for organizations. Especially in times of economic downturn, when the demand levels seem to drop down behind the offer levels, organizations must stay alert and keep a close eye of their inventory to sales ratio.

6 % Capital acquisition ratio

Tracking capital acquisition ratio is a key area of focus for shareholders. This indicator allows them to better understand the extent at which internal funding sources are available to finance their capital needs. It comes as no surprise that tracking internal funding sources was of special interests, since they are less expensive and less risky.

5 # Time to fill a vacant position

As 2011 was marked by an increase in workforce availability for many markets around the world, this KPI had a decreasing trend especially for junior and middle management job openings. However, for top management positions, the targets required to reach are still challenging for most of the recruiters. This makes it a popular KPI for both in-house recruiting processes and for external recruitment agencies.

4 % All commodity volume (ACV) distribution

Marketers and retailers are especially interested in this KPI as it helps them get a better understanding of the customer traffic in stores that sell a certain brand or product, which can further impact decisions regarding product portfolios and distribution channels, key elements of the marketing mix.

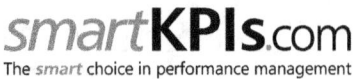
3 % Realization rate

Tracking the realization rate is one of the major focus areas for organizations delivering professional services. In challenging economic times, discounted rates are common practice, however they put further pressure on profit rates. Professional services companies achieving high realization rates usually have a strong company presence on the market and are recognized for their service quality.

2 % Call setup success rate (CSSR)

In today's competitive telecommunication environment, the emphasis has shifted towards delivering high quality services while keeping them at an affordable level. Improving call setup success rate by increasing the radio signal coverage, expanding the network capacity and optimizing the performance of its different elements was therefore seen as one of the greatest priorities for telecom operators in 2011.

1 % Hospital bed occupancy rate

This healthcare KPIs reflects the high level of interest in the sector in improving the performance of healthcare facilities. Driven by increasing pressure from patients for improved quality and volume of service and government regulatory compliance requirements, the use of KPIs in the healthcare industry makes it one of the most measured in the professional spectrum.

Top 10 KPIs of 2011-2012 List

KPI name	Functional Areas	Industries
% Hospital bed occupancy rate	-----	Healthcare
% Call setup success rate (CSSR)	-----	Telecommunications / Call Centre
% Realization rate	-----	Professional Services
% All commodity volume (ACV) distribution	Sales and Customer Service	-----
# Average time to fill a vacant position	Human Resources	-----
% Capital acquisition ratio	Finance	-----
# Inventory to sales ratio (ISR)	Supply Chain, Procurement, Distribution	-----
# Units per man-hour	Production and Quality Management	-----
% Cannibalization rate of new product offering	Sales and Customer Service	-----
% Production schedule attainment	Production and Quality Management	-----

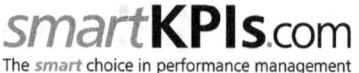
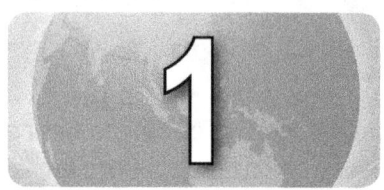

Functional Areas	Sub-categories	Industries
N/A	Hospitals	Healthcare
KPI record	**Indicator type**	**Unit type**
sK41	smartKPI	%

Name

% Hospital bed occupancy rate

Definition and variations

Definition

Measures the percentage of beds in the hospital that are occupied by patients, from overall number of hospital beds.

Variations

% Bed occupancy rate - long-term patients
% Bed occupancy rate - short-term patients

Related KPIs

% Alternate level of care days (ALC)

Tags

hospital, occupancy

Calculation

Subordinate measures used for calculation

A = # Hospital inpatient beds occupied
B = # Hospital inpatient beds

Calculation formula	Formula type	Trend is good when
(A/B)*100	Rate	Within range

Focus

Purpose

To indicate the hospital's efficiency regarding bed management and its spare capacity.

BSC perspective	Measurement focus	Impact stage
Customer	Volume	Process
Indicator focus	**Measurment type**	**Level**
Leading	Quantitative	Strategic

Data profile

Data capture period	Standard reporting frequency	Data integrity
Spot	Daily	High

Automation fit	Limitations	
Recommended	Accurate reporting for this KPI requires real-time registration of inpatients, so that no lag exists between the actual hospitalization (and the occupancy of the bed), and registering it in the bed management system.	

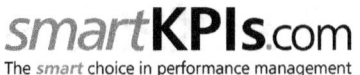

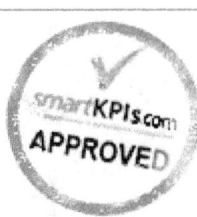

Targets

Benchmarking fit
Suitable

Notes
Given the universality of the measure, it suits benchmarking very well. High levels of bed occupancy reflect the ability of a hospital to provide safe patient care and indicate an efficient use of a hospital's capacity.

Threshold example
Red: <70% ; >95%

Yellow: 70-85% ; 90-95%

Green: 85-90%

Analysis and resources

Overall notes
Bed occupancy rate is used to assess the demands for hospital beds and hence to gauge an appropriate balance between demand for health care and number of beds available. Managing the bed occupancy rate can be a difficult task due to the demand that cannot be controlled by postponing (like in the case of a guest house, for example).

Additional resources
http://news.bbc.co.uk/2/hi/health/5370336.stm

http://www.nscb.gov.ph/glossary/terms/indicatorDetails.asp?strIndi=134

References

1. Adeyi, O. , Smith, O., Robles, S. and World Bank (2007), Public policy and the challenge of chronic noncommunicable diseases, available at: http://siteresources.worldbank.org/INTPH/Resources/PublicPolicyandNCDsWorldBank2007FullReport.pdf
2. Health Policy Research Associates and Institute for Health Policy (2007), Performance Reviews of Provincial and Line Ministry Healthcare Services, available at: http://203.94.76.60/AHF/pdf/CD03/Assesment_Overall_Perfor_bw_Districts02_35-54.pdf
3. Republic of the Philippines, Department of Health (2004), Other Health Facilities Statistical Report, available at: http://www.google.com.au/url?sa=t&rct=j&q=republic%20of%20the%20philippines%2C%20department%20of%20health%20(2004)%2C%20other%20health%20facilities%20statistical%20report&source=web&cd=5&ved=0CDkQFjAE&url=http%3A%2F%2Fwww.formsphilippines.com%2Fforms%2Fdoh11.pdf&ei=AzGiUOrUFc2LswbDsYClDQ&usg=AFQjCNEFzXqCO4NfGAg8XSEqKpWR_fr_lw

Additional fields recommended for internal use

Ownership and expertise

Organizational area
Subject Matter Experts

Measure owner (title)
Measure owner (name)

Data custodian (title)
Data custodian (name)

Interdependencies

Organizational KPI ID number
Related objective

KPI origin
Priority

Other users of source data
Reports containing the KPI

Data

Current status (active/inactive)
Activation date
Target activation date

Data source (report or system)
Earliest data available as of (date)
Latest data available as of (date)

Data source area
Timing of data production
Lead time for data availability

KPI evaluation

Reporting effort rating

Cost of using the KPI

KPI maturity level

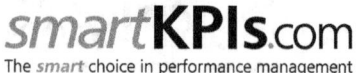
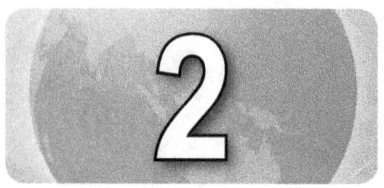

Functional Areas	Sub-categories	Industries
N/A	Telecommunications	Telecommunications / Call Center

KPI record	Indicator type	Unit type
sK865	smartKPI	%

Name
% Call setup success rate (CSSR)

Definition and variations

Definition
Measures the percentage of call attempts that result in a connection to the dialed number, out of the total number of call attempts.

Variations
% Successful call attempts
% Ratio of successful call set-ups
% CSSR

Related KPIs
% Calls not routed due to internal congestion

Tags
calls

Calculation

Subordinate measures used for calculation
A = # Successful call attempts
B = # Call attempts

Calculation formula	Formula type	Trend is good when
(A/B)*100	Rate	Increasing

Focus

Purpose
To assess the service accessibility of the telecommunication network.

BSC perspective	Measurement focus	Impact stage
Internal Processes	Quality	Process

Indicator focus	Measurment type	Level
Leading	Quantitative	Operational

Data profile

Data capture period	Standard reporting frequency	Data integrity
Day	Monthly	High

Automation fit	Limitations	
Recommended	Accurate data gathering requires sound call management systems to monitor call attempts made by all agents.	

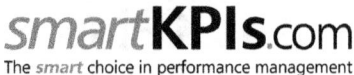

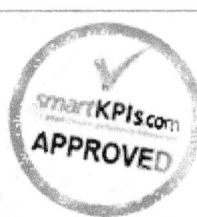

Targets

Benchmarking fit
Suitable

Notes
Low levels of call set-up success can be due to telecommunication lines issues caused by lack of radio coverage, radio interferences between subscribers or limited capacity of the network.

Threshold example
Red: <95%   Yellow: 95-98%   Green: >98%

Analysis and resources

Overall notes
This KPI reflects the accessibility of the telecommunications services used. A call attempt is considered to be successful even when the dialed number is recorded as busy.

Additional resources
http://www.call-center.net/Scorecard-mod3.pdf

http://www.iaeng.org/publication/WCECS2009/WCECS2009_pp393-398.pdf

References

1. Das, S. K. et al. (2002), Performance Optimization of VoIP Calls over Wireless Links Using H.323 Protocol, available at: http://citeseerx.ist.psu.edu/viewdoc/download?doi=10.1.1.16.9164&rep=rep1&type=pdf
2. Kho, W., Baset, S. A. and Schulzrinne, H. (2006), Skype Relay Calls: Mesurements and Experiments, available at: http://www1.cs.columbia.edu/~salman/publications/skyperelay-gi08.pdf
3. Kollar, M. (2008), Evaluation of Real Call Set Up Success Rate in GSM, Acta Electrotechnica et Informatica, Vol. 8, No. 3, pp. 53-56, available at: http://www.degruyter.com/view/j/aeei.2011.11.issue-3/v10198-011-0031-x/v10198-011-0031-x.xml

Additional fields recommended for internal use

Ownership and expertise

Organizational area	Measure owner (title)	Data custodian (title)
Subject Matter Experts	Measure owner (name)	Data custodian (name)

Interdependencies

Organizational KPI ID number	KPI origin	Other users of source data
Related objective	Priority	Reports containing the KPI

Data

Current status (active/inactive)	Data source (report or system)	Data source area
Activation date	Earliest data available as of (date)	Timing of data production
Target activation date	Latest data available as of (date)	Lead time for data availability

KPI evaluation

Reporting effort rating	Cost of using the KPI	KPI maturity level

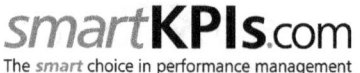
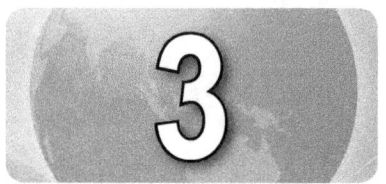

Functional Areas	Sub-categories	Industries
N/A	Engineering	Professional Services
	Recruitment / Employment Activities	
	Legal Practice	
	Business Consulting	
	Accounting Services	

KPI record	Indicator type	Unit type
sK321	smartKPI	%

Name

% Realization rate

Definition and variations

Definition

Measures the percentage of revenue actually earned relative to the potential revenue represented by list prices.

Variations

% Rate realization
% Billing realization rate

Related KPIs

% Consultants generating revenue

Tags

revenue

Calculation

Subordinate measures used for calculation

A = $ Revenue actually earned
B = $ Potential revenue represented by the list prices

Calculation formula	Formula type	Trend is good when
(A/B)*100	Rate	Increasing

Focus

Purpose

To indicate the company's ability to bill at its list prices, as clients usually tend to negotiate for price reductions.

BSC perspective	Measurement focus	Impact stage
Financial	Money	Outcome

Indicator focus	Measurment type	Level
Lagging	Quantitative	Operational

Data profile

Data capture period	Standard reporting frequency	Data integrity
Month	Monthly	High

Automation fit	Limitations	
Recommended	Accurate reporting for this KPI is dependent on a well maintained register of the pricing list and billing rates applied.	

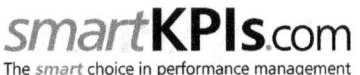

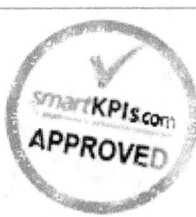

Targets

Benchmarking fit

Suitable

Notes

A high realization rate indicates a strong competitive position in the market, usually based on the premium quality of services. Despite the benchmarking suitability, data regarding realization rates for companies are rarely available to the public.

Threshold example

Red: <70%   Yellow: 70-90%   Green: >90%

Analysis and resources

Overall notes

Lower levels of results achieved for this KPI are due not only to discounted prices, but oftentimes to bad-paying customers, that do not pay the entire bill value. It can be applied at organizational level, by calculating an average billing realization rate, including operational and individual level.

Additional resources

http://www.smartkpis.com/blog/2010/03/16/performance-measurement-in-the-business-consulting-industry-measures-and-more/

References

1. Greene, A. G. (2009), The lawyer's guide to governing your firm, Chicago: American Bar Association
2. Hildebrandt International (2004), Anatomy of a law firm merger: how to make or break the deal, Chicago: American Bar Association
3. Mabey, S. and MacKay, K. (2010), Key Performance Indicators: Understanding How to Keep Your Eye On The Dashboard, Law Practice Journal, American Bar Association, Vol. 36, No. 2, pp. 57-59

Additional fields recommended for internal use

Ownership and expertise

Organizational area	Measure owner (title)	Data custodian (title)
Subject Matter Experts	Measure owner (name)	Data custodian (name)

Interdependencies

Organizational KPI ID number	KPI origin	Other users of source data
Related objective	Priority	Reports containing the KPI

Data

Current status (active/inactive)	Data source (report or system)	Data source area
Activation date	Earliest data available as of (date)	Timing of data production
Target activation date	Latest data available as of (date)	Lead time for data availability

KPI evaluation

Reporting effort rating	Cost of using the KPI	KPI maturity level

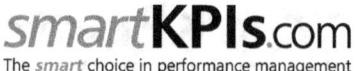
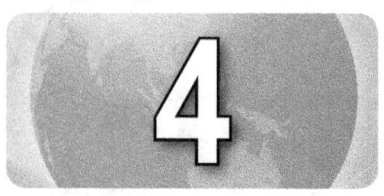

Functional Areas	Sub-categories	Industries
Sales and Customer Service	Sales	Any
KPI record	**Indicator type**	**Unit type**
sK2313	Key Performance Indicator	%

Name

% All commodity volume (ACV) distribution

Definition and variations

Definition

Measures the brand or product availability as a result of numeric distribution, weighted by its share of all commodity sales.

Variations

% ACV distribution

Related KPIs

% Adjusted trial rate

Tags

offer

Calculation

Subordinate measures used for calculation

A = $ Sales of stores that stock the brand
B = $ Sales of all stores

Calculation formula	Formula type	Trend is good when
(A/B)*100	Volume	Increasing

Focus

Purpose

To indicate the customer traffic in stores that sell the brand.

BSC perspective	Measurement focus	Impact stage
Customer	Volume	Output
Indicator focus	**Measurment type**	**Level**
Lagging	Quantitative	Strategic

Data profile

Data capture period	Standard reporting frequency	Data integrity
Month	Monthly	Medium
Automation fit	**Limitations**	
Recommended	Accurate reporting requires access to sales data of all stores, which can be difficult to have.	

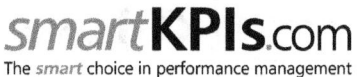

Targets

Benchmarking fit
Suitable

Notes
The higher the results, the more exposed the product to the customers visiting the stores.

Threshold example
Red: <40%   Yellow: 40-60%   Green: >60%

Analysis and resources

Overall notes
When sales data is not available for calculation, marketers can use the square footage of the stores, as an approximation of their sales levels.

Additional resources
http://jan.ucc.nau.edu/~rml/adv311/process/research/lesson/sld009.htm

References

1. Absoluteastronomy.com (2011), All commodity volume, available at:
http://www.absoluteastronomy.com/topics/All_commodity_volume
2. Baye, M. R. (2001), Proposed Merger Between Heinz and Beech-Nut Scrutinized, Managerial Economics and Business Strategy, available at:
http://faculty.lebow.drexel.edu/HammoudehS/Managerial/Heinz_case.pdf
3. Farris, P. W., Bendle, N. T., Pfeifer, P. E. and Reibstein, D. J. (2006), Marketing Metrics: 50+ Metrics Every Manager Should Master, NJ: Wharton School Publishing

Additional fields recommended for internal use

Ownership and expertise

| Organizational area | Measure owner (title) | Data custodian (title) |
| Subject Matter Experts | Measure owner (name) | Data custodian (name) |

Interdependencies

| Organizational KPI ID number | KPI origin | Other users of source data |
| Related objective | Priority | Reports containing the KPI |

Data

Current status (active/inactive)	Data source (report or system)	Data source area
Activation date	Earliest data available as of (date)	Timing of data production
Target activation date	Latest data available as of (date)	Lead time for data availability

KPI evaluation

| Reporting effort rating | Cost of using the KPI | KPI maturity level |

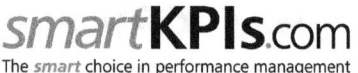
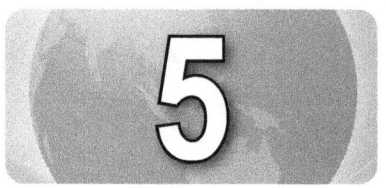

Functional Areas	Sub-categories	Industries
Human Resources	Recruitment Recruitment / Employment Activities	Professional Services

KPI record	Indicator type	Unit type
sK688	smartKPI	#

Name

Time to fill a vacant position

Definition and variations

Definition

Measures the average number of days between the moment when a job requisition is raised to when a new employee fills the role.

Variations

\# Average time to recruit
\# Time to fill a vacant position
\# Time-to-hire

Related KPIs

\# Employment brand strength

Tags

time

Calculation

Subordinate measures used for calculation

A_i = # Time to fill position 'i', where i=1 to n
n = # Positions filled

Calculation formula	Formula type	Trend is good when
$(A1+A2...+An)/n$	Average	Decreasing

Focus

Purpose

To indicate the efficiency of the recruitment process.

BSC perspective	Measurement focus	Impact stage
Internal Processes	Duration	Process

Indicator focus	Measurment type	Level
Leading	Quantitative	Operational

Data profile

Data capture period	Standard reporting frequency	Data integrity
Rolling average	Monthly	Medium

Automation fit	Limitations
Not recommended	Measurement requires data from all recruitment projects, across all teams and sections, which can make it difficult to automate the collection process.

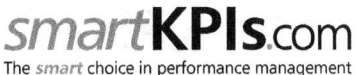

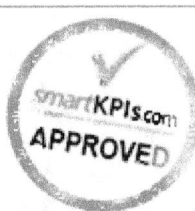

Targets

Benchmarking fit
Suitable

Notes
Targets are very useful for recruitment managers to establish expectations based on a reasonable level of service. In addition, recruiting agencies may find useful for comparison to competition, as clients demand on-time services.

Threshold example
Red: >60   Yellow: 40-60   Green: <40

Analysis and resources

Overall notes
It can be used by both Human Resources departments and recruitment agencies. For HR departments, "# Recruitment lag time" may be a more relevant KPI, as this measures the time it takes to actually replace an employee, which can affect the company's productivity.

Additional resources
http://www.ere.net/2004/07/27/understanding-time-to-hire-metrics-can-time-to-fill-be-too-low/

References

1. Montgomery County (2008), FY08 Operating Budget and Public Services Program, available at:
http://www.montgomerycountymd.gov/content/omb/FY08/psprec/human_resources.pdf
2. Pricewaterhouse Coopers (2007), 2007 Global Metric List, available at:
http://www.pwc.com/en_CA/ca/tax/saratoga/publications/saratoga-07-global-metric-en.pdf
3. Washington State Department of Labor and Industries (2007), Human Resource Management Report, available at:
http://www.accountability.wa.gov/reports/safety/20071113/LNIFullHR.pdf

Additional fields recommended for internal use

Ownership and expertise

Organizational area	Measure owner (title)	Data custodian (title)
Subject Matter Experts	Measure owner (name)	Data custodian (name)

Interdependencies

Organizational KPI ID number	KPI origin	Other users of source data
Related objective	Priority	Reports containing the KPI

Data

Current status (active/inactive)	Data source (report or system)	Data source area
Activation date	Earliest data available as of (date)	Timing of data production
Target activation date	Latest data available as of (date)	Lead time for data availability

KPI evaluation

Reporting effort rating	Cost of using the KPI	KPI maturity level

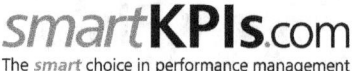
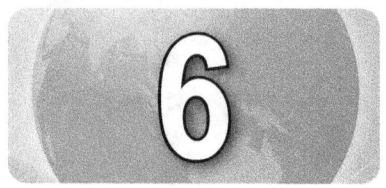
6

Functional Areas	Sub-categories	Industries
Finance	Financial stability	Any
KPI record	**Indicator type**	**Unit type**
sK3101	Key Performance Indicator	%

Name

% Capital acquisition ratio

Definition and variations

Definition

Measures the ability of a company to finance capital expenditures from internal sources.

Variations

% Capital acquisition

Related KPIs

$ Operating cash flow (OCF)

Tags

capital

Calculation

Subordinate measures used for calculation

A = $ Operating cash flows
B = $ Dividends
C = $ Cash paid for acquisitions

Calculation formula	Formula type	Trend is good when
[(A-B)/C]*100	Rate	Increasing

Focus

Purpose

To indicate the extent at which internal funding sources are available to finance the capital needs, as these are considered to be less expensive and risky.

BSC perspective	Measurement focus	Impact stage
Financial	Risk	Input
Indicator focus	**Measurment type**	**Level**
Leading	Quantitative	Operational

Data profile

Data capture period	Standard reporting frequency	Data integrity
Spot	Quarterly	Low
Automation fit	**Limitations**	
Not recommended	Measurement requires accurate and functional cash management and accounting systems.	

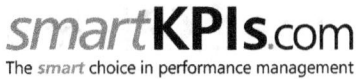
Targets

Benchmarking fit
Suitable

Notes
Targets depend on the shareholder's preference for dividend payout, or their commitment to reinvest.

Threshold example
Red: <50%   Yellow: 50-70%   Green: >70%

Analysis and resources

Overall notes
Although it might be safer to resort to internal financing sources, organizations should also consider balancing with external sources (such as loans), when being able to obtain high levels of leverage and returns.

Additional resources
http://financialratios.blogspot.com/2008/04/capital-acquisition-ratio.html

References

1. Bizwiz Consulting (2011), Capital Acquisition Ratio, available at: http://www.bizwiz.ca/leverage_ratio_calculation_formulas/capital_acquisition_ratio.html
2. Bouwman, C. H. S. (2009), Bank Capital, Monitoring and Bank Performance, available at: http://www.google.ca/url?sa=t&rct=j&q=&source=web&cd=5&ved=0CDkQFjAE&url=http%3A%2F%2Fweb.mit.edu%2Fcbouwman%2Fwww%2Fdownloads%2FBouwmanBankCapMonitorAndBankPerf.pdf&ei=eyuiUIThF4nDswaY5IHIDg&usg=AFQjCNEzcgXzpJ1TSU1jlqufDQpBK9o0eQ
3. Reserve Bank of India (2008), The Role of Domestic Savings and Foreign Capital Flows in Capital Formation in India, available at: http://www.rbi.org.in/scripts/BS_VIEWContent.aspx?ID=1919

Additional fields recommended for internal use

Ownership and expertise

Organizational area	Measure owner (title)	Data custodian (title)
Subject Matter Experts	Measure owner (name)	Data custodian (name)

Interdependencies

Organizational KPI ID number	KPI origin	Other users of source data
Related objective	Priority	Reports containing the KPI

Data

Current status (active/inactive)	Data source (report or system)	Data source area
Activation date	Earliest data available as of (date)	Timing of data production
Target activation date	Latest data available as of (date)	Lead time for data availability

KPI evaluation

Reporting effort rating	Cost of using the KPI	KPI maturity level

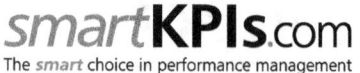
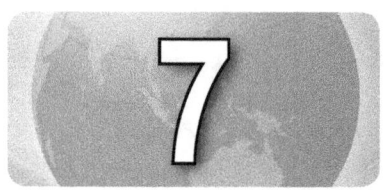

Functional Areas	Sub-categories	Industries
Supply Chain, Procurement, Distribution	Inventory Management	Retail
KPI record	**Indicator type**	**Unit type**
sK4808	smartKPI	#

Name

Inventory to sales ratio (ISR)

Definition and variations

Definition
Measures the ratio between the retailer's inventory value and the sales revenue.

Variations
Inventory-to-sales ratio
ISR
Inventories to sales ratio
Inventory-sales ratio

Related KPIs
Days sales of inventory (DSI)

Tags
inventory, sales, retail

Calculation

Subordinate measures used for calculation
A = $ Inventory value
B = $ Sales revenue

Calculation formula	Formula type	Trend is good when
A/B	Ratio	Within range

Focus

Purpose
To determine whether or not the company is carrying too much inventory, by indicating the inventory on hand.

BSC perspective	Measurement focus	Impact stage
Internal Processes	Money	Output
Indicator focus	**Measurment type**	**Level**
Leading	Quantitative	Operational

Data profile

Data capture period	Standard reporting frequency	Data integrity
Month	Monthly	Medium

Automation fit	Limitations
Recommended	Accurate reporting for this KPI is dependent on a well maintained inventory and sales register. Reporting frequency should match the speed of the inventory turnover.

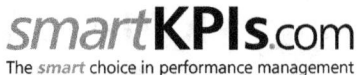
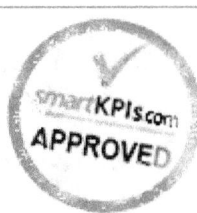

Targets

Benchmarking fit
Suitable

Notes
A high value of this ratio indicates a large amount of inventory on hand or stagnation of sales. Caution should be taken when benchmarking this indicator, as it varies based on industry, market and product type.

Threshold example
Red: <1; >1.6

Yellow: 1-1.2; 1.4-1.6

Green: 1.2-1.4

Analysis and resources

Overall notes
Carrying too much inventory on the company's books can be an obstacle for operational and organizational growth, as this creates hesitation to produce or hire more, until inventory drops down to a more comfortable level.

Additional resources
http://www.ressex.com/pankajressexppt.pdf
http://seekingalpha.com/article/193439-speaking-of-durable-how-s-that-recovery
http://www.activemedia-guide.com/invstats.htm
http://research.stlouisfed.org/fred2/series/ISRATIO

References

1. Bassin, M. W., Marsh, M. T. and Walitzer, S. (2003), A Macroeconomic Analysis Of Inventory/Sales Ratios, Journal of Business & Economic Research, Vol. 1, No. 10, pp. 37-46, available at: http://journals.cluteonline.com/index.php/JBER/article/view/3059
2. Financial Forecast Center (2011), U.S. Inventory to Sales Ratio Forecast, available at: http://www.forecasts.org/inventory-to-sales-ratio.htm
3. U.S. Census Bureau (2012), Total Business Inventories/Sales Ratios: 2003 to 2012, available at:
http://www.google.com.au/url?sa=t&rct=j&q=%20u.s.%20census%20bureau%20(2006)%2C%20total%20business%20inventories%2Fsales%20ratios%3A%202001%20to%202010&source=web&cd=1&ved=0CBoQFjAA&url=http%3A%2F%2Fwww.census.gov%2Fmtis%2Fwww%2Fdata%2Fpdf%2Fmtis_current.pdf&ei=uDyiUJKjIM3PsgblyoGQDg&usg=AFQjCNG9frxwjKlhyztCA0deud7e91clpQ

Additional fields recommended for internal use

Ownership and expertise

Organizational area
Subject Matter Experts

Measure owner (title)
Measure owner (name)

Data custodian (title)
Data custodian (name)

Interdependencies

Organizational KPI ID number
Related objective

KPI origin
Priority

Other users of source data
Reports containing the KPI

Data

Current status (active/inactive)
Activation date
Target activation date

Data source (report or system)
Earliest data available as of (date)
Latest data available as of (date)

Data source area
Timing of data production
Lead time for data availability

KPI evaluation

Reporting effort rating

Cost of using the KPI

KPI maturity level

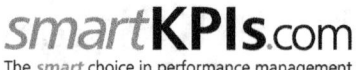

Functional Areas	Sub-categories	Industries
Production & Quality Management	Production	Any

KPI record	Indicator type	Unit type
sK443	smartKPI	#

Name

Units per man-hour

Definition and variations

Definition

Measures the number of completed units realized per hour of work. A man-hour is the amount of work done by one person in one hour.

Variations

Units/MH
Pieces per labor hour

Related KPIs

% Production first time yield (FTY)

Tags

construction, man-hour, productivity

Calculation

Subordinate measures used for calculation

A = # Production units
B = # Man-hours

Calculation formula	Formula type	Trend is good when
A/B	Average	Increasing

Focus

Purpose

To assess labor productivity in terms of output per man-hour.

BSC perspective	Measurement focus	Impact stage
Internal Processes	Volume	Output

Indicator focus	Measurment type	Level
Leading	Quantitative	Operational

Data profile

Data capture period	Standard reporting frequency	Data integrity
Day	Monthly	Medium

Automation fit	Limitations	
Recommended	Accurate reporting for this KPI is dependent on a well maintained system for tracking production outputs and man-hours.	

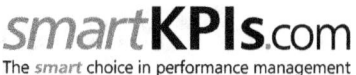
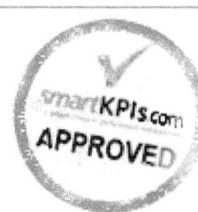

Targets

Benchmarking fit
Suitable

Notes
Targets may vary based on the industry. In some industries, man-hour estimates are based on the type of project and experience from similar projects.

Threshold example
Red: <15   Yellow: 15-20   Green: >20

Analysis and resources

Overall notes
Along with the volume of units, the units/MH reporting method is one of the two basic reporting methods used in the construction and manufacturing industries. This KPI can be influenced by factors unrelated to the labor force, such as equipment downtime, which can decrease man-hour productivity.

Additional resources
http://www.jstor.org/pss/4225514

http://books.google.com/books?id=KQToFyMfZdYC&printsec=frontcover&dq=Production+And+Operations+Management&hl=en&ei=upw9TY6yLlaI5AbJmLzCCg&sa=X&oi=book_result&ct=result&resnum=1&ved=0CCcQ6AEwAA#v=onepage&q&f=false

References

1. Cox et al. (2003), Management's Perception of Key Performance Indicators for Construction. Journal of Construction Engineering and Management, Vol. 129, No. 2, pp. 142-151
2. Jawahar, L. and Srivastava, S. (2009), Cost Accounting, New Delhi: Tata McGraw-Hill
3. Murthy, P. R. (2005), Production And Operations Management, New Delhi: New Age International Publishers

Additional fields recommended for internal use

Ownership and expertise

Organizational area	Measure owner (title)	Data custodian (title)
Subject Matter Experts	Measure owner (name)	Data custodian (name)

Interdependencies

Organizational KPI ID number	KPI origin	Other users of source data
Related objective	Priority	Reports containing the KPI

Data

Current status (active/inactive)	Data source (report or system)	Data source area
Activation date	Earliest data available as of (date)	Timing of data production
Target activation date	Latest data available as of (date)	Lead time for data availability

KPI evaluation

Reporting effort rating	Cost of using the KPI	KPI maturity level

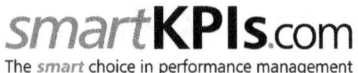
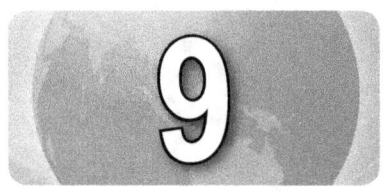

Functional Areas	Sub-categories	Industries
Sales and Customer Service	Sales	Any

KPI record	Indicator type	Unit type
sK156	Key Performance Indicator	%

Name

% Cannibalization rate of new product offering

Definition and variations

Definition
Measures the decrease in sales of existing products due to launches of new products.

Variations
% Ratio of the cannibalized sales volume

Related KPIs
$ Profits from new products or business operations

Tags
sales

Calculation

Subordinate measures used for calculation
A = $ Sales of the new product that cannibalized existing products
B = $ Sales of the new product

Calculation formula	Formula type	Trend is good when
(A/B)*100	Rate	Decreasing

Focus

Purpose
To indicate the break-even rate of cannibalization (the maximum sales volume of the new offering that could come from the company's existing offering without incurring a loss).

BSC perspective	Measurement focus	Impact stage
Customer	Volume	Output

Indicator focus	Measurment type	Level
Leading	Quantitative	Operational

Data profile

Data capture period	Standard reporting frequency	Data integrity
Quarter	Quarterly	Low

Automation fit	Limitations	
Not recommended	Accurate reporting is affected by the difficulty to measure the sales of the new product that cannibalized the existing products. It is necessary to know for sure that the decrease in sales of the existing products is due to the new product and not to competition.	

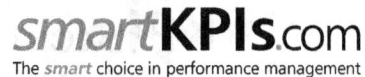

Targets

Benchmarking fit
Suitable

Notes
Cannibalization is a side effect of product line extensions, which typically aim to increase the company's revenues, or to steal market share from competition.

Threshold example
Red: >50%   Yellow: 20-50%   Green: <20%

Analysis and resources

Overall notes
A typical side effect of product line extensions is that in addition to stealing share from competitors, new offerings also take away market shares from the company's current offering. This process is commonly referred to as cannibalization.

Additional resources
http://www.goizueta.emory.edu/faculty/PeterRoberts/documents/JEBO-ResourceCannibalization.pdf

http://www.experiencefestival.com/a/cannibalization/id/1944843

http://calhoun.nps.edu/public/handle/10945/9284

References

1. Srinivasan, S. (2012), Product Cannibalization, available at:
http://www.google.com.au/url?sa=t&rct=j&q=&source=web&cd=1&ved=0CB4QFjAA&url=http%3A%2F%2Fcampus.mst.edu%2Fenggrweb%2Fseminars%2F PresentationSlides%2Ffs2003%2FSri100603.ppt&ei=kZd-UNK4IcrJswa5koDwDQ&usg=AFQjCNGItmT_bGk9pn12n1lvqDld3OGohQ
2. Mintz, O. (2012), What Drives Managerial Use of Marketing vs. Financial Metrics and Does it Impact Performance?, available at:
https://webfiles.uci.edu/omintz/Benchmark%20Report%20Template.pdf?uniq=xnhh5n
3. Leonard N. Stern School of Business (2012), Discussion Issues and Derivations, available at:
http://pages.stern.nyu.edu/~adamodar/New_Home_Page/AppldCF/derivn/ch6deriv.html

Additional fields recommended for internal use

Ownership and expertise

Organizational area   Measure owner (title)   Data custodian (title)
Subject Matter Experts   Measure owner (name)   Data custodian (name)

Interdependencies

Organizational KPI ID number   KPI origin   Other users of source data
Related objective   Priority   Reports containing the KPI

Data

Current status (active/inactive) Data source (report or system)   Data source area
Activation date   Earliest data available as of (date) Timing of data production
Target activation date   Latest data available as of (date)   Lead time for data availability

KPI evaluation

Reporting effort rating   Cost of using the KPI   KPI maturity level

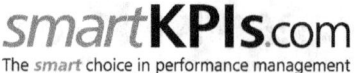
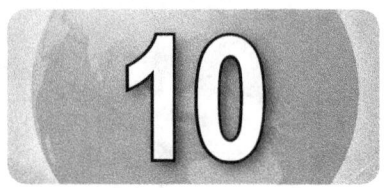

Functional Areas	Sub-categories	Industries
Production & Quality Management	Production	Any

KPI record	Indicator type	Unit type
sK1744	Key Performance Indicator	%

Name
% Production schedule attainment

Definition and variations

Definition
Measures how much of the production schedule is actually achieved.

Variations
% Schedule attainment in production

Related KPIs
% Production delays due to raw material shortage

Tags
production plan tracking

Calculation

Subordinate measures used for calculation

A = # Actual production
B = # Scheduled production
C = # Actual production time
D = # Scheduled production time

Calculation formula	Formula type	Trend is good when
[(A/B)*(D/C)]*100	Composition	Increasing

Focus

Purpose
To evaluate the production schedule attainment and accuracy.

BSC perspective	Measurement focus	Impact stage
Internal Processes	Quality	Process

Indicator focus	Measurment type	Level
Leading	Quantitative	Operational

Data profile

Data capture period	Standard reporting frequency	Data integrity
Week	Monthly	Medium

Automation fit	Limitations	
Recommended	Difficulties can occur if no clear production schedule is developed and tracked.	

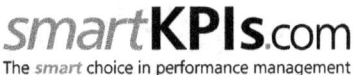

Targets

Benchmarking fit

Suitable

Notes

Targets should be set taking into consideration the risks and other unplanned situations that can occur during the production process, that can influence either the duration or the volume of production (e.g. unplanned maintenance).
A high level of this indicator shows rigorousness and effectiveness in attaining the production volume and duration.

Threshold example

Red: <70%   Yellow: 70-90%   Green: >90%

Analysis and resources

Overall notes

Monitoring this KPI supports improvement in production planning and schedule attainment. Production changes should be monitored and documented for root cause analysis, understanding accuracy and developing a plan for improvements.

Additional resources

Bragg, S. M. (2002), Business ratios and formulas: a comprehensive guide. John Wiley and Sons

http://www.ohcow.on.ca/press_release/RSI/RSI_day/2009/ROI.pdf

References

1. APQC (2007), Supply Chain Definitions and Key Measures, available at:
http://www.apqc.org/knowledge-base/documents/supply-chain-definitions-and-key-measures
2. Bakar, A., Hakim, L., Chong, S. and Binshan, L. (2004), Measuring supply chain performance among public hospital laboratories, International Journal of Productivity and Performance Management, Vol. 59 Iss: 1, pp.75 - 97, available at:
http://www.emeraldinsight.com/journals.htm?articleid=1829560&show=html
3. Bragg, S. (2002), Business Ratios and Formulas A Comprehensive Guide, New Jersey: John Wiley & Sons, Inc.

Additional fields recommended for internal use

Ownership and expertise

Organizational area	Measure owner (title)	Data custodian (title)
Subject Matter Experts	Measure owner (name)	Data custodian (name)

Interdependencies

Organizational KPI ID number	KPI origin	Other users of source data
Related objective	Priority	Reports containing the KPI

Data

Current status (active/inactive)	Data source (report or system)	Data source area
Activation date	Earliest data available as of (date)	Timing of data production
Target activation date	Latest data available as of (date)	Lead time for data availability

KPI evaluation

Reporting effort rating	Cost of using the KPI	KPI maturity level

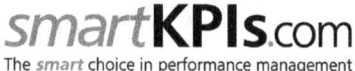
Appendix A: Related reports

- Extensive collections of the most visited KPIs on smartKPIs.com, across functional areas and industries;
- Thorough analysis of each KPI according to smartKPIs.com documentation forms and standards;
- Proof-of-concept of relevant KPIs, documented at best practice standards.

2010 Top KPIs reports

Reports by Functional Area

Reports by Industry

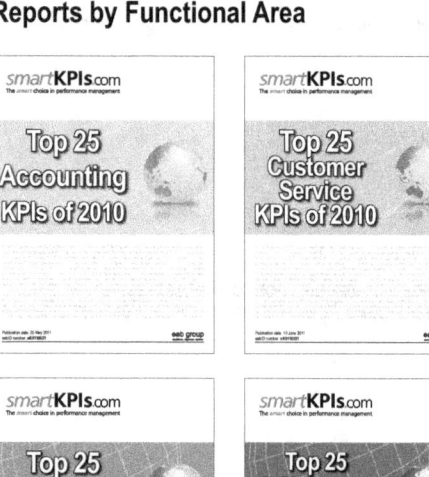
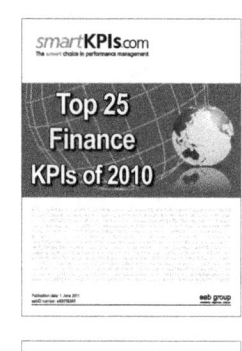
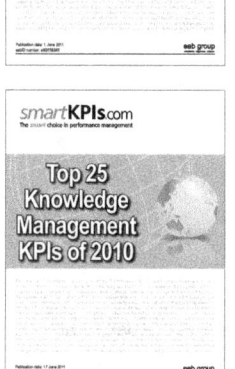
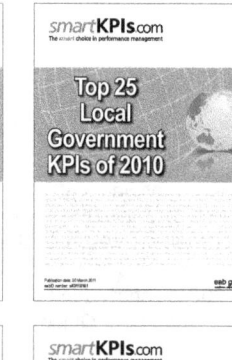
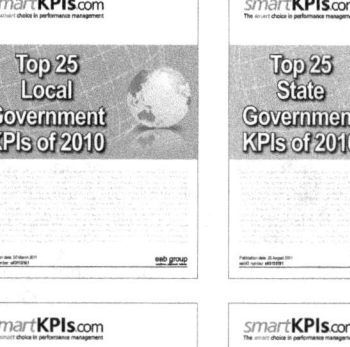
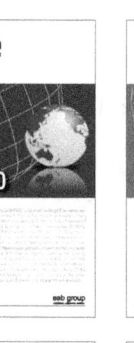
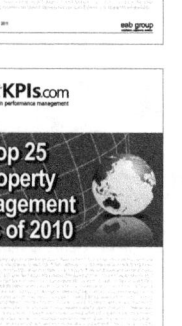
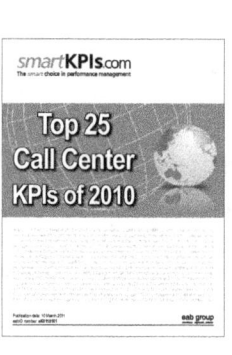
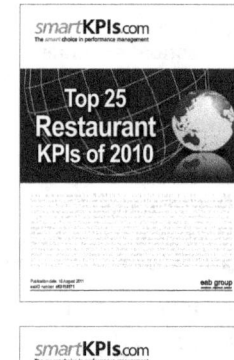
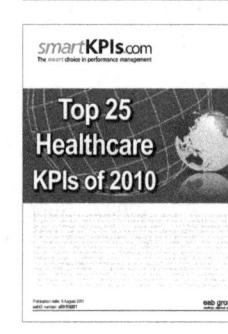
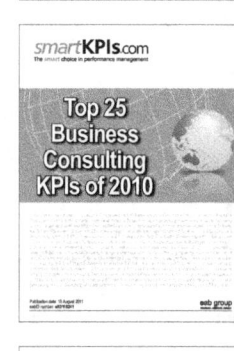
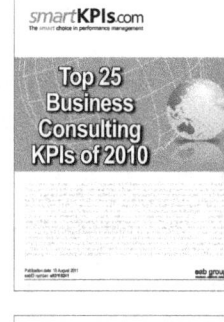
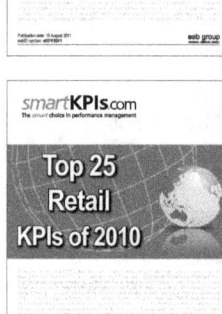
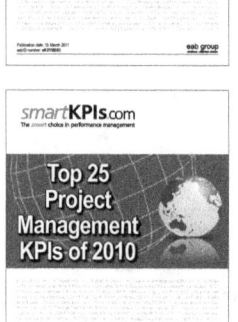
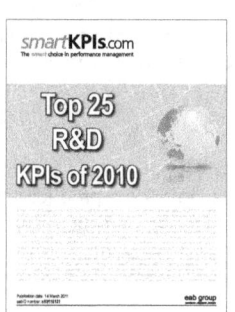
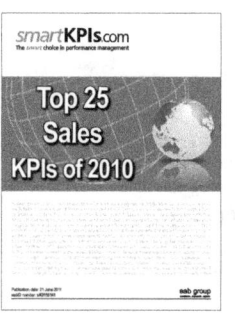
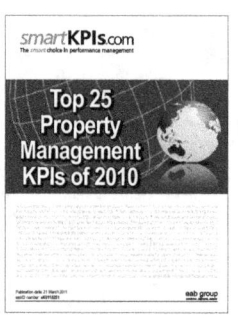
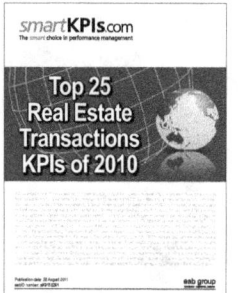

www.smartkpis.com/premium/products/reports/browse-top-kpis-reports

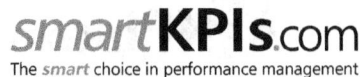
2011-2012 Top KPI reports

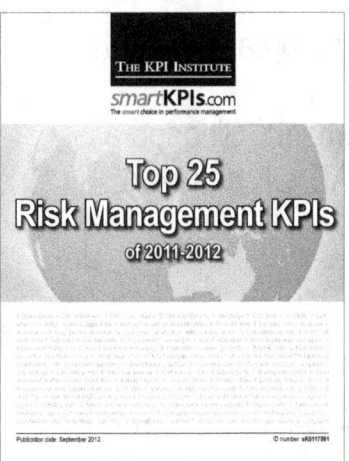 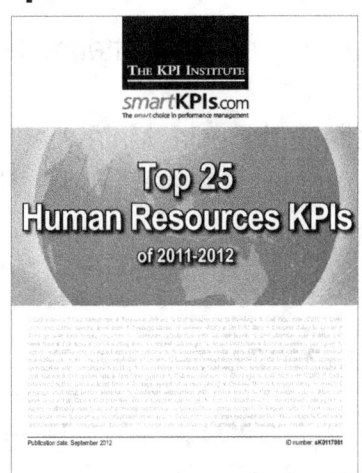 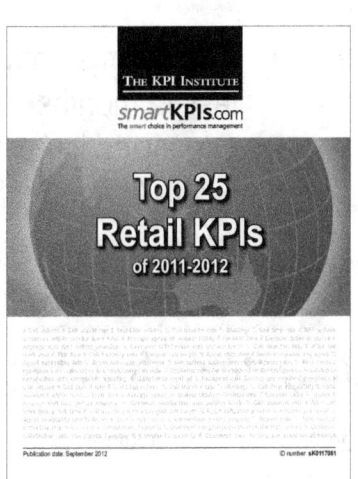 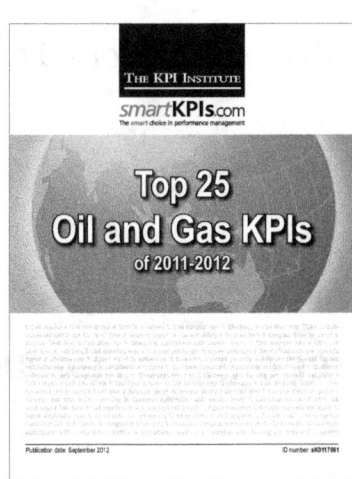

By Functional Area

Top 25 Accounting KPIs of 2011-2012	Top 25 Governance KPIs of 2011-2012	Top 25 Public Relations KPIs of 2011-2012
Top 25 Accounts Payable and Receivable KPIs of 2011-2012	Top 25 Human Resources KPIs of 2011-2012	Top 25 Quality Management KPIs of 2011-2012
Top 25 Advertising KPIs of 2011-2012	Top 25 Information Technology KPIs of 2011-2012	Top 25 R&D KPIs of 2011-2012
Top 25 Application Development KPIs of 2011-2012	Top 25 Innovation KPIs of 2011-2012	Top 25 Recruitment KPIs of 2011-2012
Top 25 Compensation and Benefits KPIs of 2011-2012	Top 25 Inventory Management KPIs of 2011-2012	Top 25 Retention KPIs of 2011-2012
Top 25 Compliance and Audit Management KPIs of 2011-2012	Top 25 IT Security KPIs of 2011-2012	Top 25 Risk Management KPIs of 2011-2012
Top 25 Contract Management KPIs of 2011-2012	Top 25 Knowledge Management KPIs of 2011-2012	Top 25 Sales KPIs of 2011-2012
Top 25 Corporate Travel KPIs of 2011-2012	Top 25 Logistics / Distribution KPIs of 2011-2012	Top 25 Service Delivery KPIs of 2011-2012
Top 25 CSR KPIs of 2011-2012	Top 25 Maintenance KPIs of 2011-2012	Top 25 Service Management KPIs of 2011-2012
Top 25 Customer Service KPIs of 2011-2012	Top 25 Marketing KPIs of 2011-2012	Top 25 Supply Chain Management KPIs of 2011-2012
Top 25 Data Center KPIs of 2011-2012	Top 25 Network Management KPIs of 2011-2012	Top 25 Supply Chain, Procurement, Distribution KPIs of 2011-2012
Top 25 eCommerce KPIs of 2011-2012	Top 25 Portfolio Management KPIs of 2011-2012	Top 25 Talent Development KPIs of 2011-2012
Top 25 Enterprise Architecture KPIs of 2011-2012	Top 25 Procurement / Purchasing KPIs of 2011-2012	Top 25 Web Analytics KPIs of 2011-2012
Top 25 Environmental Care KPIs of 2011-2012	Top 25 Production KPIs of 2011-2012	
Top 25 Finance KPIs of 2011-2012	Top 25 Project Management KPIs of 2011-2012	

By Industry

Top 25 Academic Education KPIs of 2011-2012	Top 25 Hotel KPIs of 2011-2012	Top 25 Publishing KPIs of 2011-2012
Top 25 Accounting Services KPIs of 2011-2012	Top 25 Insurance KPIs of 2011-2012	Top 25 Railways KPIs of 2011-2012
Top 25 Airlines KPIs of 2011-2012	Top 25 Investments KPIs of 2011-2012	Top 25 Real Estate Transactions KPIs of 2011-2012
Top 25 Airports KPIs of 2011-2012	Top 25 Land Transport (Road & Rail) KPIs of 2011-2012	Top 25 Employment Services KPIs of 2011-2012
Top 25 Banking and Credit KPIs of 2011-2012	Top 25 Legal Practice KPIs of 2011-2012	Top 25 Restaurant KPIs of 2011-2012
Top 25 Broadcasting (TV and Radio) KPIs of 2011-2012	Top 25 Libraries and Archives KPIs of 2011-2012	Top 25 Retail KPIs of 2011-2012
Top 25 Business Consulting KPIs of 2011-2012	Top 25 Livestock, Hunting and Fishing KPIs of 2011-2012	Top 25 Roads KPIs of 2011-2012
Top 25 Call Center KPIs of 2011-2012	Top 25 Local Government KPIs of 2011-2012	Top 25 Shipping KPIs of 2011-2012
Top 25 Coal and Minerals Mining KPIs of 2011-2012	Top 25 Local Public Transport KPIs of 2011-2012	Top 25 Sport Club Management KPIs of 2011-2012
Top 25 Crops KPIs of 2011-2012	Top 25 Medical Practice KPIs of 2011-2012	Top 25 Sport Event Organisation KPIs of 2011-2012
Top 25 Electricity KPIs of 2011-2012	Top 25 Natural Gas KPIs of 2011-2012	Top 25 State Government KPIs of 2011-2012
Top 25 Engineering KPIs of 2011-2012	Top 25 NGO KPIs of 2011-2012	Top 25 Sustainability KPIs of 2011-2012
Top 25 Film and Music KPIs of 2011-2012	Top 25 Oil and Gas KPIs of 2011-2012	Top 25 Water and Sewage KPIs of 2011-2012
Top 25 Forestry and Logging KPIs of 2011-2012	Top 25 Ports KPIs of 2011-2012	Top 25 Telecommunications KPIs of 2011-2012
Top 25 Healthcare KPIs of 2011-2012	Top 25 Postal and Courier Services KPIs of 2011-2012	
Top 25 Hospital KPIs of 2011-2012	Top 25 Property Management KPIs of 2011-2012	

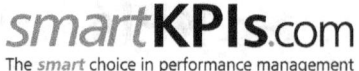

Appendix B: Training courses

Open courses of 1-3 days	• Participants from over 30 countries attended our programs over the last 12 months
	• Organized in Australia, Indonesia, Malaysia, Romania, Singapore, South Africa, Saudi Arabia, Thailand, Turkey, UAE, UK and USA
In-house programs of 2-4 days	• Customized to client needs
	• Delivered at client premises

Performance through systems training catalogue

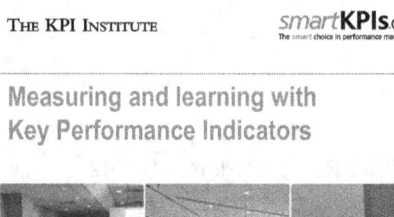

Measuring and learning with Key Performance Indicators

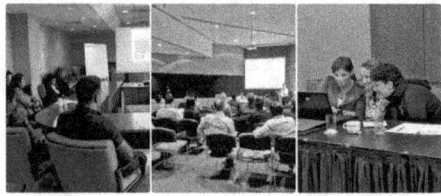

Man is the measure of all things. Protagoras of Abdera (c. 480 - 410 B.C.)

Topics covered:

• Understanding Performance Management;
• Key Performance Indicators (KPIs), performance measures and metrics;
• Selecting and documenting KPIs;
• Dashboard design;
• Rules in data visualization;
• Business analysis techniques;
• Performance review meetings;
• Establishing and implementing improvement initiatives;
• Pitfalls in performance measurement;
• Cultural and human aspects of performance;
• Performance Measurement Maturity Model;
• Insights into implementing and using KPIs smartly.

Implementing and using a Balanced Scorecard based Performance Management System

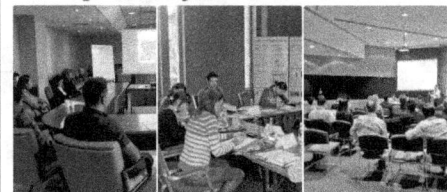

However beautiful the strategy, you should occasionally look at the results. Winston Churchill

Topics covered:

• Balanced Scorecard (BSC) evolution and current agenda;
• Architecture performance management systems;
• Desired State of Evolution;
• Strategy Map;
• Performance Scorecard;
• Key Performance Indicators;
• Performance improvement initiatives;
• BSC performance management systems implementation process;
• Using the BSC in practice;
• Linking the BSC to other organizational systems;
• Success factors and pitfalls in BSC implementations and usage.

Managing and improving individual performance

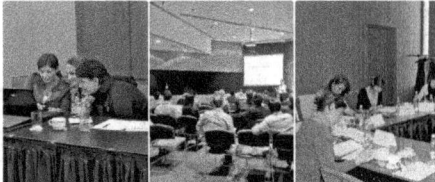

Without effectiveness there is no performance, no matter how much intelligence and knowledge goes into the work, no matter how many hours it takes. Peter Drucker

Topics covered:

• Philosophy and theory underpinning Performance Management;
• Performance Management Architecture and Integration across levels;
• Implementation of an Individual Performance Management System;
• Key Performance Indicators (KPIs) used for measuring individual performance;
• Alignment between Performance Management at strategic, operational and individual level;
• Rewarding performance: pay for performance systems;
• Cultural and human aspects of performance;
• Pitfalls and key drivers in managing and improving individual performance.

Supplier Performance Management
Maximizing the value added by suppliers

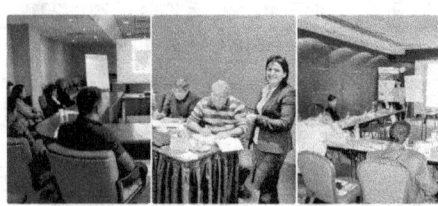

All good strategy eventually degenerates into work. Peter Drucker

Topics covered:

• Understanding supplier performance magament;
• Introduction to systems thinking and viable systems model;
• Supplier performance management systems;
• Supplier panels;
• Service Level Agreements;
• Procurement Key Performnce Indicators (KPIs) and metrics;
• Supplier Scorecards;
• Establishing and implementing improvement initiatives;
• Pitfalls in supplier performance measurement;
• Cultural and human aspects of performance;
• Supplier Performance Measurement Maturity Model.

KPIs, Dashboard & Scorecard for HR

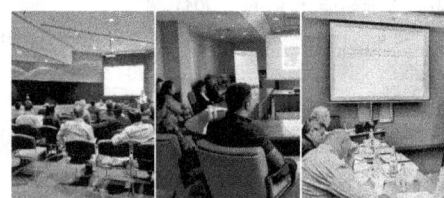

We are what we do repeatedly. Excellence is not just a simple act, bu e habit. Aristotel (384 B.C. - 322 B.C.)

Topics covered:

• Understanding Performance Management and Measurement in HR context;
• Implementing and using a performance management system in the HR department;
• Key Performance Indicators (KPIs) for HR;
• Development of an HR Dashboard;
• Selecting and documenting performance improvement initiatives in the HR department;
• Best practice in optimizing the performance in the HR department.

KPIs, Dashboard & Scorecard for Medical Centers

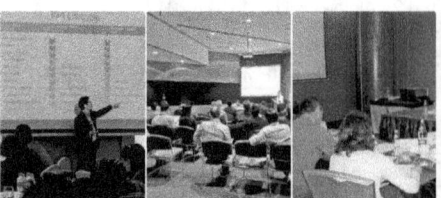

There is no substitute for knowledge. William Edwards Deming (1900 - 1993)

Topics covered:

• Understanding Performance Management and Measurement in Medical Centers;
• Implementing and using a performance management system in a Medical Center;
• Key Performance Indicators (KPIs) for Medical Centers;
• Dashboards and Scorecards for monitoring performance in Medical Centers;
• Selecting and documenting performance improvement initiatives in Medical Centers;
• Insights in optimizing the performance of Medical Centers.

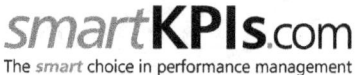
Delivery approach	• Highly interactive, numerous exercises, case studies and group discussions
	• Experiential learning simulations
All training courses include:	• Six months of free access to the premium content of www.smartkpis.com
	• Free toolkit of pre-populated templates to assist you with applying the course learnings
	• Library of relevant examples from practice

Performance through people training catalogue

THE KPI INSTITUTE — smart**KPIs**.com *The smart choice in performance management*

Implementing and Optimizing Employee Engagement Programs

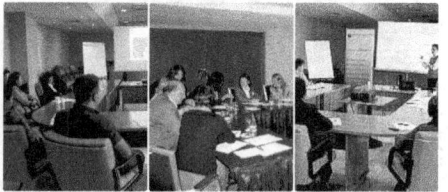

Always treat your employees exactly as you want them to treat your best customers. - Stephen R. Covey

Topics covered:
- Understanding employee engagement
- Employee engagement and performance
- Survey design and implementation
- Types of reports and how to use them
- Numbers vs. behaviors in employee engagement
- Impact Action Planning – plans and meetings
- Employee engagement as strategic priority
- Roadmap and calendar for implementations
- Training and communications plans
- Well-being

THE KPI INSTITUTE — smart**KPIs**.com *The smart choice in performance management*

Implementing Succession Management Programs

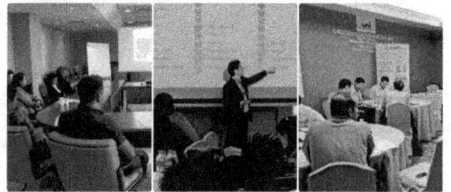

It is always wise to look ahead, but difficult to look further than you can see. - Winston Churchill

Topics covered:
- Understanding succession management
- Talent pipeline
- Succession metrics
- High performance and high potentials
- 9-Box Approach and other tools
- Talent reviews
- Career paths

THE KPI INSTITUTE — smart**KPIs**.com *The smart choice in performance management*

Integrating Talent Management Processes

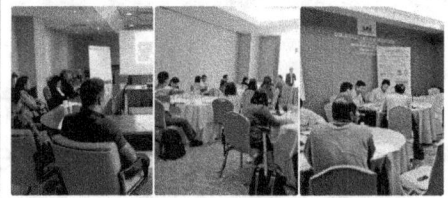

Business and human endeavors are systems...we tend to focus on snapshots of isolated parts of the system. And wonder why our deepest problems never get solved. - Peter Senge

Topics covered:
- Understanding talent management
- The talent wheel
- KPIs and Dashboards for HR
- Talent acquisition and employer branding
- On-boarding and retention
- Individual performance management systems
- Talent assessments and talent reviews
- Measuring employee engagement
- Fostering employee engagement
- Tips for integration and implementation

THE KPI INSTITUTE — smart**KPIs**.com *The smart choice in performance management*

Solutions for Managing Change in Organizations

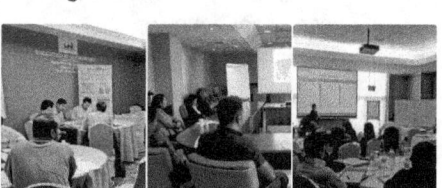

Change is the law of life and those who look only to the past or present are certain to miss the future. - John F. Kennedy

Topics covered:
- Understanding change management
- Reasons why change initiatives fail or succeed
- Breaking mental schemas
- Addressing resistance to change and organizational inertia
- Building a learning organization
- Selecting change management frameworks
- Stages of change and how to prepare for them
- Change management – design and implementation
- Roles in change management
- Assessing impact of change efforts

THE KPI INSTITUTE — smart**KPIs**.com *The smart choice in performance management*

Fish Banks Business Simulation Workshop

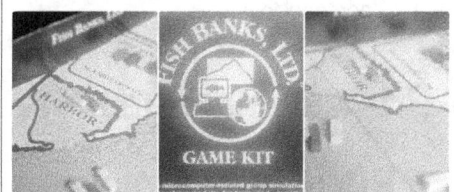

The transition to a sustainable society requires a careful balance between long-term and short-term goals and an emphasis on sufficiency, equity, and quality of life. - Denis L. Meadows

Topics covered:
- Effective Management - manage your organization and compete with others
- Resource Allocation- understand how to best allocate your resources
- Sustainability- make decisions based on a long-term plan
- Maximizing Resources- effective co-operation and negotiation
- Strategy Design- build strategy using data
- Performance- measure and manage performance
- Collaboration- cooperative learning and group problem solving
- Conflict Resolution- manage interdependence and scarce resources
- Systemic Thinking- understand the impact and complexity of actions
- Decision making- systemic analysis and accountability

THE KPI INSTITUTE — smart**KPIs**.com *The smart choice in performance management*

Friday Night at the ER Business Simulation Workshop

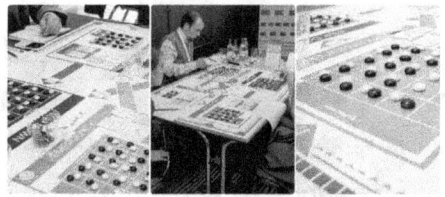

A system is a network of interdependent components that work together to try to accomplish the aim of the system. A system must have an aim. Without an aim, there is no system - W. Edwards Deming. The New Economics

Topics covered:
- Systems Thinking, managing interdependence, complexity, delay
- Collaboration, shared accountability, coordinated action
- Innovation, mental models, openness to redesign
- Use of Data, system performance data, measurement
- Structural Thinking, designing for performance

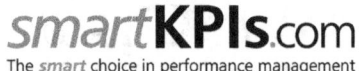
Appendix C: Advisory services

The KPI Institute performance improvement architecture

PERFORMANCE is about achieving a desired level of results in a domain of human activity

PERFORMANCE

A coherent strategy is essential in achieving desired state and continuous improvement

STRATEGY

Performance improvement efforts require a mix of people management practices, process-oriented improvements and innovation

PEOPLE

Managing performance through people focuses on solutions such as:
- workforce planning
- talent acquisitions
- compensation and benefits
- learning and development
- employee engagement
- organizational culture

SYSTEMS

Managing performance through systems relies on utilizing a performance architecture in alignment with strategic priorities at:
- organizational level
- operational level
- team level
- individual/employee level
- personal level

INNOVATION

Managing performance through innovation requires organizational capabilities in areas such as:
- research
- knowledge management
- design thinking
- innovation management
- competitive intelligence
- consumer behavior

In building a strong foundation for performance, organizations should leverage systemic thinking and excellence in managing change, projects, risks and processes

Process Management

Risk Management

Project Management

Change Management

Systems Thinking

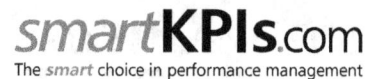

INTEGERPERFORM

the consulting arm of The KPI Institute, dedicated to assisting organizations in deploying best practice performance improvement solutions

European office: +40 721 233 084 / +40 369 801 650
Australian office: +61 42 456 8088 / +61 3 9670 2979
Email: office@integerperform.com, www.performanceintegrators.com

Service categories

Consulting	Technology Solutions
Applied solutions clustered around the performance integration architecture developed by The KPI Institute: performance through people, systems and innovation	Software and hardware that facilitate the operation of successful performance improvement initiatives

Performance through systems - advisory services catalogue

Strategic and operational planning

- Facilitation of strategic planning sessions.
- Strategic research: environmental scans, strategic planning tools deployment (Five forces, SWOT analysis, competitor review).

Organizational Performance Management Systems Implementations

- Integrated performance management systems based on the Balanced Scorecard.
- Application at all organizational levels, or limited to strategic level, operational level or individual level.

Key Performance Indicators Advice

- Overhaul of existing KPIs, by reviewing and updating them in accordance to organizational strategy and best practice.
- Assistance with KPI selection.
- KPI documentation support – customization of smartKPIs Premium templates to reflect organizational needs.
- Development of customised KPI catalogues.
- Assistance in identifying reliable benchmarking resources.

Operational performance management solutions

Supplier performance management – Development and implementation of supplier scorecards for both products and services suppliers

Portfolio performance management
- Development of Portfolio Dashboards and Project Scorecards
- Identification of Key Risk Indicators and establishment of Risk Scorecards

Benefits realization management
- Development of benefits management plans
- Project or program evaluation

Alliances performance
- Establishment of Alliances Scorecards
- Development of Service Level Agreements

Assessment / Audit / Review

Audit of organizational performance management systems at strategic, operational or individual levels.
Organizational capability assessment using TKI's proprietary tools:
- Performance Management Maturity Model
- Performance Measurement Maturity Model

Performance through people - advisory services catalogue

Workforce Planning • Succession management system implementations, talent reviews facilitation, workforce needs assessment • Talent assessments (personality, individual challenges and values), implementation of 360 feedback solutions	**Talent Acquisition** • Audit of recruitment and selection practices • Recruitment processes mapping and optimization • Job analyses and career paths identification
Employee Engagement • Survey design and implementation, organizational and team level reports • Guidance in impact action planning implementation	**Compensation and benefits** • Review and benchmarking of compensation and benefits plans • Pay-for-performance implementations
Learning and Development • Guidance in developing organizational learning and development plan • Integration of individual performance management system with organizational learning initiatives	**Organizational culture** • Organizational culture assessments • Organizational network analyses • Change management planning and guidance

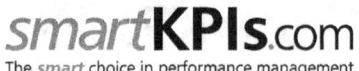

Appendix D: Technology solutions

smartKPIs Key Performance Indicators Online Database

20,000 KPI examples
7,100 KPIs defined
2,700 KPIs documented in detail
15 Functional areas
24 Industries
3 Contexts

EXPLORER
$39
6 months access

Features

- ✓ Basic access
- ✓ Explore the complete catalogue
- ✓ Use advanced search
- ✓ View KPI definitions
- ✓ Save KPI examples

Numbers

- ✓ Browse 7000+ KPI examples
- ✓ Access 17 documentation fields
- ✓ View 200 documented KPIs

Research

One research report:
- ✓ Top 20 KPIs of 2010

Most Popular

PREMIUM
$249
12 months access

Features

- ✓ Explorer benefits plus
- ✓ Export of KPI examples in PDF format
- ✓ Edit the number of KPIs listed per page
- ✓ Filter by views, rating and documentation status
- ✓ Access to all documentation fields

Numbers

- ✓ Browse 7000+ KPI examples
- ✓ Access 17 documentation fields
- ✓ View 200 documented KPIs

Research

Two research reports:
- ✓ Top 20 KPIs of 2010
- ✓ Top 25 KPIs of 2010 report of your choice

INSIGHT
$999
12 months access

Features

- ✓ Premium benefits plus
- ✓ Online access to all research reports published in The KPI Institute's Insight Library
- ✓ There are over 25 reports published each year

Numbers

- ✓ Browse 7000+ KPI examples
- ✓ Access 40 documentation fields
- ✓ Export 1000 documented KPIs

Research

Three generic Excel templates pre-populated with over 70 KPI examples:
- ✓ Balanced Scorecard
- ✓ KPI Dashboard
- ✓ Performance Healthogram

Testimonials

On smartKPIs.com premium content

"Guys we are very thankful of the hard work you do. Your website really guides us on the daily performance management of our organization."

Omphile Macheng, Botswana

"Really a very good and useful website, I am excited about the content and comprehensiveness of data on your website, and I will recommend it to all professional in the governmental sector in United Arab of Emirates, Wish you all the best."

Mahdi El Horchi, United Arab Emirates

"Access to all smartKPIs.com research reports and advance functionality in searching the online catalogue helps my office in facilitating the understanding, selection and usage of KPIs across the organization."

Andrew Fraser, United Kingdom

On our publications

"The Top 25 Call Center KPIs of 2010 helps in understanding all the performance measures which should be taken into account to optimize performance..."

Jacob Brown, United States

"smartKPIs.com provided a simple yet powerful scorecard and dashboard model to start building our own with our business intelligence tools."

Humberto E Della Torre, El Salvador

"I was pleasantly surprised of the level of experience and knowledge of the smartKPIs.com team. The toolkit delivered was what I had anticipated to be."

Alex Giammona, Australia

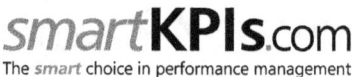

INTEGERPERFORM Business Intelligence Software

Scoreboard and QuickScore by Spider Strategies, ideal anywhere in the world

TRY THE LIVE DEMO	TEST	BUY
www.software.integerperform.com Username: **view** Password: **demo**	Contact: info@integerperform.com for a 30 days trial of the software	Administrator licence: **$99/month** Communication (edit) license: **$30/month** View only license: **FREE**

Characteristics

✓ Intuitive, robust, fully live and interactive

✓ Reliable in any economic environment

✓ Offers optimal return on investment

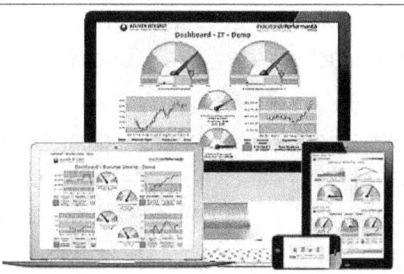

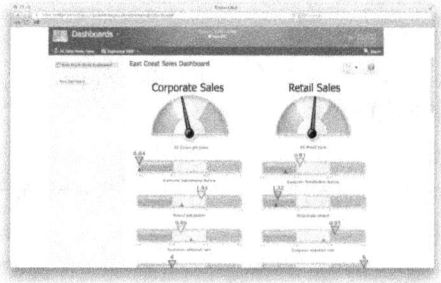

Benefits

✓ Real time control of your business

✓ Easy monitoring, analysis and reporting of KPIs

✓ Perfect for Balanced Scorecard automation

✓ Fast consolidation of information

Configuration

✓ Easy to access and to use, fully web-based

✓ Possibility of external, in-cloud hosting, as well as on-site

✓ Easy to access from any device or location having Internet access

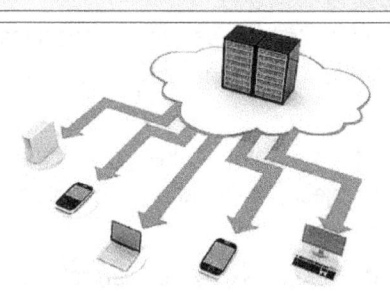

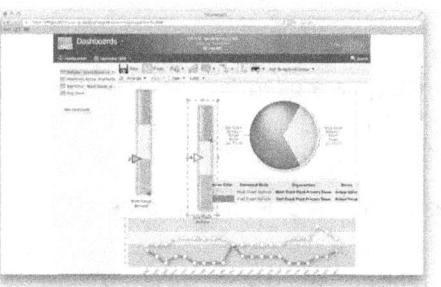

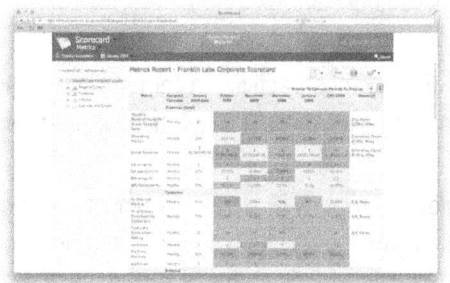

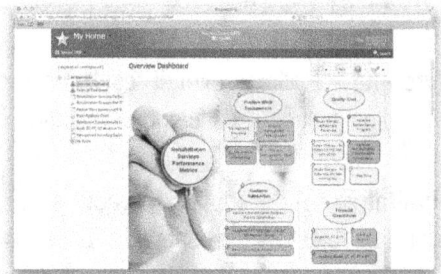

Who uses it?

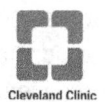
Cleveland Clinic

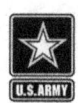
U.S. ARMY

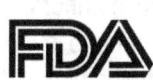
FDA

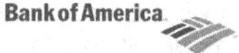
Bank of America

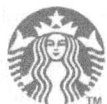

unicef

Walmart
Save money. Live better.

www.integerperform.com/kpi-dashboard-balanced-scorecard-software

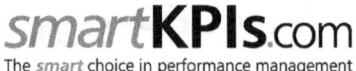

Appendix E: Glossary of Terms

The following list provides an explanation of several popular terms characterizing KPIs:

Rate – A specific type of ratio expressed in many cases as part to whole. Examples of rates are the natality or mortality rate, expressed as the number of births or deaths per a certain number of population or the currency exchange rate, where the value of one currency is compared to the value of the other currency.

Ratio – A relation between two measures that might be distinct, but which are part of the same category of elements, such as the ratio of boys to girls, teachers to students, doctors to patients, revenues to expenditure.

Composition – A composite indicator is formed when individual indicators are compiled into a single index, on the basis of an underlying model of the multi-dimensional concept that is being measured. It measures multi-dimensional concepts (e.g. competitiveness, e-trade or environmental quality) which cannot be captured by a single indicator.

Index – A number computed from a specific formula or calculation methodology, used to characterize a complex set of data.

Leading – Drive the performance of the outcome indicators, being predictors of success or failure. Examples of leading indicators are: "% Employees involved in the innovation process", "% Conversion rate" or "% Inventory quality ratio (IQR)".

Lagging – Type of indicators that reflect the success or failure after an event has been consumed. Examples include: "$ Operating profit per room", "$ Earnings before interest and taxes (EBIT)" or "$ Cost avoidance savings".

Input – Reflects assets and resources invested in or used to generate business results. Examples include: "# Headcount", "$ Cost per broadcast hour" and "# Knowledge materials distributed to employees".

Process – Refers to the efficiency or productivity of a business process. Examples include: "% On time delivery", "# Conflicts arisen during the project", "# Average call handling time" and "# Mean time to repair".

Output – Measures the financial and nonfinancial deliverables or results of business activities. Examples include: "% Passenger seats sold", "# New customers acquired" or "$ Revenue per successful call".

Outcome – Reflects overall results or impact of the business activity in terms of generated benefits, as a quantification of performance. Examples include: "% Customer retention", "% Employee turnover", "$ Net income after taxes (NIAT)" or "% Brand awareness".

Qualitative – A descriptive characteristic, an opinion, a property or a trait. The most common ones gauge customer or employee satisfaction through subjective assessments. Based on a subjective interpretations of a customer's or employee's opinions. Oftentimes these type of indicators are not expressed numerically, but as narrative text. Sometimes a rating is allocated to rank between levels (i.e. Likert scale).

Quantitative – A measurable characteristic, resulted by counting, adding or averaging numbers. Quantitative data is most common in measurement and therefore forms the backbone of most KPIs. Operational systems that manage inventory, supply chain, purchasing, orders, accounting, financial systems, all gather quantitative data by means of KPIs. Other examples of quantitative KPIs are "# Employee tenure", "# Units per man-hour" or "# Maintenance backlog".

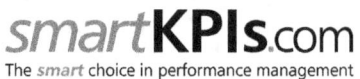

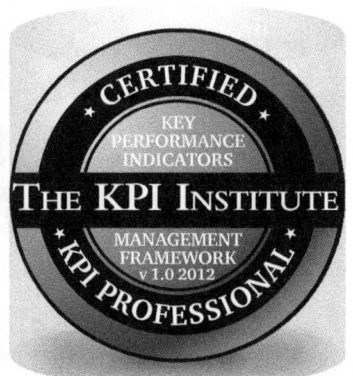

Certified KPI Professional Training Course

- Understand the complexities of working with KPIs and learn how to address them
- Develop a working knowledge of the Key Performance Indicators Management Framework
- Use over 30 performance measurement tools to facilitate the deployment and value added by KPIs.

Getting Key Performance Indicators (KPIs) right by using a rigorous KPI management framework

Over the last 3 years, the team at The KPI Institute:
- Documented 7,000+ KPIs from 15 functional areas and 24 industries;
- Reviewed 1,000+ performance reports from 125 countries;
- Referenced 20,000+ resources (books, articles, performance reports) as part of the documentation process;
- Developed over 20 KPI Dashboards and Balanced Scorecards.

With the insights gained we:
- Assisted over 5,000 organizations in finding solutions for their KPI needs;
- Trained over 400 participants in 30 countries on how to work rigorously with KPIs.

Upcoming course dates:
Europe, Middle East, Asia and Australia

More details at:
www.training.smartkpis.com

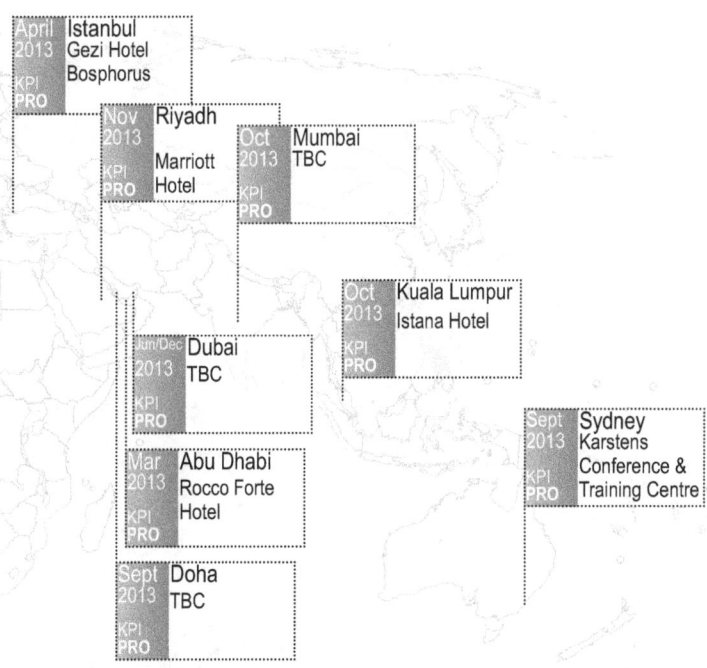

Testimonials from around the world

Great! So glad I found it. Gave me everything I need to do my job properly and with confidence. **Leonne, Australia**

Thank you so much for your effort and your contribution to this workshop. I'm very pleased to have you as facilitator of the topic. **Settha Y., Cambodia**

It was indeed a great opportunity to be able to participate at the KPI training course. Look forward for other future programs with Aurel. **Aini, Malaysia**

It was a good program, through which I got a clear idea about modern practices in using KPIs. **Shamima, Bangladesh**

Good program, well organized. Well experienced trainer. Great job. Definitely recommendable. **Raech, India**

I contacted smartKPIs.com for an in-house training with my team. We found both the material and the way of explaining concepts by doing examples invaluable. I would also say that this is a great value for money if you want to build the competency within your organization. **Fahad, Saudi Arabia**

Thank you for the excellent training workshop on KPIs. It was an eye-opening experience and provided much needed guidance and clarification. The information gained has provided focus and depth. **Parsa, Bahrain**

The feedback from the participants was gratifying and positive, and we are glad that we took the time and effort to develop such a program to meet the need of our staff for extending their knowledge in the area of KPI and all related. **Hanan, Qatar**

Aurel is knowledgeable of all KPI aspect and answers all questions. We were never bored as the course was very interactive. The course was beyond what expected. **Nahla, Abu Dhabi**

The trainer was excellent. I look forward to attend more sessions with him in the future. My knowledge in the area has improved significantly. Great job! **Neeti, Dubai**

I became a lot more knowledgeable about the KPI concept now. **Manzuma, Nigeria**

"I really learned a lot from the program. As a result, I am more equipped in installing performance management systems, by being able to integrate the concepts of the MBO, Balanced Scorecard, KPI and Competencies into the system. Thanks so much for the knowledge you shared during our 3 days of training." **Tess, Philippines**

www.ingramcontent.com/pod-product-compliance
Lightning Source LLC
Chambersburg PA
CBHW081237170526
45165CB00009B/3091